EMERALD STREET

EMERALD

A History of

STREET

Hip Hop in Seattle

DAUDI ABE

FOREWORD BY SIR MIX-A-LOT

UNIVERSITY OF WASHINGTON PRESS   *Seattle*

Emerald Street was made possible in part by the Northwest Writers Fund, which promotes the work of some of the region's most talented nonfiction writers and was established through generous gifts from Linda and Peter Capell, Janet and John Creighton, Michael J. Repass, and other donors.

4 CULTURE   This publication was also supported by a grant from the 4Culture Heritage Special Projects program.

Additional support was provided by gifts from Krist and Darbury Novoselić and Michael T. Wing.

Design by Thomas Eykemans
Composed in Bodoni*, typeface designed by indestructible type*;
Impact, typeface designed by Geoffrey Lee; and
Helvetica, typeface designed by Max Miedinger
Map by Ben Pease, Pease Press

24 23 22 21 20   5 4 3 2 1

Printed and bound in the United States of America

UNIVERSITY OF WASHINGTON PRESS
uwapress.uw.edu

LIBRARY OF CONGRESS CATALOGING-IN-PUBLICATION DATA ON FILE
ISBN 978-0-295-74757-6 (hardcover)
ISBN 978-0-295-74756-9 (paperback)
ISBN 978-0-295-74783-5 (ebook)

The paper used in this publication is acid free and meets the minimum requirements of American National Standard for Information Sciences—Permanence of Paper for Printed Library Materials, ANSI z39.48-1984.∞

To my wife, Danielle;
my children, Dana, Leila, and Elijah;
my mother, Joan, and father, Ben;
my brother, Peter, and sister, Angela;
and the entire Abe and White families

CONTENTS

FOREWORD

Emerald Street: A History of Hip Hop in Seattle by Daudi Abe is a title that speaks directly to someone like me, since the legendary Emerald Street Boys were my first local inspiration. Their vocal delivery, sense of spacing and organization on stage, and professionalism were ahead of the curve and inspired me to take making music seriously. This book is the first detailed account of the rich history that is almost four decades of hip hop in Seattle—a story I have had a unique view of for nearly the entire time. Dr. Abe's thorough research and straightforward writing has created a well-rounded narrative that allows readers from anywhere to get a true sense of Seattle flavor.

What is Seattle flavor? The uniqueness of being yourself. During the early and mid-1980s there was so much local talk about who would be the first to "make it" from Seattle. In a lot of ways, at the time I think that carrot being out there pushed the entire scene to try new things. I was fortunate enough to have my music break into the mainstream by doing something different. "Square Dance Rap" and "Posse on Broadway" weren't about New York or living the gangster life; they were about being from Seattle.

As hip hop continued to grow in Seattle, it wasn't just about rap. DJs from Seattle have gone on to produce for some of the biggest names in music. Massive Monkees from Beacon Hill are world-champion breakers, and local graffiti artists have had their work shown in galleries. Over the years this community has continued to challenge and support the creative energy of its young people.

I am proud to have a place in *Emerald Street*. A big part of hip hop is representation, and I have always done my best to let people know where I'm from. When my records first started selling, I had the opportunity to tour with legends like Public Enemy, NWA, and Ice-T; they constantly told me what a great place Seattle was. Performing live and in videos was a chance to highlight the city. Look at the "Baby Got Back" video and see all the gear with the names of local teams.

Things have definitely changed throughout the years. When I won the Grammy Award for "Baby Got Back" in 1993, that presentation was not a part of the televised ceremony. Since then, hip hop has become more of a cultural force, not only in the United States but around the world with Seattle a definite contributor the entire time. Locally, hip hop has remained connected to what's going on at home. From 206 Zulu to the Seattle Hip-Hop Summit Action Network (SHHSAN) to Pro Brown's 2012 op-ed in the *Seattle Times* responding to a number of shootings in the city's South End, the consciousness of local hip hop has remained an important part of the scene.

In 2011, I literally handed a baton to Macklemore on stage at a show and told him to run with it. Man, did he ever! But so have many others. Although it was symbolic, he and I know that one person could never fully represent all of hip hop in Seattle. Although lots of people from the outside looked at Mack and me as overnight successes, both of our stories are rooted in the Seattle hip-hop experience, which, just like every other local scene, is unique. What the rest of the world suddenly heard was simply a product of all the people, places, sounds, and ideas that made up our environment.

Hip hop's competitive spirit can get in the way of the cooperation that is necessary for any scene to thrive, and at times this was the case in Seattle. But it's that same sense of competition that has pushed the culture to such incredible levels. Dr. Abe does a great job of capturing the details of local hip hop that contributed both to what worked and what did not. I love my hometown of Seattle, and after all of the history found in *Emerald Street*, I can't wait to see what we come up with next.

ANTHONY "SIR MIX-A-LOT" RAY
Auburn, Washington, USA

ACKNOWLEDGMENTS

This project would not have been possible without the amazing assistance I received from numerous members of the community. Thank you all for making the effort and sharing your time, insights, expertise, and stories. Props and respect to the journalists and writers (whether cited here or not) who put in work covering the scene, and a special shout-out to anyone not mentioned enough or at all—still an important part of this great history.

These incredible people and organizations include: Anna Banana Freeze, Ante Up, Art Primo, BPC at Monroe, Roc "Select-A-Roc" Caldwell, James "Captain Crunch" Croone, Casey Carter and MissCaseyCarter.com, Cedric Prim, Colleen Ross, Damico Parker, Dan Satterberg, David Toledo, Derrick X (aka Silver Shadow D), Eric "Professor E" Davis, Guy "DJ Uncle Guy" and Chris "Ferl" Davis and Another Record Store, DeVon Manier, Draze, DV One, DVS, Earl Debnam, Fever One, Bob Fisher, Fleeta Partee, John "Frostmaster Chill" Funches, Funk Daddy, Gabriel Teodros, Jason Gavin, Georgio Brown, Ghetto Prez, Gifted Gab, Chul Gugich and 206UP, Heidi Jackson, Ish, Jace, Jazmyn Scott, J. Moore, Jake One, Jeromeskee, Julie C, Kelli Faryar, Erika "Kylea" White, Omari Tahir-Garrett, Kevin Gardner, Susan Giffin, King Khazm, Kun Luv and Seaspot, Larry Mizell Jr., Lisa Loud, Logic Amen, Mac Slug, Massive Monkees, Andrew Matson, Megan Jasper, Meli Darby, B-Mello, Mike Clark, the City of Seattle Office of the Mayor, MOHAI (the Museum of History and Industry), Charles Mudede, Nissim, Notework, Northwest African American Museum, Northwest Folklife Festival, Patrick Lagreid, Pablo D, Paul de Barros, Alison Pember, Prometheus Brown, "Nasty" Nes Rodriguez, Rachel Crick, Rell Be Free, Robert Newman, Georgia Roberts, Porter Ray, Ricardo Frazer, Sam Chesneau, Samson S, Sean Malik, the Seattle Police Department, Seattle Public Library, Sheila Locke,

"Shockmaster" Glen Boyd, Simon Robinson, Sir Mix-A-Lot, Sista Hailstorm, Jeff "Soul One" Higashi, SPECSONE, Spin Nycon, Steve Sneed, Sub Pop Records, Edward "Sugar Bear" Wells, Supreme, The Station Café, Third Andresen, Tony B, Topspin, Keith Tucker, Damisi Velasquez, Vitamin D, Vivian Phillips, Akil Washington, the University of Washington Hip Hop Student Association (UWHHSA), Aaron Walker-Loud, the Wing Luke Museum of the Asian Pacific American Experience, Inye Wokoma and Wa Na Wari, Kitty Wu, Wyking Garrett, Yirim Yiddim Seck, Zach Quillen, Zeb "ESTEEM 1" Hill, and 206 Zulu.

Love to Sheba, Simone, Savannah, Damico Jr., Harlowe, Alex Jr., Alexis, Grayson, Dr. Quintard Taylor and BlackPast.org, Kevin Powell, Tonya Mosely, Florangela Davila, David Shields, Brian Coleman, Mike Gastineau, Garfield High School Class of 1988 and the 88 Posse, Zaki Barak Hamid, Humanities Washington, Keith Ervin, and the families Canty, Woo, Hall, Monterrosa, Allah, Phillips, May, Seraile, McDonald, Harris, Williams, Breland, Hill, Andresen, Leong, Hubbard, Robinson, Griswold, Parker, Puzzo, Salisbury, Harden, Frank, Weeden, Parnell, Paige, Stewart, Mosley, Arunga, Cunningham, Forrest-Parramore, Nowell, Burns, Small, Nelson, and DeCuire. Also, love to my supervisory committee members in the College of Education at the University of Washington—Dr. Geneva Gay, Dr. James Banks, Dr. Ed Taylor, and Dr. Albert Black—and to my people in the Cultural and Ethnic Studies Department at Bellevue College and the Arts, Humanities and Social Science Division at Seattle Central College.

Much love and respect to Elizabeth Wales and Wales Literary Agency, Larin McLaughlin and the entire staff at the University of Washington Press, and Charles Mudede, whose request in 2006 to write an article for *The Stranger* on early Seattle hip hop became the beginnings of this work. Shoutout to all my students—former, current, and future: you're the reason I love what I do.

Rest in peace Demetri High, Hugh Harris, Roosevelt Hubbard, Chris "Big Boss" Cross, Edward "Sugar Bear" Wells, Jeff "Soul One" Higashi, Eric "E-Double" Jerricks, Jonathan "Wordsayer" Moore, Randy Hubbard, Dorian "Solo Doe" Dinish, "Big" Mike Nowell, Wayne "Lover B" Burton, Pastor Eugene Drayton, and Zion Preparatory Academy.

And last, I say peace to the Central District, the South End, and the entire 206. Let's find that HBM (Hated By Many) tape, please . . .

DAUDI ABE
Seattle, Washington, USA

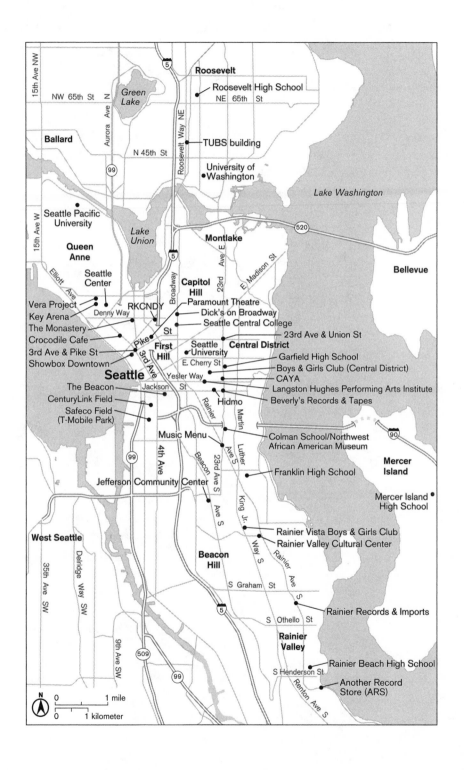

EMERALD STREET

"I'm the man they love to hate, the J. R. Ewing of Seattle"

EAST Coast, West Coast, and the "Dirty" South have all become well-marked regions on the hip-hop map. In hip-hop parlance the "Northwest Coast," as it is sometimes referred to, geographically represents the portion of the United States that borders the Pacific Ocean, specifically north of California. This book tells a story of hip hop in Seattle, the capital of this vast, and until relatively recently, largely unfamiliar region. Its purpose is twofold: (1) to shine light on a rich but often overlooked and underappreciated aspect of Seattle's cultural history, and (2) to position Seattle's contribution within the larger national and international narrative of hip hop. *Emerald Street* represents a first-of-its-kind record of the intersection of Seattle, a culturally distinguished, world-class city, and hip hop, the foremost youth culture of the post–civil rights era. Sonic and conceptual innovations from the Pacific Northwest have coexisted with the ability to hold on to not just rap music, or MCing, but also the remaining three basic founding elements of hip hop—DJing, graffiti, and breaking—in ways that other, more well-known regions have failed to maintain.

Hip hop entered the mainstream in the 1980s, became the driving force behind popular culture in the 1990s, and remained both a social fixture and economic dynamo in the 2000s. During these four decades the scope of hip-hop scholarship has increased significantly, thanks to contributions such as *Black Noise: Rap Music and Black Culture in Contemporary America* (1994) by Tricia Rose, *Making Beats: The Art of Sample-Based Hip-Hop (Music/Culture)* (2000) by Joseph Schloss, *Rap Music and Street Consciousness* (2004) by Cheryl Keyes, and *Prophets of the Hood: Politics and Poetics in Hip-Hop* (2004) by Imani Perry. Numerous books, including *Can't Stop Won't Stop* (2005) by Jeff Chang, have been written about the overall history of hip-hop culture. *Emerald Street* is part of the next phase of hip-hop scholarship:

3

the historic examination of specific regions or cities, which has already seen several contributions, including *Third Coast: Outkast, Timbaland and How Hip-Hop Became a Southern Thing* (2007) by Roni Sarig, *Bounce: Rap Music and Local Identity in New Orleans* (2012) by Matt Miller, *6 'n the Morning: West Coast Hip-Hop Music 1987–1992 and the Transformation of Mainstream Culture* (2013) by Daudi Abe, and *Hip-Hop in Houston: The Origin and the Legacy* (2013) by Maco Faniel.

Best known nationally for software, coffee, and grunge, Seattle may seem an unlikely place for a thriving hip-hop scene, with artists like Sir Mix-A-Lot and Macklemore viewed by the mainstream as "surprising" success stories. One recent jab from a cable music channel drives this point home: while the 2012 song "Same Love" by Macklemore and Ryan Lewis, featuring Mary Lambert, played on the channel Hit List, the following graphic appeared:

> DID YOU KNOW?
> Macklemore grew up in the spoken word community
> due to Seattle's barely-there hip-hop scene.

These dismissive attitudes from outside sources about hip hop in Seattle are almost as old as hip hop itself. In 1986, *Billboard* magazine mockingly referred to Seattle as a "hip-hop hotbed." This perception persisted despite the fact that nationally and internationally recognized figures from various aspects of the local hip-hop scene have emerged from the Northwest Coast over the course of nearly forty years.

Any discussion about the roots of Seattle hip hop must begin in the Central District (CD), the traditional home of Seattle's African American community. As Dr. Quintard Taylor wrote in his book *The Forging of a Black Community: Seattle's Central District from 1870 through the Civil Rights Era,* "Black Seattle through much of the twentieth century was synonymous with the Central District, a four-square-mile section near the geographic center of the isthmus that constitutes the city."[1] Although Seattle's first Black resident, Manuel Lopes, from Cape Verde, arrived in 1858, the city did not have a significant African American presence until the World War II migration, which increased the population from 3,789 in 1940 to 15,666 in 1950. By 1970, Seattle had 37,868 African Americans, with the vast majority living in the Central District. Beginning in 1970, Seattle's Black population expanded south into the Rainier Valley, doubling the geographic area but not the population of African Americans in the city. As those Blacks moved south, they integrated previously white neighborhoods. They were joined by new immigrants from Southeast Asia, Latin America, and the African continent.

By 2000 southeast Seattle, known locally as the South End (zip code 98118), had become one of the most racially diverse neighborhoods, not only in Seattle but in the entire United States. Hip hop arrived in the city in the 1980s amid these rapidly changing ethnic and racial dynamics. In many ways the rise of Sir Mix-A-Lot in the 1990s or Macklemore in the 2010s reflects the unique social climate in which each emerged. Beginning with the release of "Rapper's Delight" by the Sugarhill Gang on New Jersey–based Sugar Hill Records in 1979, hip hop sent cultural shockwaves through young people in the CD and the South End, which would eventually travel to other parts of the city. As neighborhoods transformed and gentrification became an issue, local hip hop documented the changes.

Over time, MCing, or rapping, became the most commercially viable aspect of hip-hop culture. This was also true in the Pacific Northwest, and several local artists have achieved mainstream hip hop's ultimate symbol of validation—a rap Grammy, first awarded in 1989. In fact, Seattle-bred artists claimed back-to-back rap Grammys, in 1993 when Sir Mix-A-Lot's "Baby Got Back" won the Grammy for Best Solo Rap Performance and in 1994 as Ishmael "Butterfly" Butler and Digable Planets won the Grammy for Best Rap Performance by a Duo or Group for their song "Rebirth of Slick (Cool Like Dat)." At the Fifty-sixth Grammys in 2014, Macklemore and Ryan Lewis walked away with four awards, including Best Rap Performance and Best Rap Song for "Thrift Shop," Best Rap Album for *The Heist*, and Best New Artist. Macklemore's run of independently released music eventually reached number one on the charts, gained supporters worldwide, and won accolades as the ultimate do-it-yourself rags-to-riches music story. However, this was not exactly uncharted local territory. Although Sir Mix-A-Lot was signed to Rick Rubin's Def American Recordings at the time he won his Grammy, he'd already made his bones at NastyMix Records.

Formed in 1985, NastyMix became perhaps one of the most unlikely success stories in the history of music. In an era when New York City was still the center of the hip-hop universe, serious doubts were cast on the legitimacy of nearly all material that came from elsewhere. The fact that an independent rap label, based in Seattle of all places, had released two platinum Mix-A-Lot albums in the late

1980s shocked the hip-hop world. In addition to a do-it-yourself ethos, Mix-A-Lot and Macklemore also shared a willingness to musically go against the grain of their respective eras. In his breakout hit "Posse on Broadway," Mix-A-Lot reversed field on the rising popularity of super-macho West Coast "gangsta" rap by calling out domestic violence in his reference to using mace to defend a woman from her abusive boyfriend. Similarly, Macklemore and Ryan Lewis's songs "Thrift Shop" and "Same Love" countered two of hip hop's most popular and oldest norms: bling (the celebration of expensive jewelry and name-brand clothing) and homophobia.

In addition to its lyrical diversity, the unique nature of hip hop from Seattle has continued to defy any particular label or sonic aesthetic. Whereas New York hip hop, for example, had traditionally been associated with Roland 808 drum machines, and California hip hop relied heavily on synthesized and funk-based samples, no dominant style ever took hold in Seattle. It has long been maintained there is no specific way to categorize Seattle hip hop. This is in stark contrast to the grunge rock movement of the 1990s, which initially was known as the "Seattle sound."

Although Grammy Awards function as a standard means of recognition, this book also explores the radio booths, community centers, social protests, nightclubs, immigrant communities, and dance studios in Seattle that made all of this possible. The full story of hip hop in Seattle reflects the variety of activities and achievements that formed the fabric of community and helped to create the music. In the mid-1990s, for example, local legend B-Boy Fever One became the first breaker from Seattle to join the pioneering, world-famous New York–based Rock Steady Crew. Fever eventually returned to the Seattle area, and while spending time mentoring young people at Jefferson Community Center, he met young Jerome "Jeromeskee" Aparis. Fever saw a special quality in Jeromeskee, who in 1999 co-created and led the Beacon Hill–based breaking crew Massive Monkees. Massive went on to win world championships at international break-dance competitions in London in 2004 and Seoul in 2012.

Seattle has also produced a stable of DJs and producers who have collaborated with and created songs for some of the biggest names in music. Central District legend Vitamin D has worked with many local and national hip-hop acts as well as rhythm and blues artists. An incredibly versatile producer, Vitamin D has such diverse credits as arranger, audio engineer, audio production, executive producer, horn arrangements, keyboards, mixing effects, cutting, and piano. Among younger generations, he is known for producing the theme song for *Power*, a popular cable TV urban drama series. Vitamin D protégé Jake One has produced for the likes of De La Soul, E-40, 50 Cent, Cypress Hill, T.I., Ghostface Killah, Snoop Dogg, G-Unit, Wale, and Drake. Jake One received Grammy nominations in 2012 for production credits on the album *Some Nights* by the group Fun and the single "3 Kings" from the Rick Ross LP *God Forgives, I Don't*, nominated for Best Rap Album.

In addition to world-renowned artists, Seattle also produced *The Flavor*, an internationally read hip-hop magazine, published by Alison Pember and Rachel Crick between 1992 and 1996. Beginning as a quarterly before becoming a monthly, *The Flavor* at its peak distributed more than ten thousand free copies every month at record stores across the United States as well as in Denmark, Great Britain, and the Netherlands.

Since hip hop's beginning, fashion and style have been signature aspects of the culture. From Run DMC's shell-toe Adidas sneakers to baggy jeans and hoodies, the physical presentation of clothing choices was a way to express an allegiance with hip hop. Seattle natives Tony Shellman and Lando Felix helped define street fashion when they launched the urban clothing company Mecca USA with Evan Davis in 1994. Creative differences with their corporate partners in 1996 led Shellman, Felix, and Davis to walk away from Mecca USA, after which they simply turned around and started the fashion line ENYCE in 1997.

Despite the rap stars, the Grammy Awards, break-dance championships, magazines, and fashion boutiques, the true foundation of the Seattle scene is something different. Grassroots organizing and engagement of the community by individuals and organizations has been the defining element of local hip hop. In the early 1980s a young Sir Mix-A-Lot made a name for himself playing parties at the Boys & Girls Club in the Central District. In the late 1990s the event known as Sure Shot Sundays, produced by Jonathan "Wordsayer" Moore in response to a lack of live all-age hip-hop events in Seattle, created a space for youth, including a young Ben "Macklemore" Haggerty, to perform on stage for the first time. The Seattle chapter of Russell Simmons's Hip-Hop Summit Action Network (HHSAN) was created in 2002 by Wyking Garrett, and in 2004 Daniel "King Khazm" Kogita established the local chapter of Afrika Bambaataa's New York–based

Universal Zulu Nation. For more than a decade, 206 Zulu has partnered with numerous schools and nonprofits in Seattle providing youth-centered activities, informational forums, educational workshops, leadership development, and documentation of local hip-hop history.

Hip hop in Seattle offers a lens for some of the changes that have shaped the region over the past several decades. For example, gang violence that accompanied the crack epidemic of the mid-1980s was discussed in "Union St. Hustlers" by Ice Cold Mode. Draze used "The Hood Ain't the Same" to outline the gentrification of the Central District. The growing local East African and Asian/Pacific Islander immigrant populations were represented by such artists as Malitia MaliMob and Prometheus Brown, respectively. Although Referendum 74 legalized recreational marijuana in Washington State in 2012, local hip hop had long before embraced cannabis culture with songs like DMS's "Sunshine," album titles such as Nacho Picasso's *Blunt Raps*, and groups like the Stay High Brothers. Also on that ballot in 2012 was the same-sex marriage measure Initiative 502, which passed using Macklemore and Ryan Lewis's "Same Love" as the theme song.

Ultimately, the story of *Emerald Street* is the story of community. The compilation albums, hip hop–themed forums and conferences, countless talent shows and open mic sessions, willingness to collaborate with potential competitors, and an emphasis on serving youth have all combined to produce a vibrant, diverse hip-hop scene in Seattle on nearly every level. The range of this community exists not only in a racial and socioeconomic sense but also in the various styles, energies, and ideologies that different participants have continued to bring to the collective.

1

"Welcome to Seattle where the sun don't shine"

SEATTLE, THE CENTRAL DISTRICT, AND THE ARRIVAL OF HIP HOP

SEATTLE, located in Martin Luther King County in Washington, was named after the Duwamish tribe leader Sealth, who made contact with the first white settlers that arrived in 1851. When Seattle was incorporated on Duwamish land by the Territorial Legislature in 1869, the city had two thousand inhabitants, with the primary industries being lumber, coal mining, and fishing. Following the completion of the Northern Pacific Railway in 1883, Seattle gained an estimated one thousand new residents per month during the late 1880s, and by the early 1900s nearly 250,000 people called Seattle home. In the 1930s the Great Depression hit the Seattle area hard; however, the United States' entry into World War II revitalized the local economy as such businesses as Todd Pacific Shipyards, the Pacific Car and Foundry in nearby Renton, and the Boeing Company flourished.

Cultural and racial diversity in Seattle came gradually as more white and nonwhite residents, attracted by increasing job opportunities, began moving to the area in the early 1900s. Scandinavians found work in fishing and lumbering, while Japanese immigrants operated truck gardens and hotels. Communities of Chinese, Filipino, Italian, and Jewish immigrants slowly took root and began to grow.[1] Early on, African Americans in Seattle primarily worked service jobs. Men were often employed as railroad porters and waiters or in construction, while women frequently worked as domestic servants or owned small boardinghouses or stores. Expanded professional opportunities gradually became more available in the relatively progressive social atmosphere of the Northwest.[2]

Seattle's Early Black History

Seattle's first Black resident, Manuel Lopes, arrived in 1858 and became the town's first barber. Lopes was born in the Cape Verde

Islands and settled in New Bedford, Massachusetts, before coming to Seattle. He was followed in 1861 by William Grose (Gross), who opened Our House, a restaurant and hotel located on the Seattle waterfront, and eventually added a barbershop. Grose's hotel was destroyed in the Seattle Fire of 1889, but during the same period he settled on a piece of land in what was then Northeast Seattle near what is now Twenty-third Avenue and East Madison Street in the Central District. This became the neighborhood of settlement for the city's earliest Black middle-class residents.[3]

African American settlers who first came to Seattle in the mid-nineteenth century were drawn by the region's "free air," meaning the absence of the most blatant policies and practices of racial discrimination that were a part of everyday life for Black people in the southern United States. African American men, for example, routinely participated in civic life in Seattle at a time when voting prohibitions and terrorist tactics drove post–Reconstruction era African Americans away from the polls in other regions of the country. Black men in Washington voted throughout the Territorial period, and the Washington Territorial Suffrage Act of 1883 briefly made it possible for Black women to cast ballots until that law was struck down by the Territorial Supreme Court in 1887. Although it would be incorrect to claim that racism and discrimination in the Pacific Northwest was never an issue, those dynamics certainly looked different in Seattle than they did in other parts of the United States.[4]

The development of early hip hop in Seattle took place primarily in the South End and the Central District, the longtime center of the city's Black community. The turning point for Seattle's African American population can be traced to 1940, when Black people made up about 1 percent of the city's total population. The start of World War II meant that jobs were available in the defense industries at companies like Boeing, and between 1940 and 1950 the Black population grew from just under four thousand to nearly sixteen thousand, an increase of 413 percent. This trend continued over the next several decades, and by 1960 the numbers rose to almost twenty-seven thousand. In 1970 there were just under thirty-eight thousand, and by 1980 roughly forty-seven thousand African Americans called Seattle home.[5]

The US Supreme Court case of *Brown v. Board of Education*, decided in 1954, helped consolidate the emerging push for civil rights around the United States. Galvanized by Dr. Martin Luther King Jr.'s only visit to Seattle in November 1961, the local civil rights establishment prepared to join the wave of change that swept the nation.

Unlike in the Deep South, Black people in Washington State had been voters for almost a century and thus did not have to struggle for the ballot. However, Seattle's Black community had traditionally faced three interrelated issues: job discrimination, housing discrimination, and de facto school segregation, which held back collective educational and economic progress.[6]

Two predominant civil rights organizations in Seattle were the National Association for the Advancement of Colored People (NAACP), founded by Letitia Graves in 1913, and the National Urban League, founded by bacteriologist Lodie Biggs in 1930. As the civil rights movement gained momentum both nationally and locally, more groups and movements began to appear, such as the multiracial nonviolent Congress of Racial Equality (CORE). In 1961 CORE began targeting supermarkets around Seattle known for engaging in racist employment practices. The Drive for Equal Employment in Downtown Seattle (DEEDS), organized by CORE, ran a four-month boycott of such downtown businesses as Seattle-based department store Nordstrom, J.C. Penney, and the Bon Marche (which later became Macy's, now closed). These businesses faced protests and picket lines over discriminatory hiring practices. The direct action protests were credited with helping to create hundreds of job opportunities for African Americans in Seattle's downtown retail core. As a result of this campaign, Nordstrom became the first major retailer in the nation to create a voluntary affirmative action program.[7]

While efforts to end employment discrimination met with some success, the fight against housing discrimination in Seattle continued. By the mid-1960s, eight of every ten Black residents in the city lived in the Central District. As more Blacks moved to Seattle, they faced individual discrimination; neighborhood associations, which maintained restrictive covenants; and "redlining" by the Federal Housing Authority (FHA), which actively encouraged disinvestment in Black neighborhoods by discouraging loans in those areas by banks and other financial institutions.[8] After years of demonstrations and civil disobedience, "open housing"—the right of individuals to live where they wished, regardless of their race—finally became law in Seattle on April 19, 1968. The legislation was sponsored by Sam Smith, the first African American member of the city council, and passed by the council two weeks after Martin Luther King Jr.'s assassination in Memphis. In some ways, open housing helped set the stage for the eventual fragmentation of Seattle's Black community. By the early 1970s, thanks in part to open housing legislation at both the local and national levels,

African Americans began to reside in previously all-white communities. These newcomers to suburban cities of western Washington—such as Kent, Federal Way, and Auburn—included former inner-city residents as well as those who moved to Seattle from across the nation who had no prior ties to the traditional African American community.[9]

As Black people made important gains with respect to where they could work and live in Seattle, the issue of education for African Americans proved more difficult to reconcile. De facto school segregation (racial isolation despite the absence of formal segregation laws or public officials who openly supported racial separation) became among the most challenging issues facing the Black community in Seattle, lasting long after the tumultuous 1960s. In 1889, Washington had been one of the few states in the nation to enter the Union with a constitution that barred racial segregation in public schools. However, the overwhelming concentration of African Americans in the Central District from the World War II era and continuing through the 1950s ensured that Seattle schools would be racially segregated. In 1950 none of the city's elementary and secondary schools were predominantly Black.

Seattle school district census information from 1962 indicated that Garfield High School had become the first predominantly Black high school in the state, with African American students making up 51.4 percent of the student body. Franklin High School, Garfield's closest neighboring high school to the south, was second with 9.2 percent African American students. Meanwhile, six of Seattle's remaining nine high schools had five or fewer Black students on campus. Seattle's civil rights establishment, operating under the premise that quality education for Black children meant sending them outside the Central District, successfully pushed to have these students bused to mostly white schools in the northern part of the city. The Seattle School District officially ended its busing program in 1997, although issues such as the racial achievement gap and disproportionate discipline rates among African American students in the city's schools remain to this day.[10]

Black Power in Seattle

Until the mid-1960s, Seattle's middle-class civil rights establishment, including organizations such as the NAACP and the Urban League, operated as "the voice" of the Black community. The pushback against these groups emerged from what became known as the Black Power movement. The term was coined in 1966 by Stokely Carmichael, leader of the Student Nonviolent Coordinating Committee (SNCC).

Almost overnight, the phrase shifted the discourse among African Americans all over the United States, primarily along generational lines.[11] Carmichael came to speak in Seattle on April 19, 1967, at the University of Washington and Garfield High School in front of an estimated four thousand people. His message resonated with younger African Americans as well as many white and Asian high school and college students. Bold and unapologetic, Carmichael attacked institutionalized racism, the white press, and integrationists while encouraging Seattle's Black community to take control of their destiny.[12]

By the late 1960s a number of Black Power groups had formed in Seattle, including SNCC, the Central Area Committee for Peace and Improvement (CAPI), and the United Black Front (UBF). However, none of these groups resonated with a small core of UW student activists—Aaron Dixon, Larry Gossett, and Carl Miller—who had led protests at Franklin High School. The Franklin incident began on March 29, 1968, when word spread that two Black female students had been sent home for wearing their hair in an "Afro" style. UW Black Student Union (BSU) members Gossett and Dixon, along with Seattle SNCC chairman Miller, arrived at Franklin with a list of demands, including the addition of a Black history curriculum, the hiring of a Black teacher and administrator, and the students' right to wear hair as they pleased. The district superintendent agreed to the demands, but Gossett, Dixon, and Miller were later arrested and convicted on charges of unlawful assembly. Their six-month jail sentence, which was later dropped, prompted an uprising at Garfield High School, leading to six arrests following several hours of unrest.[13]

The Black Panther Party for Self-Defense was formed in 1966 by Huey P. Newton and Bobby Seale in Oakland, California. By 1967 the Panthers had emerged as the most recognized "Black militants" in the country after they walked into the California State Capitol in Sacramento with loaded shotguns. Dixon met with Seale during a March 1968 trip to the Western Black Youth Conference in San Francisco and invited the Panther leader to Seattle. Seale subsequently visited the Northwest and appointed nineteen-year-old Dixon as captain of the Seattle chapter of Black Panther Party, the first outside of Oakland.[14]

One of Dixon's first acts was monitoring the Seattle police in the Central District—a move that won the Seattle Panthers support in a community that had long felt victimized by law enforcement. However, in doing so, they subsequently became the target for intense police surveillance and harassment. On July 29, 1968, the Seattle police raided the Panther's Central District headquarters. Dixon and

Panther co-captain Curtis Harris were arrested on suspicion of possession of stolen property: a typewriter. The raid triggered the first race riots in the Central District, resulting in sixty-nine arrests and injuries to seven police officers and two civilians, despite jailhouse pleas for calm by Dixon and Harris, who were later acquitted on charges related to the typewriter.[15]

Seattle's young Panthers were not intimidated. In February 1969 armed Panthers, mirroring what happened in Sacramento in 1967, joined with members of CORE and the UBF to deliver a list of Central District demands at the State Capitol in Olympia to the Senate Ways and Means Committee.[16] Confrontational actions marked the Panthers as thugs and terrorists in the eyes of many people, including a number of African Americans not only in Seattle but across the country. Far less attention was paid to the Black Panthers as they launched a free health-care service, which eventually evolved into the Central District's Odessa Brown Clinic, initiated testing for sickle-cell anemia, set up prison visitation programs, and ran a free breakfast program for children in need.[17] This legacy of local action by the Black Panthers and numerous others helped inform a new generation of activists, who would approach community service through a hip-hop lens.

Similar to numerous other African American neighborhoods in the United States, as the Central District moved into the 1970s, the community dynamics began to change. The end of the Civil Rights and Black Power movements intersected with gentrification and other social and economic factors that signaled changes in the Central District as the center of Black Seattle. Deteriorating buildings, crime, drugs, cyclical intergenerational poverty, and welfare dependency combined to generate growing levels of alienation, despair, and anger among Black residents of the CD. In addition, relatively low property values and the close proximity to downtown brought increasing numbers of upwardly mobile white people to the area. The resulting increase in housing prices and rents slowly pushed the Black population of the CD south to the Rainier Valley and even farther to the outlying southern suburbs of Renton, Kent, and Federal Way. By 1980 Black people in the Rainier Valley outnumbered those in the Central District, and only 38 percent of Seattle's African American population lived in the CD.[18] Meanwhile, Seattle overall had slowly shifted demographically, with a population that was 80 percent white, 9.4 percent Black, 7.8 percent Asian/Pacific Islander, 2.5 percent Latino/ Chicano, and 1.4 percent Native American.[19]

Black Music in Seattle before Hip Hop

The city's expanding multicultural environment was also reflected in local arts scene. Before the arrival of hip hop, Black music in the Seattle area had a long and rich tradition. By the 1930s, African Americans in the city had created a leisure culture centered on music and sports. Black musicians and performers, dating back to Bertran Philander Ross Hendrix and Zenora Moore, the grandparents of Jimi Hendrix, ushered in a music scene in the 1920s that included local acts like the Edythe Turnham Orchestra, Oscar Holden, and the Black and Tan Jazz Orchestra. These musicians played mostly on Jackson Street and at venues in the south end of downtown like the 908 Club and the Black and Tan nightclub. As one observer recalled: "You could see almost as many people at 12th and Jackson at midnight as you'd see on 3rd and Union [the center of Downtown Seattle] in midday." Seattle's mostly Black jazz musicians often played in Asian American–owned clubs, which in turn introduced them to a trans-Pacific jazz circuit that eventually included Shanghai and Manila.[20]

World War II introduced Seattle jazz to an even wider audience, and in 1948 the scene attracted eighteen-year-old Ray Charles from Tampa, Florida. Charles, who began playing music at age three, lost his sight when he was seven to glaucoma. He learned to read and compose music in Braille and mastered several instruments, including the piano, clarinet, and saxophone. Charles made a name for himself in Seattle playing gigs for diverse audiences at the Black Elks Club on Jackson Street, the all-white Seattle Tennis Club, and after-hours establishments such as the Black and Tan Club and the Rocking Chair, where he was eventually discovered and offered a recording contract. Charles went on to record more than sixty albums, win twelve Grammy Awards, and earn induction into the Rock & Roll Hall of Fame in 1986. He was awarded the Presidential Medal of the Arts in 1993.[21]

Quincy Jones moved with his parents in 1943 from Chicago to the Seattle area, where he gained his first musical experiences doing gigs and writing arrangements while a student at Garfield High School. As a teenager, he played backup for some of the biggest names in music, including Louis Jordan, Billie Holiday, and Nat King Cole when they performed in Seattle during the postwar years. Jones's big break came when he was asked to join jazz great Lionel Hampton's band after moving to Boston. Jones accepted and over the next four decades received twenty-seven Grammy Awards, an Academy Award, and an Emmy Award. He produced Michael Jackson's 1982 album *Thriller*, one of the highest selling studio albums of all time.[22]

One of Black Seattle's best known musical talents came into the world in 1942. Born in Seattle, Jimi Hendrix came of musical age in the city. At fifteen he was playing guitar in a local jazz combo, but he left Seattle in 1961 after enlisting in the United States Army. Upon receiving an honorable discharge, Hendrix moved to London, where his career took off. After scoring several hits in the United Kingdom, he reached number one in the United States with his 1968 album *Electric Ladyland*. Hendrix headlined the Woodstock Festival in upstate New York in 1969, where he introduced his groundbreaking electric guitar rendition of the "Star Spangled Banner." Already known among rock musicians and their fans, Hendrix was exposed to a worldwide audience as a result of his Woodstock performance. Widely recognized as one of the greatest guitarists of all time, he died in London of drug-related complications on September 17, 1970, at age twenty-seven. His body was flown back to Seattle, where the Hendrix family resided, and buried at Greenwood Cemetery in Renton.[23]

Seattle's Geographic and Cultural Distance from Hip Hop's Urban Centers

In comparison to more established urban centers such as New York or Los Angeles, Seattle's relatively young urban identity was still emerging during the 1980s. For many people in the United States the region was "a veritable hinterland known best for its mountains, rivers, and forests and as home of Boeing's corporate manufacturing headquarters," wrote author and scholar Murray Forman in his essay "Represent: Race, Space, and Place in Rap Music." Aside from Jimi Hendrix, "the city was otherwise not regarded as an important or influential center for musical production or innovation."[24] By the end of the 1980s hip hop had begun to develop in Seattle in ways that were both similar and different to the scenes in established urban areas. Where television shows and films gave New York and LA broad national exposure, cultural representations of Seattle had not yet become widespread. Seattle's rap music, not weighed down as much by a deep history of existing imagery, thus presented a unique opportunity for innovative lyricists to reimagine and re-present the city.

Bruce Pavitt, cofounder of the alternative-oriented Sub Pop label, argued: "One advantage Seattle has is our geographical isolation. It gave a group of artists a chance to create their own sound, instead of feeling pressured to copy others."[25] This comparative independence was on display beyond music and lyrics. Seattle's failure to imitate New York or Los Angeles in any significant manner sprung from the fact that in a post–civil rights urban cultural sense, Seattle was in many ways a work in progress. Geographic seclusion combined with the region's still evolving multiethnic identity to create a fertile environment within which organic, community-based approaches to the various aspects of hip-hop culture eventually flourished.

Seattle's regional isolation has another dimension—its sheer geographic and cultural reach. Aside from Portland, Oregon, the next biggest city south is San Francisco, eight hundred miles away. Minneapolis is the next major city due east, nearly 1,700 miles away. Although most of the areas in between are not known as population centers, nonetheless there are consumers of culture at every point along the way. In *Bad Land: An American Romance*, Seattle author Jonathan Raban documented his drive east through Washington into Idaho and Montana to determine where Seattle's influence ends and Minneapolis's begins.[26] While Raban never determined an exact point, using allegiance to professional baseball teams as a measurement, he found that Mariners fans outnumbered Twins fans as far east as North Dakota. The book showed that Seattle is actually the capital of a vast country, one that identifies with its professional sports teams and other aspects of its cultural life such as glass art, newspapers, alternative rock scenes, and urban styles—that is, Black urban entertainment such as R&B, rap music, hip-hop fashions, and so on.

Charles Mudede, longtime writer and editor for *The Stranger*, a Seattle alternative weekly newspaper, noted that the African and African American populations of Seattle and Tacoma combined to form the largest Black community north of San Francisco and west of Milwaukee. "Because small towns like Twin Falls, Idaho, have young people who are familiar with Black entertainment via national networks like BET," Mudede argued, "they are ripe markets for entrepreneurs who produce events and music within Seattle's black community."[27]

Hip Hop's Early Days in New York City

Culturally and geographically, a place like Twin Falls, Idaho, with a population under fifty thousand, could not have been further from hip hop's origins. The foundations of hip hop were formed in the South Bronx during the 1970s. The four original elements of hip-hop culture included the musical aspect of DJing, the visual art component of graffiti, the kinetic dance portion of b-girling/b-boying (breaking), and the verbal action of MCing or rapping. Different fundamental aspects of these elements can be directly traced to long-held cultural traditions, primarily from Africa and the Caribbean.

A new style of DJ that rocked block parties and community centers around New York City in the 1970s initially evolved from Clive "DJ Kool Herc" Campbell, a native of Jamaica who immigrated to the United States in 1967. These gatherings inspired other aspiring local DJs, such as Grandmaster Flash, who began manipulating two turntables with copies of the same record and a mixer to prolong a favorite section of a favorite song for as long as he chose. The Grand Wizzard Theodore, another local DJ, was credited with inventing the practice of scratching records. Afrika Bambaataa exemplified the diverse nature of early hip hop by sampling a wide and eclectic variety of music, including Kraftwerk, James Brown, Captain Sky, and the score from the film *The Good, the Bad, and the Ugly.*[28] These pioneers and others provided a blueprint that tens of thousands of DJs all over the world still follow today.

Graffiti, the visual artistic portion of hip-hop culture, was one of the first elements of hip hop to make an impression on the general public. In 1971 the message "TAKI 183" began appearing on so many subway cars in New York City that the *New York Times* assigned a reporter to investigate. A July 21, 1971, story reported that TAKI was an unemployed seventeen-year-old Greek kid named Demetrios with nothing better to do than spray his name wherever he happened to be. TAKI was his nickname, and he lived on 183rd Street.[29] Graffiti writers or "bombers" began breaking into train yards at night and painting massive colorful grand design "burners" or "pieces" that would take up entire sides of subway cars. The message changed from TAKI simply saying "I was here" to "I am here, and I'm leaving this behind to show you that I have style; that I am a style master. . . . That I was the first ever to paint a cloud above my 'piece' [short for 'masterpiece']. . . . That I am king, and my style will influence all you 'toys' [shorthand for 'novices']."[30] When trains pulled into a station, writers such as Kase 2 and Dez literally had "captive" commuter audiences all over New York City. Respect within the graffiti community was earned by those who "hit up" the most daring locations or created the most intricate and original designs.

If graffiti is the visual arts component of hip hop, b-girling/ b-boying (or breaking) is the dance component of hip hop. Borrowing elements of various dance styles such as jazz, tap, and lindy-hopping, breaking also sampled from disciplines like Eastern martial arts and capoeira, a Brazilian martial art that combines dance, acrobatics, and music. Early breaking was significantly influenced by Puerto Rican culture and traditions present in New York City during the 1970s.[31] Popping and locking, a primarily upright style of hip-hop dance is more associated with the West Coast and also has roots in Latino dance traditions. Dance historian, writer, and critic Sally Banes theorized that breaking, like other forms of street culture, including graffiti, verbal dueling, and rapping, is a public display of virility, wit, and skill—in short, of style. Breaking serves as a way of using the body to inscribe one's identity on streets and trains, in parks and high school gyms. Most of all, "breaking is a competitive display of physical and imaginative virtuosity, a codified dance-form-cum-warfare that cracks open to flaunt personal inventiveness."[32] Mainstream media seized upon the early massive popularity of breaking as no fewer than three major studio films featuring break dancing—*Beat Street, Breakin'*, and *Breakin' 2: Electric Boogaloo*—were all released in 1984. Breakers were featured in commercials for McDonald's and the closing ceremonies of the 1984 Summer Olympics in Los Angeles.

Although it eventually became the public face of hip hop, MCing or rapping, the verbal facet of hip-hop culture, initially did not receive significant attention. MCs were present at early block parties, but they generally got on the microphone only when the DJ gave permission. Even then the MCs job was to simply tell everyone how great the DJ was and announce any upcoming events.[33] However, the creativity and storytelling of MCs like Busy Bee and Lovebug Starski, who would rap while he was DJing, soon brought the vocalist to the forefront of hip-hop culture.

In the mix of hip hop's birth in the South Bronx and subsequent migration to other boroughs around New York City came Sylvia Robinson. A former recording artist herself in the 1950s and 1960s, Robinson launched her own label, Sugar Hill Records, with her husband, Joe, in 1979. After hearing a DJ rap at a birthday party for a younger relative, Robinson displayed historic forethought by embracing this new music early on. Her visionary sample of the 1979 disco smash "Good Times" by the group Chic as the music behind "Rapper's Delight" was widely credited as one of the keys that made this record so accessible to so many people. Def Jam Records cofounder Russell Simmons noted: "'Good Times' reflected the new aesthetic even if Chic's Nile Rodgers and Bernard Edwards didn't know it when they made the track. It had simple melody, a memorable hook, and an incredible bass, guitar, and drum arrangement that b-boys could instantly relate to."[34]

Robinson herself assembled Wonder Mike, Big Bank Hank, and Master G, collectively known as the Sugarhill Gang. Hank began rapping while working as a bouncer at a local hip-hop club where Double Trouble, featured in the 1983 hip-hop movie *Wild Style*, and others performed. Robinson heard Hank reciting rhymes at his other job in a pizza shop in New Jersey and invited him to join the group on the spot. Wonder Mike, a friend of Robinson's son, was already part of another group from New Jersey, as was Master G. Robinson was impressed enough after hearing both audition to offer them the opportunity to round out the Sugarhill Gang.

Until 1979 hip hop's mobility was essentially limited generally to crude, low-quality cassette tapes. Certainly the people at Sugar Hill Records were not the first ones with the idea of putting hip hop on wax; they simply had the means. "Rapper's Delight" by the Sugarhill Gang, released in the fall of 1979 on New Jersey–based Sugar Hill Records, is widely acknowledged as the song that introduced most of the world to rap music. However, it was not the first rap record. The Fatback Band released a single earlier in 1979 called "You're My Candy Sweet" on Spring Records, with a B side that was a rap called "King Tim III (Personality Jock)." The single became a hit when record stores around New York began playing the rap in preference to the A side, and radio station WKTU followed up with airplay. Unlike "King Tim III," "Rapper's Delight" was a nationally distributed record, which allowed people all over the world to hear the result of what had been building up in New York City.[35]

Once "Rapper's Delight" started getting play, the reception from New York's established hip-hop community was less than enthusiastic. Many felt that Robinson had simply taken their rhymes, attitude, and culture and made a record. "All of us—MCs, DJs, promoters—resented it," Russell Simmons later said. "I personally was wrecked. I had so much animosity toward the Sugarhill Gang. They sure weren't known where the real MCs hung out." Some even thought that "Rapper's Delight" would be hip hop's one-and-only shot at serious exposure. "At first we thought that record had shut the door," Simmons said, "when in reality that door was about to swing wide open."[36]

Hip Hop Arrives in Seattle

For most people in the Pacific Northwest, hip-hop culture first arrived when KYAC, a Seattle-based rhythm and blues/soul music AM radio station that had been around since the early 1970s, began to play

"Rapper's Delight." Robert L. Scott, KYAC program director and a veteran of local radio, took a bold step playing the song when no other station in town would. "Rapper's Delight" quickly received increased radio play, and the twelve-inch vinyl single was sold at Seattle record shops such as Dirt Cheap Records and Music Menu. As early consumers of hip hop began to digest this first offering of rap to the mainstream, a couple of things stood out. First was a line delivered by Wonder Mike in the opening verse of the song:

> You see I am Wonder Mike
> and I'd like to say hello
> to the black to the white
> the red and the brown
> the purple and yellow.[37]

This purposeful shout-out to all the races was significant. The lyric sent the message that everyone was welcome, no matter your skin color. Second, this countered what would become the mainstream version of the hip-hop narrative. In the mind of the general public, hip hop started out as (and today is still) primarily a Black thing. Although hip hop was born out of the African American experience and culture, in practice it has always been as multicultural as the United States itself. Early examples of hip-hop media such as the independent film *Wild Style* and the documentary *Style Wars*, both released in 1983, illustrate this diversity of characters. *Wild Style* held immense power: it allowed many people for the first time to see what hip hop looked and sounded like from a grassroots perspective, instead of as an oddity in a news story. Also, it showed the interconnectedness of the four elements of hip hop for the first time.

Another significant aspect of the lyrical content from "Rapper's Delight" is found in these lines delivered by Big Bank Hank:

> So after school
> I take a dip in the pool
> which is really on the wall
> I got a color TV so I can see
> the Knicks play basketball.[38]

This geographic reference to the New York Knicks, the city's NBA team, was a subtle but important way for the MC to communicate specific allegiances to the listener. At its core, rap music has always been about telling who you are and what it's like where you're from. That type of discourse builds community, and in this way the genre has separated itself from nearly every other form of music. Pioneering Los Angeles rapper Ice-T addressed the practice of representing a city, a neighborhood, or even a street. "That's what you do; as a rapper, you're kinda like a cheerleader for a neighborhood," he said. "That's what a lot of people will ask, 'Why do you always say the name of your [record] label or your street?' Because that's what the rapper does, it's about shoutin' out. You're reppin' a group."[39]

As rap music began to travel, people from different locations figured out that in order to make their own attempts at rhyming relevant, they had to rap about themselves and their environment. Therefore most of those who rapped in the Northwest found themselves pulling from the regional cultural stockpile as it existed at that time. Because New York was the center of this exciting new culture, there were examples of performers who were Seattle natives suddenly claiming to have New York roots, hoping to gain credibility. This inferiority complex was not necessarily unique to Seattle, but remnants of it would continue to shape some local attitudes for decades to come.

By the early 1980s enough people in Seattle had become interested in hip hop that a local scene took root. As it had in New York, Seattle's early hip-hop landscape grew out of three primary sources: nightclubs, community centers, and local events and activities. Some clubs in the area—Club Broadway, Skoochies (later Oz and then DV8), Spectrum, Omni, Encore, Castle Rock, and the Skate King locations in suburban cities such as Bellevue and Burien—simply incorporated the ever-increasing amounts of rap records released into the musical rotation played on Friday and Saturday nights. Other venues actively courted participants by advertising and holding specialized contests and competitions. One example of this was a club called Lateef's, located near the intersection of Rainier Avenue and Rose Street in South Seattle. Lateef's was one of the first local establishments to host regular open mic nights on Fridays and Saturdays. Aspiring rappers would come to show and prove their skill in front of crowds for a $100 first prize. The novelty of rap at this time combined with the relatively limited number of people who would actually get up and perform in front of an audience made these events stand out from the average nightclub scene.[40]

Although older teens were able to get into some clubs like Lateef's, younger teenagers did not have access to these venues. For this underserved demographic, hip hop could also be found within the community at all-age locations such as the Rainier Vista Boys & Girls Club off the northeast corner of Empire Way (now Martin Luther King Jr. Way) and Alaska Street. As an early hub for hip hop–related activities in Southeast Seattle, Rainier Vista had regular dance and rap contests and held dances on the weekends featuring local DJs, including a young Sir Mix-A-Lot. Prime all-age locations in the Central District included the Langston Hughes Performing Arts Institute on Seventeenth Avenue South and Yesler Way as well as the Rotary Boys & Girls Club located at the corner of East Spruce Street and Nineteenth Avenue. In addition, several community and city events showcased different aspects of hip hop. These included the Black Community Parade and Festival held at Judkins Park, the Funfest talent competition at Garfield High School, the annual Festival Sundiata, Folklife Festival, Bumbershoot, and 4H events all held downtown at the Seattle Center. Other gatherings at house parties, school dances, and in church basements also served as outlets for Seattle's expanding hip-hop scene.

A variety of media delivery methods—including films, record stores, newspapers, and cable television—also contributed to the spread of hip-hop culture in Seattle. The producers of *Wild Style*, the first hip-hop movie, released in 1983, cast people who were actively involved in New York's hip-hop movement instead of professional actors, like graffiti writers Lee Quinones, Fred "Fab 5 Freddy" Brathwaite, and Sandra "Pink" Fabara as well as MC Busy Bee, which gave the film a documentary feel as it made its way around the country. Although *Wild Style* was received warmly by young people eager to take in anything hip hop related, the mainstream regarded it with uncertainty. "The film looks to be a partly improvised piece of fiction, about the cheeky, high-spirited art of the south Bronx, that is, subway graffiti, also known as 'writing,' and about rapping and breaking," wrote critic Vincent Canby in the *New York Times*. "The slight narrative of *Wild Style* is about Raymond (Lee George Quinones), a skinny, outwardly mild-mannered Bronx teen-ager by day and, by night, the notorious 'Zorro,' a celebrated but unidentified spray-paint artist for whom every subway car is an empty canvas."[41]

While the movie underscored the utter desolation and urban decay that was the South Bronx in the early 1980s, it also captured the creative vibe and desire to innovate that characterized hip hop from the start. The film allowed the visual component of evolving hip-hop style to be seen and imitated by Seattle youth eager to match a look with the sound. This included iconic accessories like Puma and Adidas sneakers with fat shoelaces; sweatsuits, Kangol bucket hats, oversized belt buckles, and Cazal glasses; names emblazoned on T-shirts and sweatshirts with iron-on letters; giant, colorful graffiti "pieces" spray-painted around the city; and the practice of carrying around a piece of linoleum that would serve as a surface to break-dance on outdoors instead of simply spinning on concrete or dirt.[42]

As key social and cultural community spaces, record stores played an important role in hip hop's entry and spread throughout Seattle. Scattered around the city in various locations, these independently owned outlets filled a space in the still infant rap market that the larger chain stores such as Tower Records and Musicland did not. Dirt Cheap Records on the corner of Twenty-second Avenue and East Union Street was one of the first in town to carry "Rapper's Delight" in the fall of 1979. Another early adopter was Music Menu, near the intersection of Rainier Avenue South and Twenty-third Avenue. It was operated by "Shockmaster" Glen Boyd, who would go on to write for *The Rocket,* the Seattle–based free monthly newspaper that covered arts, culture, and music, and cohost the program *Rap Attack* with "Nasty" Nes Rodriguez on radio station KCMU. Music Menu developed a reputation around the greater Seattle area for stocking the latest and hottest in rap music. Other independent outlets included Beverly's Records & Tapes located at the corner of Twenty-third Avenue and Jackson Street, Little Record Mart on East Madison Street, and Rainier Records and Imports at the corner of Rainier Avenue South and South Holly Street.

Despite an active local print media landscape, initially there were a limited number of print outlets that devoted space to Seattle hip hop. In fact, essentially the only local publication that consistently covered hip hop in the Pacific Northwest during the 1980s was *The Rocket,* published from 1979 through 2000. At its peak *The Rocket's* circulation approached one hundred thousand between Seattle and Portland, and the paper had a staff of twenty. One of the first writers to cover hip hop for *The Rocket* was senior editor Robert Newman. *The Rocket* devoted column space to the likes of the dance/rap crew the Emerald Street Boys and became the rare local media outlet to deliver news of early Seattle hip hop to the entire city.[43]

At the same time, the rise of cable television and the resulting need for programming also offered occasional opportunities for the public to experience hip hop. Although MTV was launched in 1981, the network initially ignored most African American artists not named Michael Jackson or Prince. However, by 1983 alternatives began to appear. One example was *Night Tracks,* a late-night weekend show introduced by Atlanta-based superstation WTBS that featured a number of the Black artists MTV would not play. In addition, the fledgling USA network carried a four-hour evening music video show called *Night Flight,* which had recurring episodes focusing on hip hop. A description of the program in the *Seattle Times* television guide at the time said: "Take Off to Street Music—The Phenomena of 'Hip-Hop,' 'Rapping,' and 'Break Dancing' are portrayed in videos featuring The Gap Band, The New Edition, Gladys Knight, Malcolm McClaren, *Flashdance,* and others."[44]

— —

Nearly from the start, the Black experience that initially informed hip hop in Seattle was considerably different than in other areas of the United States. Local African Americans voted in the 1880s, and during the 1960s institutional issues such as housing and employment discrimination were for the most part effectively addressed amid the Civil Rights movement by organizations such as the Urban League, the NAACP, and CORE. Groups like the Black Panthers remained active addressing numerous other grassroots issues within the community. Racism and prejudice were present, just without the firehoses and lynchings that became symbolic in places like the Deep South. This relatively progressive atmosphere and a still developing urban identity was nurtured within the geographic isolation of the Pacific Northwest, and a new culture of innovation that spanned from business to the arts began to emerge.

As hip hop's first generation became active in Seattle during the 1980s, DJs and MCs, like the Emerald Street Boys and the Emerald Street Girls, "Nasty" Nes Rodriguez, and Sir Mix-A-Lot emerged alongside such entities as the Boys & Girls Club in the Central District, Lateef's, among the first nightclubs in Seattle to cater to hip hop, and radio station KKFX 1250 AM to lay a dynamic local foundation. Meanwhile, the activity of numerous breakers and graffiti writers in the area ensured that all four of the original elements of hip hop would be well represented in Seattle moving forward. That forward movement provided the necessary opening for the hip hop–based exportation of local culture. Within the decade Seattle hip hop would be heard not just nationally but internationally as well.

2

"Go back the other way, we'll stop and eat at Dick's"

SEATTLE HIP HOP IN THE 1980S

BEFORE they even met as teens, James Croone and Edward Wells had heard of each other. In the Wild West atmosphere of hip hop that was Seattle's Central District in the early 1980s, word spread quickly once it became known that someone could rap or dance. Young hip-hop kids became like traveling gunfighters going from town to town looking for a duel. Countless "battles" took place in parks, on sidewalks, and in backyards all over the CD. Croone and Wells had both become hooked on hip hop after hearing "Rapper's Delight." They worked on their dance moves and rap skills, practicing on the way to school and entering talent shows. When Wells heard that there was another kid in the neighborhood who might be able to take him out, he went on a mission. Wells and Croone met and battled, each leaving impressed with the other. It was this confrontation that introduced Eddie "Sugar Bear" Wells and James "Captain Crunch" Croone.[1]

Wells and Croone formed their first group together, The Terrible 2, in 1980. By this time, some Seattle nightclubs had started to offer open mic nights in response to the surging popularity of rap music. However, few people were ready to perform in public, and nearly all of them were teenagers like Wells and Croone. Despite this, popular club Lateef's in South Seattle was holding regular open mic nights as well as actual rap contests.[2] The Terrible 2 entered their first rap contest at Lateef's and lost to another duo, Gary Jam and Big Boss Cross, known collectively as Jam Delight. Croone and Wells then met Robert "Sweet J" Jamerson, whose addition to the group meant the name would have to be changed. After a naming competition held in the summer of 1981, the Seattle-King County Convention and Visitors Bureau adopted the nickname "The Emerald City" in an effort to promote tourism. Since Croone, Wells, and Jamerson had all grown up on the streets of Seattle, Wells came up with the group's new name: the Emerald Street Boys.[3]

Emerald Street Boys Develop the Rap Scene

As the Emerald Street Boys became more polished, they began performing at venues like the Empire Plaza on Empire Way (today's Martin Luther King Jr. Way), the Nighthawk in South Seattle, and various
events for the Central Area Motivation Program (CAMP), which promoted institutional and community change through advocacy. Soon
the group started playing spots that catered to more traditionally
white audiences, such as Fisherman's Restaurant on Pier 57 and the
Dragon Palace on Broadway, where the Emerald Street Boys appeared
on the bill with an assortment of new wave bands. In addition, the
group made appearances at community events such as the Black Community Festival in Judkins Park and the cultural and music festivals
Bumbershoot and Festival Sundiata, both held at the Seattle Center.[4]

By early 1982, the Emerald Street Boys had started to generate
some buzz in the local media. In February the group performed a
benefit at the National Guard Armory on Elliot Avenue, which was
reviewed by journalist Robert Newman in *The Rocket*. "The Emerald
Street Boys lived up to their reputation," Newman wrote. "Seattle may
not be the Bronx, but the Boys are great. They did a mighty job of
rapping and rocking the house." After noting their ages (at the time
Croone and Jamerson were sixteen, Wells fifteen) Newman continued: "Although the word cute does come to mind, the Boys are both
talented and sophisticated in both dancing and rapping. Rapping
in unison is this group's strength, and they use it to good effect."
He ended the review this way: "The Emerald Street Boys have been
together for about a year and a half, playing clubs and parties around
Seattle, and the word on the street is that they're this city's best."[5]

The June 1982 issue of *The Rocket* featured a review of a mix performed by Wells (aka Sugar Bear). Writer Karl Kotas lamented the fact
that Sugar Bear, like numerous other DJs at the time, had made Tom
Tom Club's 1981 hit "Genius of Love" the focus of his mix. After label-
ing the Emerald Street Boys "the best known of local rap ensembles,"
Kotas explained: "While unable to wax rhapsodic due to overexposure
to the underlying material, I must note that it is an interesting rework-
ing . . . executed with technical competence. The realization that this
had been cut 'live' with two turntables and a mixing board made for a
more appreciative listening." Kotas mentioned Sugar Bear's inclusion
of vocal samples from such celebrities Ed McMahon, Steve Martin,
and Richard Pryor, concluding that while "sometimes eerie and often

witty, this is as good as similar East Coast material." Kotas noted that although Sugar Bear's mixes were not available commercially, they could be heard on radio station KRAB's (107.7 FM) weekday afternoon drive program *Urban Renewal* hosted by Herb Levy.[6]

The Emerald Street Boys won the All City Rap-Off at the 1982 Black Community Festival and also opened for the Gap Band at the Seattle Center Arena. They performed with the Silver Chain Gang (Duke of Earl, Sir Wesley, and Jazzy D) and the Emerald Street Girls (formed as a duo about a year after the debut of the Emerald Street Boys) at the high-profile fifth anniversary party of the performing arts theater On the Boards. By now, the competitive climate of hip hop in Seattle had begun to take shape with acts like 3D, West Coast Funk Brigade, Deputy Rhyme, West Side Threat, and Duke & Double Rock contributing to the depth of local talent. Most of this music reflected the traditional Roland 808 drum machine–based New York style, the techno/funk-centric sound of early Los Angeles hip hop, or a combination of both.[7]

Soon after formation of the Emerald Street Boys, "Nasty" Nes Rodriguez, a Filipino American DJ and radio personality on station KKFX (KFOX) 1250 AM, became their DJ. At live events Rodriguez would play instrumentals from popular twelve-inch singles for the group to rhyme and dance to. The Emerald Street Boys also performed the introduction for Nes's show on KFOX.[8] This early African American–Asian American collaboration in a rap group wasn't entirely unique to Seattle but set multiethnic collaborative work as part of the foundation of the Seattle hip-hop scene.

In 1983 the Emerald Street Boys continued to play local events like Bumbershoot and the Seafair Parade. Newman, who had written several articles on the Emerald Street Boys for *The Rocket*, marched in the Seafair Parade with the group. They "danced and performed along the parade route, attracting a giant crowd of adoring teens," he recalled. "Their soundtrack consisted of me carrying a giant boombox and playing the instrumental side of [Grandmaster Flash & the Furious Five's hit 1983 song] 'The Message' over and over."[9] The Emerald Street Boys were doing shows not only in the Seattle area but also in Portland, Oregon, and Canada. Also that year the group recorded Seattle's first rap record, *Christmas Rap* (B side "The Move"), produced by Tony "Tony B" Benton and released by his label Telemusic Productions. Benton had learned the music business in 1978 while working at Music Menu record store. He had formed an R&B group named Teleclere, and their single "Ultra Groove," written about in *The Rocket,* became the number one song on "C-89" KNHC 89.5 FM. Benton supervised the live instrumentation that served as the music for "Christmas Rap" and "The Move." As the first local artists to release a rap record, the Emerald Street Boys emerged as one of the early faces of the Seattle hip-hop scene.[10]

In 1984 the New York group the Treacherous Three—Special K, L.A. Sunshine, and Kool Moe Dee—was one of the best known rap groups in the world. Run DMC had yet to truly take off, having just released their self-titled debut album. As Newman noted in *The Rocket*: "Now that Grandmaster Flash and the Furious 5 have splintered, there's no group that can touch the [Treacherous] 3's track record." Coming into their performance at the Seattle Center Exhibition Hall, the Treacherous Three were fresh off their scene-stealing appearance in the iconic hip-hop movie *Beat Street*, where they performed the memorable song "Santa Rap." In addition, the Treacherous Three had a starring role in the pilot for the new hip-hop television variety show *Graffiti Rock*. Event promoter Ed Locke billed the Seattle show as the "Beat Street Breakdown."[11] Before the show the two crews hung out together as the Emerald Street Boys showed the Treacherous Three around Seattle. The groups played basketball against each other and even held an impromptu dance battle while downtown, which the Emerald Street Boys claimed to have won.[12] Newman echoed this likelihood in his review of the concert in *The Rocket*. "As dancers," he wrote, "they [the Treacherous Three] couldn't match the popping pyrotechnics of the opening act, the Emerald Street Boys."[13]

The range of the Emerald Street Boys soon extended beyond recording songs and preparing dance routines. Local director Steve Sneed had worked on community programs at the Central District Boys & Girls Club in 1981. With a background in theater, he started collaborating with Reco Bembry to produce *Street Life*, an original play written by James Lollie. The play, which included members of the Emerald Street Boys, ran at the Broadway Performance Hall on the campus of Seattle Central Community College in 1985. Sneed and Bembry, who helped manage the Emerald Street Boys and would eventually form a production company called Sneeco, developed the connection between local theater and hip hop with 1986's *Boys Will B-Boys*. Housed at On the Boards and originally set to feature the Emerald Street Boys, internal conflicts and disagreements within the group forced the producers to recast the Silver Chain Gang in the starring role. This essentially marked the beginning of the end for the Emerald Street Boys as the face of early Seattle hip hop. As more local artists emerged amid the quickly expanding cultural landscape, fresh and new options became increasingly available. In time, the Emerald Street Boys, and most other early groups, disbanded and went on to do other things.

Sneed continued his work at the Langston Hughes Performing Arts Institute in the Central District in 1988. The Langston Hughes facility was largely vacant at the time, did not have an overseeing board, and there was talk from the city of tearing down the building. Sneed organized the center and focused on making space available to community artists, musicians, and other performers in need of venues and practice space. The idea was based on the "late night" basketball model employed by community centers across the country, which made gyms available for teenagers to drop in and play at such nontraditional hours as Friday and Saturday nights. Similarly, Sneed made Langston Hughes available for drop-in rehearsals and performances. Combined with classes on acting, theater, and music production, the program allowed hundreds of local youth to develop skills and interests in the arts in an era when these programs were being eliminated in schools. Another example of Sneed's work at Langston Hughes intersecting with hip hop was a play called *Peer Pressure*, which featured Derrick "Vitamin D" Brown.[14]

As the Emerald Street Boys moved on, many things about the group and its significance reverberated throughout the local scene for decades. The initial mixed racial composition of the group, engagement with other non–hip-hop community arts associations, the endorsement of performers who reflected gender diversity, and the dedication to growing community spaces for youth and others to create opportunities for supporting hip-hop arts and culture in a grassroots way all carried on in Seattle's hip-hop world for years to come.

Seattle Breaking and Graffiti in the Early 1980s

Although Seattle rappers received a good deal of attention early on, local participants in other areas of hip hop were also laying foundations. In 1984 the *Seattle Times* ran a feature story on breaking in its Arts and Entertainment section. In the largest and oldest daily newspaper in town, this story introduced many in Seattle to hip hop for the first time. "Break dancing, or 'breaking,' has broken out of the ghetto and on to prime-time television, ballet stages, even Seattle streets," the article began. It described breaking as "an athletic dance form that originated a decade ago on the sidewalks of New York. Practiced mainly by Black and Hispanic boys, it has developed as part of an East Coast urban subculture called 'hip hop' characterized by its own slang, graffiti, clothing styles and music." The *Times* also expanded on the musical context of breaking. "Breakers perform to the sounds coming from a 'box'—a bulky portable radio and cassette player—blaring 'rap music,' characterized by hypnotic, controversial lyrics backed by a rhythmic, usually electronic, beat." [15]

Later the same year activist, singer, and actor Harry Belafonte and the New York–based Rock Steady Crew arrived to promote their movie *Beat Street* at the Seattle Film Festival. Belafonte was a show business giant with Emmy, Grammy, and Tony Awards, and *Beat Street* represented the first time he produced a film in which he did not star. Belafonte explained that many young people attracted to breaking had been relegated to a "life of deprivation; the absence of opportunity, and they've become victims of the promises of leaders who represent power and influence and allude to their supposed humanity. This whole idea of this emergence, this force, from this rather oppressed, bleak world is like a phoenix rising from the ashes." While on tour supporting *Beat Street*, Belafonte claimed to have witnessed breakers in such cities as Berlin, Copenhagen, Rio de Janeiro, and Tokyo while arguing the positive benefits of the culture. "It crosses social-economic lines, and it's very much what rock music used to mean. The hip-hop culture is real folk art, like gospel music. It had no place in the mainstream at the beginning, and it set its own standards, its own taste." [16]

Fans of breaking got another boost on June 30, 1984, when local NBC affiliate KING television aired the pilot for the Michael Holman–produced hip-hop variety show *Graffiti Rock*. The program featured the New York City Breakers along with the Treacherous Three and Run DMC. [17] Meanwhile local dance continued to expand as the West Side Crew and Seattle Circuit Breakers performed at the Broadway Performance Hall on the campus of Seattle Central Community College as guests of the Ewajo Dance Workshop. The competitive atmosphere around local breaking took on a New York feel as downtown Seattle became a prime area for b-girls and b-boys to meet up and battle. Two primary spots emerged as hubs for local breakers. One was the Seattle Center. Located at the northern end of downtown, the seventy-four-acre campus was dedicated in 1962 as part of the "Century 21" World's Fair, and included the now iconic Space Needle. [18]

The open spaces and festive atmosphere made the Seattle Center a natural environment for spontaneous battles between rival crews. The fact that the Space Needle was a major tourist destination, combined with several large-scale community events every spring and summer at the Seattle Center, meant there were always plenty of people around to watch. The other location was in front of the McDonald's on the corner Third Avenue and Pine Street. This intersection specifically represented a significant center of activity in an already busy and growing downtown area. Pine Street ran east to west and brought large amounts of traffic directly from Broadway and Capitol Hill to Westlake Center and the heart of downtown. In addition, Third Avenue was one of the few two-way north-south streets in downtown Seattle, which gave the corner a unique, centralized feel.

Local crews and individuals frequently roamed these areas and others in search of a battle. However, the rules of competition were not always rigid. It was not uncommon to have random dancers form a spontaneous crew and battle another just-made-up crew on the spot. This dynamic was similar to a pick-up basketball environment where teams form organically to play against each other. The romanticized version of hip-hop history states that during a time when street gangs were on the rise, breaking came and offered a peaceful, competitive alternative that dramatically reduced gang violence. While this may have been true to a certain extent, trying not only to defeat but publicly humiliate your opponent within a testosterone-laden environment led to a fair amount of animosity and physical confrontation beyond simply dancing.

Soon more organized and formal events began to appear around the area. One example was *Summer Break*, a 1984 exhibition cosponsored by the Seattle Department of Parks and Recreation and televised by local ABC affiliate KOMO. The event received advance press in the *Seattle Times*, with preliminary rounds held at the Langston Hughes Performing Arts Institute, followed by fifteen groups and fifteen individuals advancing to compete at the Seattle Center. The broadcast of the competition also featured an accompanying report by the host, veteran local weatherman Steve Poole, as he attempted to simultaneously learn and explain the basics of breaking and hip-hop fashion to the Seattle viewing public.[19]

Early local dancers included such individuals as "Seattle's first break dancer" Jonathan "Junior" Alefaio, Flex, 3D, Special T, Junior Bopper, Leland, Ziggy "Zig Zag" Puaa, Rafael Contreras, Carlos "Sir

Slam-A-Lot" Barrientes, Danny Molino, Dave "Pablo D" Narvaez, David
Toledo, and Spencer Reed. There were numerous active dance crews,
including the Emerald City Breakers, West Side, Seattle Circuit Breakers, DeRoxy Crew, 1st Degree Breakers, Breaking Mechanism, Fresh
Force, and Seattle City Breakers. Lateef's, Stallions, Club Broadway,
Spectrum, Buzzy's, Skoochies, and Club Fremont were all popular
clubs for breakers and breaking contests in the area. Community
centers, YMCAs, and school assemblies also provided opportunities for
breaking exhibitions. Other styles of hip-hop dance in the mid-1980s
such as the "Pee-Wee," based on comedian Pee-wee Herman, enjoyed
brief spells of popularity, and the "Prep" even spawned dance-specific
crews such as the Ducky Boys and PPIA (Party People In Action).[20]

As the early local scene developed, it became visibly apparent
that graffiti was another aspect of hip hop that was putting down local
roots. The 1983 premiere of the landmark documentary film *Style
Wars*, on Seattle's PBS affiliate KCTS Channel 9, delivered a spectacle
of street art to eager young eyes. *Style Wars* taught the rest of the
world a lesson about graffiti that New Yorkers already had learned
from TAKI 183—if you "get up" enough in the right places, people
will know your name. The film followed several notorious graffiti
writers including Min One, Dez, Iz, and Seen as they snuck through
New York's subway tunnels to train yards, avoiding the deadly electric
third rails. Armed only with cans of spray paint, they outran transit
police to "create mural masterpieces with block letters and cartoon
figures, all in the name of fame. *Style Wars* documents the thrill of
seeing their so-called 'wild style' graffiti tags on passing subway
trains throughout the city."[21]

Immediately following the airing of *Style Wars*, early examples
of oversized aerosol art began to appear on various walls around
the Central District. The overall size of these initial paintings was
relatively small in contrast with the works that took up entire sides of
train cars in New York City. This changed in 1984 when a block-long
"burner" was painted on the side of Nordstrom's flagship department
store in downtown Seattle by DC3 and Kuo "Mr. Clean" Yang. In New
York graffiti artists used the subway as not only a canvas but also a
mobile exhibit to show off their work to each other and the general
public. Without this option Seattle artists chose walls that were easily
visible on the most traveled roads, such as Twenty-third Avenue and
Martin Luther King Jr. Way in the Central District, Rainier Avenue,
and downtown locations like First Avenue, Pine Street, the old City

Light building, and both ends of the Alaskan Way Viaduct. Another way to ensure graffiti would be seen by young people was to target schools, which gave rise to competitive painters trying to go "all-city" by having pieces at every junior high and high school in the city. Meanwhile others, known as "daytime bombers," chose to paint on several "legal walls" located around town.[22]

Without a formal strategy to combat it, Seattle police rarely caught graffiti in-progress. Detectives were sometimes assigned to the most prolific cases, and the city itself would not have a dedicated graffiti clean-up squad until 1994. Throughout the 1980s a growing group of local graffiti artists (including Spraycan, DadOne, Fleeks, Spaide, KeepOne, Skreen, Faze, Sam Sneke, Shylo, Shame, Danny Molino, Bizlove, Michael "Specs Wizard" Hall, Bazerk, and Dorian "Solo Doe" Dinish) were leaving increasingly complex and advanced designs for the public to digest. Two seminal aerosol pieces would be a forty-foot mural along the athletic track at Garfield High School in 1985 by David "Image 8000" Toledo and Bobby "Vision" Charles as well as a piece titled *ImageNemo* at Gas Works Park by Toledo and Sean "Nemo" Casey completed in 1987.[23]

"Nasty" Nes Meets Sir Mix-A-Lot and the Local Rap Scene Grows

As it had in New York, radio played an early and crucial role in building a community around hip hop in Seattle. Without a doubt, the first person most responsible for this dynamic locally was "Nasty" Nes Rodriguez, who had arrived in the United States from the Philippines in 1970. Following his graduation from Roosevelt High School in 1979, Rodriguez studied media communications at Bellevue Community College. Rodriguez loved "Rapper's Delight," and after visiting his sister in New York City, he requested she start recording local radio shows for him. The cassette tapes that arrived in the mail included pioneers like Jellybean Benitez and The Latin Rascals on WKTU, Frankie Crocker on WBLS, and the first rap radio show, *Mr. Magic's Rap Attack* on WHBI.

In the late 1970s, KYAC (1250 AM) was Seattle's leading radio source for Black music. Rodriguez landed an internship at the station and was charged with answering the request line. When KYAC underwent an ownership change in 1980, it switched its call letters to KKFX, informally known as KFOX. Rodriguez applied for a job at the new station, and program director Steve Mitchell hired him to host a show from 7:00 to 9:00 on Sunday nights called *FreshTracks*.

Initially the format of the show was to spotlight new music, primarily rhythm and blues or rap. However, the number of requests for rap songs dominated all others, and by 1981 *FreshTracks* became the first rap radio show west of the Mississippi River.

From the beginning, *FreshTracks* was a game changer. Live mixing and scratching on two turntables was completely new to Seattle radio. This foreign sound of Nasty Nes "in the mix" along with the rapid rise in popularity of hip hop created a diverse cross-section of listeners. Nes introduced his "Mastermix," a thirty-minute nonstop blend of popular songs. While based primarily in rap, these mastermixes followed in the footsteps of Afrika Bambaataa and pulled music from an eclectic variety of genres and artists, including Kraftwerk, Hall and Oates, and Los Angeles–based Egyptian Lover. After achieving sky-high ratings, *FreshTracks* was extended to Monday through Friday. This new weeknight program was called *Night Beat* and ran from 7:00 to midnight. Even though KFOX was an AM music station, *Night Beat* became one of the highest rated shows in the city, outperforming competitors on the FM side of the dial.

In 1984, Nasty Nes heard about a series of parties being held at the Boys & Girls Club in the Central District and went to investigate. Every weekend, someone who called himself Sir Mix-A-Lot was packing the gym, and for a dollar per person he gave the crowd a complete one-man show. Mix-A-Lot, who could cut, mix, and scratch records as well as rap, commanded the crowd. Thoroughly impressed by what he saw, Nes invited Mix-A-Lot onto KFOX to air his music. Mix's underground material, which included songs like "7 Rainier," "Square Dance Rap," and "Let's G," now got wide airplay. Sir Mix-A-Lot became the most popular artist on KFOX, receiving more phone-in requests than even Michael Jackson and Prince. This exercise in musical democracy indicated Seattle pride in a local artist who seemed poised to take the baton from the Emerald Street Boys.[24]

A Seattle native, Anthony "Sir Mix-A-Lot" Ray, grew up in the Bryant Manor Apartments on East Yesler Way in the Central District. He graduated from Roosevelt High School in 1981 without any formal musical training but had an ear and a passion for music. He also possessed a knack for working with machines and systems. This led Mix-A-Lot to begin experimenting and creating music with machines like the Roland 808 drum machine, Korg and Moog synthesizers, and a Commodore 64 computer. Mix-A-Lot drew inspiration from the Emerald Street Boys, the first hip-hop performers in town to draw extended attention in the local media. He briefly DJd for the group Jam Delight and by 1983 was making songs and DJing on weekends at the Rainier Vista Boys & Girls Club in South Seattle. Mix-A-Lot moved locations and began playing at the Rotary Boys & Girls Club in the Central District. Word-of-mouth spread throughout the CD about these parties, and while Mix-A-Lot was busy setting up his equipment inside the gymnasium, hordes of excited young people gathered for impromptu preshow breaking and rap battles.

From the start, Sir Mix-A-Lot's material was completely self-composed and arranged. One song attacked people who copied his tapes without permission with new "boom boxes" that had two-cassette tape decks. This technology enabled anyone to copy music and essentially gave rise to a homegrown form of musical bootlegging. "Square Dance Rap," with its digitized Alvin and the Chipmunks–like vocals, built on the tradition of hip-hop producers sampling from other musical genres. Another song, "Cap Rap," drew directly from the Black oral folk tradition of delivering humorous and clever insults. By 1985 the attention Mix-A-Lot generated brought bookings at more diverse venues around the city. As his star began to rise, so did his confidence. Although he had performed at Club Broadway, the Seattle Center Exhibition Hall, and the Mountaineers Club, he spent most of his time in his Rainier Beach apartment with a "private arsenal of synthesizers, computers and turntables."

Quoted in *The Rocket* in 1985, Mix-A-Lot said, "I come up with stuff as good, from a musician's standpoint, as anything by [New York producer] Hashim or Dr. Dre, and I do it right here in this room." However, in the already competitive world of hip hop there were inevitable critics of what local music writer Glen Boyd described as Mix-A-Lot's "funk technology." Portland, Oregon artist Chris "Vitamix" Blanchard complained: "The West Coast Sound sucks. There's no street feel to it anymore, just all these synthesizers. Well anyone can spend $4,000 on synthesizers and be the best DJ in town. But where's the talent? I'm for rawness, this is supposed to be street music."[25] Mix-A-Lot's music, sold initially out of the trunk of his car, soon became available at local record stores like Music Menu. As his popularity grew, Nasty Nes and Mix-A-Lot considered the idea of creating their own record label. Nes and partner Brett Carlson had launched a short-lived label called Cold Rock Records in 1983. Using a combination of Nes and Mix-A-Lot's names, NastyMix Records was founded in 1985 along with partners Ed Locke and Greg Jones.

As the 1980s progressed, in addition to the growing popularity of Sir Mix-A-Lot, ever increasing numbers of local participants helped deliver new ideas and creative energy to a culture that had massive appetites for both. Early figures like the Silver Chain Gang, West Side Threat, Sounds of Seattle, the Central Crew, the Emerald Street Girls, Deputy Rhyme, Duke and Double Rock, Robert "MC Le Rap" Spikes, Demetrius White, and Bill "Mr. Bill" Pleasant all helped expand the early scene. One of the first Seattle artists to reach markets outside of the Pacific Northwest was Chris "Big Boss" Cross, who, along with Gary Jam, formed the crew Jam Delight. Cross, from West Seattle, was a self-taught musician influenced by techno-funk artists like the Gap Band, Parliament-Funkadelic, and Egyptian Lover. Big Boss's first release was a mini-cassette single, "Pimpin' Wit Me," which sold poorly in stores but created substantial street buzz. Boss said his goal with the song was "to make something so loud and funky, it couldn't be ignored. You either love 'Pimpin' Wit Me' or hate it. Street people could relate to it." Boss's breakout 1986 song "Party Invader" was the result of new technological tools that more hip-hop producers were employing. He used a Korg Poly 800 synthesizer, a Linn Drum Computer, Yamaha Reverb, and Digital Delay, running everything except his vocals through a computer. Picked up for distribution by Los Angeles–based Macola Records, "Party Invader" generated attention in Chicago and New York City.[26]

Disc jockeys like Roc "Select-A-Roc" Caldwell also increased the depth of the Seattle scene by using available community spaces, such as the basement of the Madrona Presbyterian Church on Thirty-second Avenue in the Central District, to carve out underground hip-hop hotspots. These events would routinely fill the room with young people and loud music on weekend nights in an atmosphere that was relatively inexpensive, safe, and family-friendly. DJs like Brian "JOC (Jammin On Cuts)" Hatfield and John "Frostmaster Chill" Funches Jr. also represented the grassroots scene, which consisted mainly of house parties and battles such as the one Frostmaster Chill recalled from 1984 "at the Recreational Youth Center. They had DJs E.Z. Shock and Capt. Love and MCs Daddy D, Sir Lover, and Master T. I ate them on one mix." Frostmaster Chill, along with The Freeze MCs, eventually opened for the L.A. Dream Team at Seattle's Trade Center in 1985.[27]

While individual artists sought battle victories and new audiences, collectives were becoming a feature within Seattle hip hop. The Freeze MCs—Greg "Colonel G" Steen, David "Daddy D" Blanchard, and Michael "Mellow Mike" Thomas—were one early example. Alliances like Creative Choice and the Cosmic Legion, which included Sir Mix-A-Lot, "Nasty" Nes Rodriguez, Maharaji, Funk Fresh Jazz, Phantom of the Scratch, and female rapper Wicked Angel, were local performers who found strength in numbers. This phenomenon wasn't unique to Seattle hip hop and could be found in places like New York City with Public Enemy's 98 Posse and in Los Angeles, where the first album by the group Niggaz Wit Attitude was titled *NWA and the Posse*.

Another important example of local collaboration was the Emerald Street Girls, formed by cousins Mia "Angel Face" Black and Doretha "Playmate" Johnson. They performed intricate choreographed dance routines with their rhymes during live shows at places like the Black Community Festival and historic Washington Hall. Soon after, Bobbie "Luscious Lynn" Solomon and Jenell "Black Velvet" Cole joined the group as the Emerald Street Girls began to play more gigs, including sharing the bill at the high-profile fifth anniversary party of On the Boards alongside the Emerald Street Boys. Although the group soon disbanded and went their separate ways, the significance of the Emerald Street Girls cannot be overlooked. As much as the Emerald Street Boys helped innovate Seattle hip hop, Angel Face, Playmate, Luscious, and Velvet were also pioneers who ensured that an element of gender diversity was present in the early local scene.

Although there was plenty of overall activity and an artist like Boss Cross had gotten some recognition in a few out-of-town markets, by 1986 local rap music was embroiled in a crisis that seemed to be driven both by politics and identity. The question around Seattle was increasingly two-sided: (1) Who was going to be the first hip-hop artist from Seattle to "make it?"; and (2) Why hadn't it happened yet? Glen Boyd noted: "There is a myth surrounding hip-hop in the Pacific Northwest that we are one WEAK bunch of lumberjacks, and Seattle in particular has about as dead a rap as those new McDonald's commercials. Well, yes and no." Boyd argued the perceived sluggish growth of local hip hop was because "the powers that be in Seattle have not exactly been receptive to the sounds of the street. I'm talking to you, club owners, booking agents, radio programmers, 'industry types' in general." Ed Locke, president of Impact Productions and NastyMix Records, lamented the lack of opportunities for hip hop in Seattle. "The size of the market is small in the first place, and we don't have a lot of support on the radio, although Nes (Rodriguez) does what he can," Locke said. "The house DJs at the clubs get full houses on their own, so they don't want to book local artists. Club Broadway will let a rapper walk on once in a while, for free. This is due to the conservative nature of the market."[28]

Already a writer covering the scene, Boyd soon found another platform to engage hip hop with the arrival of Seattle's first FM rap radio show. AM options for hip hop had expanded with the founding of the Central District–based "Z Twins," KRIZ and KZIZ, Washington State's only African American–owned and –operated radio stations, by Chris H. Bennett, in the early 1980s. Although Nathan Hale High School station KNHC 89.5 FM, aka "C-89," was known to play some hip hop beginning in the early 1980s, it did so infrequently. In 1987, Boyd's radio program *Shock Frequency* premiered on KCMU 90.3 FM. During his debut broadcast, Boyd received a call from a friend who dubbed Boyd the "Shockmaster." The show was renamed *Rap Attack* in 1988, when "Nasty" Nes Rodriguez joined to cohost with the Shockmaster.[29]

Hip Hop and Central District Social Action

Meanwhile, an early instance of hip hop's connection with local social action began in November 1985, when the vacant Colman School building located at the southern edge of the Central District was occupied by several veteran African American activists. The group, which included Omari Tahir-Garrett, Earl Debman, Michael Greenwood, and Charlie James, was collectively known as the Citizen's Support Committee for the African American Heritage Museum/Cultural Center. They demanded that the building be used to house a Black history museum and community center. Although the water and power were soon shut off, the site was used to display books, works of art, and cultural artifacts while also hosting community events. The Seattle School District, which owned the building, notified the group that they were trespassing but took no further action in an effort to avoid a confrontation. The occupation lasted for eight years and has been cited as the longest continuous act of civil disobedience in United States history.[30]

In 1986 the Citizens' Support Committee held a benefit show featuring Los Angeles artist Egyptian Lover. He was a hip-hop pioneer, who DJd parties in the early 1980s at large-scale venues such as the LA Sports Arena before as many as ten thousand people. The techno/electro style of his most popular single, "Egypt, Egypt" (1984), helped define the sound of early West Coast hip hop.[31] Egyptian Lover played shows on consecutive nights at the Colman School gymnasium in support of the occupation. Roughly two hundred people attended each show, and, while there was no cover charge for either concert, donations were collected in support of the Citizens' Support Committee.[32]

The Teen Dance Ordinance and Seattle's Youth Music Scene

By the mid-1980s problems associated with local teen nightlife were getting increased attention, and some attributed those problems to the influence of hip-hop music and culture. Gang violence took place outside of nightclubs like Skoochies, located just southeast of the Seattle Center, and Club Broadway, with public perception shaped by the way media covered the issue. The catalyst for what would become known as the Teen Dance Ordinance (TDO) was a club/church called the Monastery located between downtown Seattle and Capitol Hill. Founded in the late 1970s by George Freeman, the Monastery featured disco lights and loud music and attracted a diverse crowd of Black and white, gay and straight, and young adults and teenagers. Soon enough, the Monastery was targeted for closure by various Seattle officials. A story in *The Rocket* included quotes from teenage supporters, not just street kids, ready to defend the Monastery. Seventeen-year-old Michael Jackson was an African American student who played basketball at Garfield High School, had no arrest record, lived at home, and had a job. "At the Monastery you can be the way you want," he said. "I'm straight but I have gay friends—it's like a family and they respect you as a person."[33]

Other media accounts and numerous police reports portrayed the Monastery as a place of drug dealers, child prostitution, and sexual predators. According to reports, Freeman did not have liquor or business licenses. One police raid resulted in the arrest of all 225 people at the club. Freeman argued that he had written letters to city officials and invited them to check out his club and help solve problems with "drunks, drug dealers, pimps, prostitutes, and queer baiters" that populated parking lots that surrounded the Monastery. Freeman alleged the city responded by saying activity in surrounding parking lots was his problem. Meanwhile, *The Rocket* reported an instance of what it described as "rednecks" in a pickup truck driving by the Monastery, yelling homophobic slurs, and at one point getting out of the truck to spit repeatedly in the face of a "new wave looking" young woman standing outside.[34]

As debate over the Monastery continued, a group calling itself Parents In Arms entered the picture. *The Rocket* described it as "a group of parents who are concerned about runaway teens, and who have spearheaded the move to close the Monastery and restrict other teen clubs." In response to an interview request by *The Rocket*, Parents In Arms founder David Crosby, an attorney, refused, saying, "*The Rocket* is a pro-drug magazine. We've gotten good press coverage so far and I don't think your magazine is going to put the emphasis where I think it should be placed." King County prosecutor Norm Maleng had already called the Monastery a "public and moral nuisance" when Parents In Arms hired Bill Dwyer, a high-profile attorney who would go on to become a federal judge, to work with the prosecutor's office against the Monastery. However, after researching the documents city officials used to build their case, *The Rocket* reported that there was more to the affidavits than details of alleged lurid activities in the Monastery. They also contained descriptions of racial mixing between teen women and men, teens of the same sex hugging and kissing, and claims that "satanic rituals" were also practiced. "None of these acts are illegal, so why are they mentioned?" The article answered this question with another question. "Could it be that the Monastery is under attack, at least partially, because of religious, homosexual and racial bias? Monastery members and members of the gay community say it is."[35]

The Monastery was eventually closed in 1985. Although Freeman maintained that there had never been any shootings or drug overdoses at the Monastery, a judge in a civil trial permanently banned Freeman from owning a nightlife establishment in Seattle.[36] That same year, city council president and future Seattle mayor Norm Rice proposed a set of regulations for dance clubs and dances held for profit, serving people under eighteen years old. These included:

- Any club operator holding five or more dances a month would have to be licensed.
- If more than thirty-five teens attend the dance, the club operator must show a plan for traffic control and crowd protection both on the premises and in the area outside the club.
- No one under fourteen would be admitted without a legal guardian.
- No one under eighteen would be admitted or allowed to remain in the club after midnight without a parent or legal guardian.

- Once in the club, a patron could not leave and be readmitted without paying a readmission fee equal to or greater than half of the admission price.
- Anyone convicted of a crime involving moral turpitude, prostitution, lewd conduct, or assault on a juvenile within the past ten years would be denied a license.
- Anyone who has failed codes or licenses or has been convicted of a felony or dependency or delinquency of a minor within five years would be denied a license.

Local civil liberties organizations questioned the law immediately. Kathleen Taylor, director of the Seattle chapter of the American Civil Liberties Union (ACLU), said, "We are looking at a series of problems we have with the (proposed) ordinance. We question whether or not there is adequate reason to severely restrict clubs."[37]

Parents In Arms exercised formidable political power in pushing through the Teen Dance Ordinance, which was passed by the Seattle City Council on July 29, 1985. Subsequent amendments to the new TDO required any club to put up a $1 million deposit for youth music events and have two off-duty Seattle Police Department officers present for security. This established a financial barrier that most local promoters of all-age events could never overcome and effectively put decisions of which functions would be allowed to proceed under control of the Seattle Police Officers Guild, which had veto power over any events its officers might work. Community fears of uneven application existed amid negative attitudes within the Seattle Police Department regarding local venues that featured hip hop and R&B. Some internal police communications, revealed later as part of a lawsuit, included:

> "Our main problem with the place is on Friday and Saturday nights when they cater to a primarily rap crowd and stay open until 3 a.m."

> "I am not sure how this problem is going to be resolved short of . . . [changing the] entertainment format, thus changing the clientele that is disruptive."

> "Is the type of music that's being played attracting the 'wrong crowd'?"[38]

In addition, dances that admitted people under eighteen would have to limit the crowd to fifteen- to twenty-year-olds. Because the ordinance never defined exactly what a "dance" was, the reach of the TDO was broad enough to cripple the youth music scene in Seattle through the 1990s.[39] Perhaps an immediate consequence of the TDO was a rise in street crime as a result of young people being left with few social options. A 1986 story in *The Rocket* by Dennis Eichhorn told of a late night/early morning assault on innocent bystanders on New Year's Eve outside a venue in downtown Seattle. The aggressors were described as "mostly young men of Asian descent . . . dressed in 'break-dancing' clothes, and one carried a beat box in his shoulder." While making no excuses for the unprovoked violence that took place, the author acknowledged that although every large city has similar problems, Seattle had yet to confront its gang-related troubles head on. Despite public relations efforts, the city had done little to provide outlets for the youth on the street. "The police have adopted a decidedly anti-youth attitude, harassing and closing down teen nightspots with brutal regularity. The lid has been clamped down, but not as tightly as the authorities would like. Incidents like these are a natural result, and the worst is yet to come."[40]

In the aftermath of the TDO, some all-age activities were driven underground and others canceled altogether. For the next decade places like community centers and churches were able to work around the ordinance somewhat, with smaller-scale gatherings not officially branded as "dances" on weekends that either ended by midnight or were held during daytime hours. By the mid-to-late 1990s organizations such as the Student Hip-Hop Organization of Washington established at the University of Washington, and events like Sure Shot Sundays hosted by Seattle MC Jonathan "Wordsayer" Moore were exclusively targeting the all-age crowd. Although crippling, artists, activists, and event promoters used such methods to continue to cultivate local hip-hop culture despite the policy restriction.

The first serious challenge to the TDO did not come until 2000. A coalition of promoters, musicians, and community members worked on a bill with City Councilmen Richard Conlin and Nick Licata that would have made it easier to hold dances. Mayor Paul Schell vetoed it, and an attempted override by the city council failed to pass. The presence of high-profile advocates such as former Nirvana bassist Krist Novoselic and the Joint Artists and Music Promotions Political Action Committee (JAMPAC) increased the pressure, and the

TDO was finally repealed in August 2002 when the council voted 6-2 to approve the All Ages Dance Ordinance (AADO). The AADO required that all venues meet city building and fire safety codes, that promoters to undergo criminal background checks, and that venues have trained security personnel on hand for any all-ages event.[41]

Gangs, Drugs, and Hip-Hop Communities

Two key linked factors that influenced the environment around Seattle hip hop were the crack cocaine epidemic and the resulting spread of street gangs. President Ronald Reagan declared a national War on Drugs in 1982 that opened the door to numerous antidrug actions, which adversely effected many urban communities over an extended period. By the mid-1980s, Seattle, like much of the country, was just beginning to come to grips with crack's destructive force as it swept through urban communities. The drug was first mentioned in the *Seattle Times* on May 28, 1986, under the headline "Crack—Cheap Form of Cocaine Spreading across Nation, into Seattle Area." The story noted: "The worst aspect of the new kind of cocaine is that it is considered exceptionally habit-forming. 'One pipe and you won't stop until your bank account is empty,' says a Seattle chemist familiar with the drug and its effects."[42]

The article outlined some of the dynamics that accompanied this new drug. One main factor was cost to the consumer: crack was generally sold in portions weighing less than a gram for between $10 and $50, while a full gram of powder cocaine cost $100 or more. "Along with a new product and a lower price, dealers have also developed a new marketing strategy: distributing small amounts of the drug over a large sales network, thus reducing arrest risks and maximizing market penetration, say police." Authorities reported instances of some residential neighborhoods that suffered traffic jams from cars lined up in front of drug sellers' houses. "It's kind of like the fast-food franchise of the drug business," said Seattle Police Department narcotics unit commander Captain Jim Deschane. A pricing structure of $25 to $40 meant a return of as much as $250 to $400 for each gram rather than the previous $100. At times those arrested for selling crack did not know the name of the supplier. Cases emerged of entire immigrant families anonymously hired to pass the drugs through the front-door mail slot of the "rock house" or "crack house" for which the dealer paid the rent.[43]

Between 1986 and 1987 the King County prosecuting attorney's office saw the number of felony drug cases related to crack explode from three hundred to three thousand, a 900 percent increase.[44] In the state of Washington, possession of 40 grams or less of marijuana was considered a misdemeanor. However, possession of any amount of cocaine was classified as a felony and fell under the Violation of the Uniform Controlled Substances Act (VUCSA). Because the penalties for "intent to deliver or sell drugs" were far greater than simple "possession of drugs," prosecutors would frequently charge defendants who possessed drugs intended to deliver or sell them regardless if the suspect was a dealer or a user. In addition, the Anti-Drug Abuse Act of 1986 established mandatory minimums for federal drug offenses, instituting the 100-to-1 crack versus powder cocaine sentencing ratio.[45] In the state of Washington, possession of crack cocaine with intent to distribute carried a mandatory minimum of five years in jail.[46]

Crack became a key part of an era of policing and sentencing, which disproportionately impacted African Americans. For example, by 2007 data indicated that 82 percent of people convicted of crack possession were Black, and 9 percent were white, despite the fact that African Americans made up only about 25 percent of total crack users.[47] Crack was the single biggest factor that accelerated the rise of street gangs across the United States in the 1980s. As Black Panther chapters across the country faded in the late 1960s and early 1970s, new groups of leaders started to assert themselves. In Los Angeles the Community Revolutionary Inter-Party Service (Crips), started by Stanley "Tookie" Williams, Jamel Barnes, and Raymond Washington, originally sought official recognition from the city as a community organization, complete with a constitution. The color blue became a signature of Crips culture. The Crips grew in membership but some, such as Eugene "Taboo" Battle in LA's Athens Park neighborhood, refused to be recruited and banded together as Bloods, adopting red as their color of choice.

By the time Crips and Bloods made their way north in the mid-1980s, street gangs already active in the Seattle area included the Triads and Yakuza, Florencia 13 and 18th Street, and the Outlaw Bikers and Aryan Brotherhood.[48] The *Seattle Times* ran a story about the growth of Crips and Bloods in the area on June 28, 1987. Under the headline "Gangs Increasing in Seattle—L.A. Toughs Leave Slums for New Turf," the article announced: "Members of Los Angeles' Crips and Bloods gangs, steeped from childhood in drug-dealing and street warfare, are moving in on Seattle. About 50 full-fledged members of California's two major Black street gangs already are here. Hangers-on and wanna-bes (youngsters who wanna-be just like them and are willing to run their errands) are being recruited." The Crips, who wore trademark blue clothing items, were reported to have staked out the Central District as their turf. The Bloods, who defied their arch rivals by wearing red, had claimed the South End, around Rainier Beach.[49]

During the 1970s and early 1980s some neighborhood tension had developed between the South End and the Central District. This rivalry sometimes manifested itself in physical confrontations but was mostly limited to things like little league sports or other competitive community events. However, the spread of various out-of-town gang affiliations in the area exaggerated these dynamics and resulted in violence, including a number of homicides allegedly connected to CD–South End "beef." A third group, the Black Gangster Disciples, represented an "alternative" to the Crips and Bloods, arriving by way of Chicago. Examples of other local groups that developed as the gang landscape evolved in the Seattle area during the late 1980s were Deuce Eight, Valley Hood Piru, East Union Street Hustlers, Genesee Blocc Crips, Yesler Terrace Bloods, South Horton, Deuce Jive Hillside, and 74 Hoover Criminals.[50] Uzis, AK-47s, and "drive-by shootings" became topics of mainstream discussion as gangs and crack swept across the country. Beginning in the mid-1980s crime, and specifically homicide rates, in Seattle reflected some of the violence associated with the crack economy.[51]

As in other cities, the grim realities of crack were absorbed and reflected in local hip hop. Musically, contributions such as "Crack Get Back" (1987) by the DI-RA Boys took a socially conscious approach to fighting the epidemic. Sir Mix-A-Lot's "Posse on Broadway" (1987) lamented "The Rockman Blues," or the bleak life of a dealer, and effects of the drug on women's bodies. Meanwhile, Ice Cold Mode's "Union St. Hustlers" (1989) specifically discussed the spread of gangs, drive-bys, and shootouts in the city associated with the crack trade. These and other examples represented Seattle hip-hop artists engaging with the contemporary issues their communities were struggling with by providing realistic grassroots perspectives for all to see and hear. Indeed, the conclusion of "Union St. Hustlers" reminded listeners the song was not a glorification of gang violence but simply the truth.

The aftermath of this period ultimately helped cast a long cultural shadow over the Central District in a demographic sense while further informing the evolution of Seattle hip hop. The economic recession that hit the United States in the early 1990s was not as severe in the Seattle area, thanks in part to the explosive growth of companies like Microsoft, Starbucks, and later, Amazon. Relatively low property values suddenly made the Central District one of the hottest real estate markets in the city, as transplants moving to town for work were attracted by the neighborhood's location. This dynamic helped accelerate the already-in-progress gentrification of Seattle's first Black neighborhood and would become a topic of discussion within local hip hop.

Early Tacoma Hip Hop

Seattle was not the only place in the Pacific Northwest where hip hop put down roots. Tacoma, thirty miles south of Seattle, also played an important role in the growth and development of local hip hop. In 1980, Glen Boyd worked at the iconic Tacoma record store Penny Lane Records. A music enthusiast, Boyd noticed almost immediately the numbers of African American military members who would come in and ask about artists he had never heard of. Boyd took note of these inquiries and requested them from New York record distributors.[52] In a piece for *The Rocket*, he wrote that although Tacoma's Black music scene had experienced numerous changes over the years, it had always maintained a close connection to the street music of the East Coast. This was due primarily to the transplanted eastern populations of the military bases in South Tacoma—McChord Air Force Base and Fort Lewis Army Base. "Tacoma's rapping, scratching and mixing DJs continue to be the center of this scene," wrote Boyd, "coming to the area from hotbeds like New York City and Washington, D.C. The action still largely revolves around the military clubs, but has recently branched out to include civilian clubs like South Tacoma's Mr. Lucky."[53]

Tacoma DJ Bobby "Galaxy" Lewis added: "The Tacoma scene keeps up to date with the East. We can get independent 12-inch records here that we can't get in Seattle." Galaxy's partner, Phillip "G-Man" Gonzales, agreed. "South Tacoma is where it's at," Gonzales said. "It mixes the East Coast hip-hop sound with the South Coast funk of groups like the Gap Band. We have the Seattle jocks coming down here to check us out, because they need to be educated." Early Tacoma club DJs like Maurice "Roots I" Holloway and Anthony "Roots II" Grant began developing their style in the mid-1970s. Roots II explained: "A good club DJ in this state must have good rapport with the crowd. It has to be continuous.

Rapping and scratching are important, but by itself, that defeats your purpose." An active and diverse hip-hop scene was alive in Tacoma, evidenced by events such as the DJ battle held at the NCO Club at Fort Lewis in September 1983. The battle featured the "Galaxy Forces," Galaxy, G-Man, and Harold "Whiz Kid" McGuire against the Roots.[54]

Tacoma's hip-hop scene expanded on multiple levels. Established military venues like the NCO club and the Tray Club at Fort Lewis as well as the Madigan Annex and the Officer's Club at McChord routinely drew several hundred people on Friday and Saturday nights. Off-base locations such as Mr. Lucky, the Rheinlander Tavern, Dynasties West, Mr. Stubbs on Broadway, and Champion Disco provided civilian alternatives to the military spots. A growing cohort of Tacoma performers—The Server, Poncho, TV Lee and Candy Rock, Jammin Green, Uncle Jam, Ron "Outlaw" Barker, J.T. Sugar Bear, Kooly Hy, DJ Hollywood, Byron Johnson, Lady K, DJ Fantasy, and DJ Julio—kept things rocking for the twenty-one and over crowd. Though not as great in number, the existence of underage venues was also important to the growth of Tacoma hip hop. Located in Federal Way, a city situated roughly between Seattle and Tacoma, Spectrum was widely regarded as one of the top underage clubs in the area. Skate King in Tacoma held special nights dedicated to popping and breaking contests, and DJs Galaxy and Roots also combined forces to open an underage nightclub. As had traditionally been the case elsewhere, radio played a key role in spreading hip hop around the south Puget Sound area. KTOY (91.7 FM) featured an urban contemporary format on weekends, while KPMA (1400 AM) broadcast the nightly show *Soul of the Sound*, which was known to turn DJs loose for scratching and mixing "marathons" that could last three hours.[55]

There was a Tacoma-based artist who made a significant national impact, although historically he has not been acknowledged. "To many of Seattle's old school DJs and MCs," Glen Boyd pointed out, "[Tacoma DJ] Whiz Kid (Harold McGuire) will always be the Godfather of Northwest hip-hop." McGuire, a native New Yorker, moved to the area for roughly eighteen months in 1983 and 1984 when his military-employed wife received orders for Tacoma. At the time Whiz's "Play That Beat Mr. DJ," released on then struggling Tommy Boy Records, was climbing up the dance charts and doing unheard-of business. "Play That Beat" became an early hip-hop classic and wound up selling 250,000 copies. "Whiz became a local celebrity," Boyd wrote, "and Tacoma briefly became the undisputed capitol of Northwest hip-hop."[56]

The trend of Tacoma as a hub for hip hop in the Pacific Northwest continued into the mid-1980s. In 1985 a show at the twenty-thousand-seat Tacoma Dome featured local artist Miztah Zelle alongside New York MCs such as T-La Rock, whose single "It's Yours" was the first song ever released on legendary hip-hop label Def Jam Records; Greg Nice, who would eventually become half of the duo Nice and Smooth; and pioneering female MC Sparky D.[57]

As part of the show, Tacoma-based High Performance Breakers battled the New York City Breakers, an all-star breaking crew assembled by New York promoter Michael Holman. In addition to touring around the country, they had appeared on television shows like *Soul Train* and *The Merv Griffin Show*. In front of a packed house, High Performance defeated the NYC Breakers. The repercussions of this victory were twofold. First, it sent the message that fresh breakdancing styles and techniques were developing outside of New York City. Second, even for those who were not at the Tacoma Dome and heard about the battle secondhand, the High Performance victory gave a healthy boost to the self-esteem of local hip hop. For the Pacific Northwest, like almost every other region of the country, New York City was still what nearly all local hip hop was measured by. Although High Performance's vanquishing of the NYC Breakers was largely symbolic, it validated the idea that the hip hop happening in places like Tacoma could in fact be just as good as, if not better than, that coming out of New York.[58]

Tacoma continued to shine as Run DMC, the self-proclaimed "Kings of Rock" and the biggest rap group in the world, became the first rappers to headline a stadium-sized show in the Pacific Northwest. Their 1986 album *Raising Hell* was the first rap record to sell a million copies. Run DMC's collaboration with Aerosmith on the song "Walk This Way" had become a smash hit on MTV at a time when precious few Black artists were in video rotation. The New Year's Eve 1986 bill at the Tacoma Dome also featured rhythm and blues crooner El DeBarge and former New Edition member Bobby Brown.[59]

Hip-Hop Grassroots Expansion

Farther down the West Coast came an example of collaboration between cities. Originally from San Francisco, Chris "Vitamix" Blanchard made a name for himself but struggled for credibility as one of the few white MCs and DJs in Portland, Oregon. Beginning in the early 1980s, Vitamix developed an eclectic reputation by mixing records such as Grandmaster Flash & the Furious Five's "The Message" and "Frog Sounds in North America" together on Portland radio station KBOO. In 1983 he connected with "Nasty" Nes Rodriguez, who began playing Vitamix's music on KFOX in Seattle. Soon Vitamix was spinning as a guest DJ on the radio program *FreshTracks*, and Rodriguez released Vitamix's song "That's the Way Girls Are" on his label Cold Rock Records. Eventually a deal was struck in 1987 to re-release the single on Profile Records. As the home of Run DMC at their peak, there were few names bigger in the rap music industry than Profile. Although the song sold a respectable number of copies, the simple fact that Profile Records had signed a Northwest artist was a major event.[60]

Despite what some perceived as a dynamic of arrested development in the mid-1980s, the cultural movement that was Seattle hip hop continued to inspire young people in different ways. These included a breaker turned DJ turned record label head, the first hip-hop performers at the venerable Folklife Festival, a mobile DJ/party unit in the Teen Dance Ordinance era, a world-class break-dancer, and a heavy dose of social consciousness. As a musical youth, Danny "Supreme" Clavesilla was drawn to hip-hop culture after going on vacation to New York City with a friend in 1983. During this visit, Supreme experienced early authentic hip hop firsthand. The next year he formed the Seattle Circuit Breakers, who were invited to participate in the televised break-dance special *Summer Break*. Eventually, he was drawn to DJing, formed a group named Incredi-Crew, and released a single in 1987 called "High Powered Hip-Hop" on his own label, Gemini Records.

Intent on getting his material out there, Supreme traveled to New York City to distribute the song at the New Music Seminar. Started in 1980, the New Music Seminar was an annual event during which artists, industry players, and record companies gathered to do business, a place where up-and-coming hip-hop artists from around the country networked and got exposure. Soon after that, Southern California–based Enigma Records approached Supreme to produce several local artists including Chenelle "Chelly Chell" Marshall. After considerable time spent producing and recording material, such as Chelly Chell's 1987 single "He's Incredible," Enigma cited various delays and deadlines in its decision not to release any of the music.[61]

Community centers, parks, and schools provided platforms for young people who had hip hop–based performance aspirations while also functioning as social gathering points. One instance was the All-City Talent Show held at Franklin High School. In 1987, DURACELL (Def Undisputed Rhymes Are Cuts Especially Long Lasting) Crew—made up of Derrick "Silver Shadow D" Seals, Clifton "Chilly C/SOZ" Seals, Bruce "Incredible B/Horton B" Griffith, Lawayne "Crazy Waves" Rainwater, and Jason "JG" Gavin—won the first All-City Talent Show. That same year DURACELL was invited to be the first hip-hop performers in the fifteen-year history of the annual Folklife Festival held at the Seattle Center, over Memorial Day weekend.[62] The festival had become a hub for diversity among numerous traditional and ethnic communities and performances, and Folklife's embrace was a clear indicator of local hip hop's growing popularity.

Another example was RICO-1, established by Reggie Brown and Robert Lomax in 1987, a mobile DJ unit that organized and played parties at various local venues. The importance of RICO-1 and other party creators and promoters like it cannot be overstated in the environment of an all-ages social vacuum created by the Teen Dance Ordinance. A fertile breaking landscape for early b-girls and b-boys in the greater Seattle area eventually produced world-class talent that rose to the top of the craft. Beginning in the early 1980s, Carter "B-Boy Fever One" McGlasson was drawn to examples of break dancing on television shows and in such films as *Style Wars*, *Wild Style*, *Flashdance*, and *Beat Street*. By his freshman year at Ingraham High School in 1984, Fever was a member of his first crew, the Grand Master Breakers. A year later, Fever's growing reputation led him to join Seattle Circuit Breakers. After high school graduation, Fever moved to New York City and impressed enough people to earn an invitation to join the hip-hop musical *Jam on the Groove*, an off-Broadway show. Created in 1995 by members of the Rock Steady Crew, the production featured a DJ, music, intricately choreographed breaking moves, and commentary about hip-hop culture by the dancers themselves.[63]

If the Rock Steady Crew represents the hip-hop equivalent of the Joffrey Ballet or the Alvin Ailey Dance Company, then Richard "Crazy Legs" Colon was its principal and director. In the 1970s, Crazy Legs was an early member of the Rock Steady Crew in the Bronx, functioning as the group's leader and helping orchestrate international tours for RSC in the early 1980s. Crazy Legs's respect for Fever grew, and after a 1998 battle that also served as an "interview,"

Fever One became the first Seattle native invited to join the vaunted Rock Steady Crew. Fever's reputation continued to grow as he developed his signature "gunz blazin" style. "Gunz blazin" not only became a Fever alias but was eventually incorporated into his routine as he would pull out imaginary weapons to "slay" his opponents.[64]

Youthful energy and social consciousness combined to inform other emergent artists in Seattle. Jamal "Jace" Farr started off as a South End b-boy who practiced on cardboard at the Brighton Elementary School playground and then ventured out to the ultimate breaking testing grounds of the Seattle Center. As rap music became more popular, Jace noticed groups like the School Boyz, DURACELL, LSR, and True Believers from West Seattle, forming and making music he liked. Taking the name Mic Master J, fifteen-year-old Jace joined forces with his brother Nigel "Demo Demone" Farr, Sean "DJ Acsean" Washington (aka DJ SeanMalik), and DJ DD to form the DI-RA Boys in 1985. DI-RA stood for Devastating Interesting Rap Alliance.

The DI-RA Boys were unique in part because of the levels of social awareness they displayed in their music. Their 1987 single "The Times" discussed President Ronald Reagan's role in the Iran–Contra scandal, a tangled affair that included allegations of an arms-for-hostage deal with Iran, illegal CIA operations in Nicaragua, and the seemingly endless supply of cocaine to US urban centers. "The Times" also tackled the proliferation of nuclear weapons. Quoted in *The Rocket*, Demo Demone said: "It's just about letting people know what's going on. How Reagan takes things like nuclear war into his hands and doesn't take it seriously. Like he's just acting out a part." Another DI-RA song, "Crack Get Back," dealt with drug abuse, addiction, and proliferation, particularly as it related to the spread of crack. Demone argued: "Whenever drugs come up in your face, you don't want it. The only time drugs understands that is when you get forceful with him." The eldest of the three at seventeen years old, Demone represented DI-RA's impressive levels of social maturity and self-awareness. In 1987 the DI-RA Boys attracted enough attention to be the only rap group included on a compilation album for the National Black United Front (NBUF), a project organized by longtime African American Seattle civil servant Charles Rolland, and performed at the Black Community Festival and Festival Sundiata at the Seattle Center. In an era of hip hop where "hardcore" music could be defined by subject matter as much as profanity, DJ Acesean remarked: "Seattle hip-hop is too soft right now. We'd like to take it into something more hardcore."[65]

The DI-RA Boys' drive toward success came to a tragic end in 1989 when DJ DD was shot and killed. In the aftermath the remaining members disbanded the group and went their separate ways musically.[66]

Sir Mix-A-Lot Breaks Out

Within a year of its release, Sir Mix-A-Lot's 1985 independent EP *Square Dance Rap* had sold more than forty-five thousand copies. His follow-up EP, *I'm A Trip* (1986), was released on the newly formed NastyMix record label. Mix-A-Lot's style, described by Glen Boyd as "supertechno rap/funk," came from an impressive collection of equipment. "In contrast to the minimal stage gear of many hip-hop acts," Boyd wrote, "Sir Mix-A-Lot travels with an arsenal of electronic equipment that is truly impressive, hence his boast of being Seattle's 'computerized DJ.'"[67] In addition to standard turntables and mixers, Mix-A-Lot's setup included the following: three synthesizers (an Akai AX-60, a Roland Juno 2, and a Sequential Split 8); two samplers for sampling various sound effects (an Akai Sampler and Disk Drive as well as a Prophet 2000); three drum machines (a DMX, an 808, and Drumtraks); a digital reverb for "heavy drums"; an MSQ 700 Sequencer; a Harmonizer for voice modulation such as on the song "Square Dance Rap"; and an Apple II computer.

Mix-A-Lot's ability to produce material was matched by his willingness to pay dues. From the beginning, he had relentlessly sold tapes from the trunk of his car until record stores like Music Menu heard the street buzz and began carrying his music. In addition, he went on the road, doing shows in unglamorous places throughout the Deep South of the United States, opening for such artists as Cherelle, Cashflow, Jermaine Stewart, Atlantic Starr, and Too $hort. Mix-A-Lot even opened for Los Angeles–based Egyptian Lover, an artist with whom he had built competitive friction. Because both artists were from the West Coast and known for their computerized sounds, they were often compared to each other. That did not sit well with Mix-A-Lot, but it also led him to a realization. "I was doing what I'm doing before I ever heard the Egyptian Lover, so when I first started out I was obsessed with defeating him," he said. "But all that was doing was holding me under sea level. Playing with Egypt was weird at first, because we hated each other, but now we're pretty cool."

Tension between Mix-A-Lot and other Seattle rap artists had become apparent. The title of Mix-A-Lot's second EP, *I'm A Trip*, was a reference to his feeling that he was being misjudged locally. "It's all a big lie. People say 'you got a big Cadillac, you're trippin. You think you're this, you're trippin.' So I just tripped through a whole song bragging on everything I have, which ain't much. I gave the people what they always wanted." Responding to a comment in *Billboard* magazine, which sarcastically referred to his hometown as "that hip-hop hotbed Seattle," Mix-A-Lot said: "There is so much talent in Seattle. Frostmaster Chill is talented, but he needs story lines like L.L. Cool J has. That's what we were waiting for from him. We didn't work with him, because he didn't give us that and now he thinks we're trying to hold him down." In Mix-A-Lot's opinion the problem was that few people from Seattle believed in Seattle, and he cited local rappers who got onstage and claimed to be from the Bronx. "That attitude has to stop. NastyMix is ready to work with other artists. But no one's gonna make it talking about old Mix-A-Lot. They gotta get out and make it for themselves. Hell, I still got a long way to go."[68]

The popularity of the single "Square Dance Rap" helped raise Mix-A-Lot's profile outside Seattle. For five weeks it was the number one most requested song on Los Angeles radio station KDAY. Another key development occurred when a copy of the song "found its way to the United Kingdom and began getting radio play in Britain. 'Square Dance Rap' . . . became extremely popular in the United Kingdom and was released as a single by the label Streetwave." This led to an invitation to perform at England's first hip-hop festival, Fresh Fest UK in 1986. Mix-A-Lot played two sold-out shows in London's fifteen-thousand-seat Wembley Arena along with other artists on the bill—Grandmaster Flash & the Furious Five, Afrika Bambaataa, Mantronix, Lovebug Starski, The Real Roxanne and Howie Tee, Dr. Jekyll and Mr. Hyde, and the World Class Wreckin' Cru, the first Los Angeles–based rap group to release an album on a major label (CBS/Epic), who counted a young Dr. Dre among its members.[69]

Sir Mix-A-Lot's steady buildup had him well positioned for a breakout hit. Originally released in 1987, "Posse on Broadway," with vocals partly inspired by the song "Paul Revere" by the Beastie Boys, stood out in several ways. One was by name-checking specific streets and landmarks such as Rainier Avenue, the intersection of Twenty-third Avenue and Union Street, Seattle Central Community College, and Dick's Drive-In. In the same way that KRS-One of the legendary New York group Boogie Down Productions described his home in the 1986 song "South Bronx," "Posse on Broadway" sent messages about Seattle culture to the rest of the world in a way that had never been done before.

In "Posse on Broadway," Mix-A-Lot acknowledged the diversity of his crew by mentioning his white real estate investor friend Larry, he spoke out against disrespect of women, and he described using mace on a man who was about to physically assault his girlfriend. This approach was in stark contrast to the likes of Niggaz Wit Attitude (NWA), who represented the swiftly emerging strain of hip hop known as "gangsta" rap. The only white people referenced in NWA's music were the Los Angeles Police Department officers they hated. Conflicts in an NWA song always ended with a shotgun or an AK-47, and women were referred to as "bitches" or "hos" more than anything else.

The video for "Posse on Broadway," featuring Mix-A-Lot riding around in a black Mercedes Benz limousine, showcased various parts of Seattle's South End, Central District, and Capitol Hill neighborhoods. Mix-A-Lot's mention of Dick's Drive-In, a Seattle fast food institution since 1954, created massive free publicity for the local burger chain wherever the song traveled. However, the owners refused to let NastyMix Records shoot any portion of the "Posse on Broadway" video at the Dick's Broadway location. Instead, the scenes were shot at Stan's, another drive-in burger restaurant located a few miles south of Dick's at the intersection of Rainier Avenue and Dearborn Street. Twenty years later, Mix-A-Lot returned to Dick's in an orange Lamborghini while making a cameo appearance in Jake One's "Home" video, Macklemore shot the video for his song "White Walls" standing on the roof of the building, and the owner personally apologized to Mix-A-Lot for the original snub.[70]

"Posse on Broadway" experienced wide success as the single entered the national charts and the video appeared on MTV. This set the stage for the release of Sir Mix-A-Lot's debut LP *Swass* in 1988. The tone of the album radiated a unique vibe, as Mickey Hess noted in his book *Hip-Hop in America: A Regional Guide*. "*Swass* was extremely innovative and set Mix-A-Lot apart from many of his peers in rap music at the time," Hess wrote. "His rap in this album focused more on middle-class issues, using humor as an outlet, rather than depending on rage at a system or descriptions of life in the projects." Although Seattle certainly had its fair share of issues between law enforcement and the African American community, which Mix-A-Lot addressed in the song "Hip-Hop Soldier," for the most part *Swass* was about "having the most money and gold, getting the best women, and being the best rapper in the game." In a nod to the numerous rock/rap collaborations taking place, most notably Run DMC and Aerosmith's 1986 smash hit "Walk This Way," *Swass* also included a remake of the 1970 Black Sabbath song "Iron Man," featuring Seattle band Metal Church. "Bremelo" was a region-specific song about women from the city of Bremerton, across Puget Sound from Seattle.[71] Within a year of its release, *Swass* had entered both *Billboard*'s Black and Pop LP charts and sold more than five hundred thousand copies, making it the biggest-selling record released by an independent Seattle-based label in years. Despite this, *The Rocket* noted in January 1989, "Sir Mix-A-Lot would have a tough time finding a gig here [in Seattle]. Yet in cities like Miami, Houston, Phoenix, and Detroit, Mix has sold-out crowds wanting to know more about the 'Seattle hip-hop sound.'" *Swass*'s buildup was slow and steady—it took more than a year for the record to go platinum.[72]

Hardcore Rap, Race, and Seattle Youth

As hip hop grew in popularity, instances of violence at and around live shows led to questions about whether rap music was the cause. These questions were generally associated with "hardcore" acts like Public Enemy or Run DMC, who was sued by a man that was stabbed and robbed at a concert in New Jersey. However, "hardcore" was not something that Philadelphia duo Jeff "DJ Jazzy Jeff" Townes and Will "The Fresh Prince" Smith were known for; in fact, they were described as "the Cosby family of rap." By 1990, Smith was starring in the NBC network sitcom *The Fresh Prince of Bel-Air* and would go on to become one of the world's biggest movie stars. But in 1988, following a concert at Seattle's Paramount Theatre, four people were wounded in a drive-by shooting at the hotel the duo was staying in near Seattle-Tacoma International Airport.

The next day a headline in the *Seattle Times* read "Clues Hazy in Drive-by Shootings—Was Rap Music a Factor?" The story noted previous concerns over violence at rap concerts that included moving a 1987 Run DMC and Beastie Boys show from the Seattle Center to the Paramount. Although police acknowledged potential racial overtones due to the fact that each of the victims was Black and witnesses described the shooters as white, the New Jersey attorney that sued Run DMC argued: "There has been a repetitive history of violence at rap concerts. The music tends to incite violence. They should soup up security.... The music creates this environment where people go crazy."[73]

The rise in popularity of this thoroughly controversial new music and culture began to show up in different contexts. While Seattle hip hop continued to evolve and capture attention outside the city, the influence of national artists, some considered hardcore, was leaving its mark on local youth. One example of this was the 1988 Ingraham High School Ram football team. Ingraham, a predominantly white public school located at the northern edge of Seattle, featured several top African American players that lived in South Seattle but were bused nearly fifteen miles each way, per school district policy. Three senior players from the Rainier Valley, in particular, played crucial roles on the team: linebacker Wayne Burton, wide receiver/defensive back Jason Gavin, and tailback/defensive back Simon Robinson, an all-Metro League selection as a junior.

Coming into the season, Ingraham was considered the favorite in a weak Metro League, and after finishing the regular season with one loss, the Rams caught a break in their first playoff game trailing Juanita High School 14-7 late in the fourth quarter. Juanita was a perennial football power and two-time state champion in Kirkland, an eastside suburb across Lake Washington from Seattle. With Ingraham out of timeouts and unable to stop the clock, the Rebels had the ball on the Rams' twenty-yard line with less than a minute to play in the game. Then a mishandled exchange between the Juanita quarterback and running back resulted in a fumble, which Ingraham recovered and returned for the tying touchdown to send the game into overtime. Robinson rushed for 111 yards on twenty-four carries, and the Rams won the game 17-14, advancing to the state quarterfinals. A story in the *Seattle Times* stated that in the "loud and raucous" Ingraham locker room, chants of "Don't believe the hype! Don't believe the hype! Don't believe the hype!" could be heard after the game.[74]

In 1988 the phrase "Don't believe the hype" meant one thing: Public Enemy. Widely regarded with apprehension and mistrust by many Americans in the late 1980s, Public Enemy represented a number of things that made the mainstream uncomfortable. Musically, their hectic, scattered, screeching production styles perfectly complemented the equally hectic subject matters they tackled: crack cocaine, institutional racism, government corruption, media bias, and the prison industrial complex. In the process Public Enemy had run afoul of conservative commentators who labeled them "thugs" and

Jewish groups that called them anti-Semitic. Public Enemy's second album, *It Takes a Nation of Millions to Hold Us Back* (1988), became the soundtrack of rebellion for diverse groups of young people as they developed a socially conscious identity. Glen Boyd called it "a political time bomb." Lyrically the album maintained a tradition of Black pride in the face of adversity, demonstrated earlier by Grandmaster Flash & the Furious Five's 1983 song "The Message," and even earlier than that by Marvin Gaye's "What's Goin On" and Gil Scott Heron's "The Revolution Will Not Be Televised." "Musically," Boyd continued, "*It Takes a Nation* covers more territory than any rap album to date. It also signals to the world that this music is not going away, and that the time has come to take rap seriously as an art form." [75]

The Public Enemy song "Don't Believe the Hype" from *It Takes a Nation of Millions to Hold Us Back* became the theme for the Ingraham Rams. Author M. K. Asante noted its message was "essentially about being a critical independent thinker and forming your own opinions. Hype is temporary, fleeting and can change course on a dime. That's why it's important to understand that hype and talent are not synonymous." [76] When Ingraham defeated Ferris High School of Spokane 14-6 in the state semifinals, the headline in the *Seattle Times* blared "Don't Believe the Hype—Ingraham in Kingbowl—Lightly Regarded Rams Top Ferris in Semifinals." The Kingbowl, Washington State's high school football championship game, was played annually in the iconic Kingdome, located in southern downtown Seattle (SODO). Even Ingraham head coach Ron Sidenquist was on board. "All year we've read in the papers that the Metro League should be knocked out in the first round, that they're a bye for whoever has to play them," Sidenquist said. "These kids haven't believed that—that's been our rallying cry: Don't believe the hype." Ram fullback John Brown added: "They [Ferris] gave us no respect. Their coach said that they were going to win the Kingbowl and they were going to run straight over us. Coach told us coming in—Don't believe the hype. And there you go." [77]

Intent on driving home the message, several Ingraham players had small towels custom made at Sports In Action, a sports apparel boutique in South Seattle. The towels, with "Don't Believe the Hype" emblazoned across the surface, were tucked into the players' waistline for all to see. Two days before Kingbowl XII, Ingraham's opponent, Kentwood, from the Seattle suburb of Kent, dismissed several key players, including the starting quarterback and running back for violating team rules.

The Rams defeated Kentwood 21–0 on December 3, 1988, becoming the first Metro League team and first public high school from Seattle to win a state championship in football. After the game the *Seattle Times* noted: "As they were awarded the Class AAA state-championship trophy, Coach Ron Sidenquist, his players, and Ingraham's fans chanted, 'Don't believe the hype, don't believe the hype.'"[78]

Artists like Public Enemy exercised national influence and caused the mainstream considerable discomfort, but circumstances in the community were reflected in local examples of hardcore rap music. Toward the end of the 1980s, Seattle (especially the Central District) felt the brunt of the crack cocaine epidemic and all that came with it. While Sir Mix-A-Lot offered a humorous, less intense narrative than the traditions of early West Coast gangsta rap, there was also more serious street-oriented local music. One example was the 1989 single "Union St. Hustlers" by the group Ice Cold Mode (Kenyatta "Ice Cold" Thomas and DJ Ronnu McThomas). *Seattle Times* writer Andrew Matson called it "a slice of pre-gentrification Central District life on the corner of 23rd and Union."[79] The song chronicled drive-by shootings but also gave a shout-out to Ezell's, Seattle's most famous and Oprah Winfrey–endorsed fried chicken.[80] This corner was notably mentioned two years before by Sir Mix-A-Lot in "Posse on Broadway," who "rolled up to the same intersection, saw drugs and general hard times, and made a left to Capitol Hill for burgers at Dick's."[81] Ice Cold Mode released a four-song tape that was carried in local record stores, selling nearly a thousand copies. Nonetheless, Ice Cold lamented: "It's hard to find gigs in Seattle, and sometimes I feel like I put hell into this . . . this is about raising black consciousness."

The local scene expanded with Chilly Uptown's album *I Got Rules* on Ever Rap Records and groups like Ready N Willin, Brothers of the Same Mind, and The Fury out of the rural Port Orchard, Washington. As DJ Kool Kat observed, "The majority of rappers don't know what it's like in a small town." PD2, DJ Robert "3D" Stills, and MCs Donnell "2 Smooth" Jackson and Dwayne "Mellow D" Banks produced the 1989 hit "You Ain't Got No Bass." But as popular as the song was locally, few in Seattle got the opportunity to hear it in concert. When it came to performing live, PD2 would have to "leave or starve." Questions about the lack of live hip-hop shows featuring local talent had been present for some time. Music writer Glen Boyd asked, "When was the last time you saw a [non-NastyMix] Seattle-based rap act perform in a local venue?" He continued: "Rap music is everywhere. Everywhere, that is, except in the form of live music. Despite its arrival as a legitimate mass appeal musical genre, a variety of factors continue to keep it all but locked out of the clubs." These factors ranged from perpetual ignorance within the local industry of rap's impact, to an evolving but still present "sense of snobbery" from music elitists toward rap. After outlining contributing dynamics, Boyd made clear what was really at the heart of the matter. "The single greatest factor keeping rap out of these clubs is fear," he wrote. "Fear of gangs. Fear of violence. For all we know, fear of a black planet (as Public Enemy's Chuck D would say)."[82]

Social Consciousness in the Local Scene

Sir Mix-A-Lot's second album, *Seminar*, was ready for release in October 1989 on NastyMix Records. The ten-song effort was reviewed in *The Rocket* by Roberta Penn, who wrote that if Mix-A-Lot's new album were used as current events curriculum in high school, "the dropout rate would plummet." Penn said that *Seminar* was a combination of pop psychology, street sociology, and politics on top of danceable basslines. "Mix uses his own attitudes for instructional materials and examines the things that nearly every urban youth—regardless of race or economic status—must confront," she argued. "There's a tune about the teenage mom who has turned to sexual dancing for money, a chilling number about patriotism, disillusionment and national symbols and several funny take-offs on chic fads and heavy posing."

Two singles and videos simultaneously helped push sales while reinforcing Mix-A-Lot's image as an alternative to the gangsta rap that was gradually shifting the balance of power in hip hop from New York to the West Coast. One was "Beepers," which celebrated the era's emergent wireless communication technology. With its guitar sample from Prince's song "Batdance," "Beepers" was very accessible for the mainstream. The other song was "My Hooptie," a humorous story of Mix-A-Lot driving a beat-up car while his Mercedes Benz was in the shop for repairs. *Seminar* displayed a conscious side, criticizing American foreign and domestic policy on "National Anthem" and discussing reasons some young women enter the sex trade, sexual abuse in the home, and teen pregnancy, in "The (Peek-a-Boo) Game." Like *Swass*, *Seminar* sold more than a million copies, giving Nasty-Mix Records two platinum albums in its catalogue.[83]

Sir Mix-A-Lot's national profile had become substantial enough to merit a visit from *Yo! MTV Raps*, which premiered in the summer of

1988 and was hosted by Fab 5 Freddy, the New York graffiti artist who starred in the film *Wild Style*. Right away, *Yo! MTV Raps* was among the network's highest rated and most influential programs. In its second year the show traveled around the country, highlighting artists in their hometowns. The program arrived in Seattle and received a guided tour, courtesy of Mix-A-Lot and the NastyMix crew. In early 1990, Black Entertainment Television's (BET) show *Rap City* also came to Seattle to profile Mix-A-Lot. After shooting at places like the Space Needle and the downtown club Hollywood Underground, the city's first African American mayor, Norm Rice, joined Mix-A-Lot and the show's crew to tape a segment that would air as part of *Rap City*'s Black History Month celebration. Rice contended that rap music was important "because it makes you think—it's educational even though it has some controversy with it." Mix-A-Lot, reacting to criticism of his song "National Anthem," argued, "I love my car like I love my nation, but every now and then it needs a tune-up, and so does this country." Rice ended the segment by making a toast: "To our future and the future of African American youth throughout the world."[84]

In the midst of Mix-A-Lot's success, NastyMix Records added to its artist roster. Steven "Kid Sensation" Spence, a protégé of Sir Mix-A-Lot, grew up in South Seattle and graduated from West Seattle High School. Kid Sensation released his single "Back 2 Boom" on NastyMix in 1989, which sold more than one hundred thousand copies and reached the top-ten on the rap singles chart. His 1990 debut album, *Rollin' with #1*, made the *Billboard* chart during its first week of release. His first video, "Seatown Ballers," was set in Seattle's newly completed downtown Metro bus tunnel and carried a message of positivity and legal "ballin." At the end of the video a written statement read: "Our society cannot allow small interest groups to decide for the rest of us what is an 'acceptable' artistic expression, or to define what is to be considered suitable adult entertainment." Although this stance made sense in an era when groups like the Parent Music Resource Center (PMRC) seemed determined to censor certain elements of hip hop, MTV refused to play the video unless Kid Sensation allowed the network to remove the statement, which he eventually agreed to.[85]

In 1990 NastyMix Records seemed poised to be the next big thing. While celebrating its fifth birthday, the Northwest Area Music Association (NAMA) presented CEO Ed Locke and NastyMix their Outstanding Achievement Award and annual awards for Best Company of the Year and Independent Record Label of the Year.[86] In addition, the label was attempting to diversify its stable of artists by signing acts like the "self-proclaimed Kings of Splatter Rock," The Accused, "an alternative dance-music duo in the manner of Wham!" called Blue Max, and Adrienne, "a stylish R&B vocalist in the Whitney Houston vein."[87]

Despite this variety of genres, NastyMix remained true to its local hip-hop roots by signing Criminal Nation and High Performance, both from Tacoma. Composed of MC Deff, D-Rob, Pook Love, and Soundcheck, Criminal Nation released their album *Release the Pressure* in 1990. Criminal Nation's music was heavily influenced by the devastation of the crack epidemic and resulting gang activity. *The Rocket*'s Grant Alden called *Release the Pressure* "a musical document of life in Tacoma's much-storied Hilltop. It ain't Harlem, it ain't Compton, it damn sure ain't *New Jack City* . . . But it is home." Criminal Nation's songs dealt with racism ("Black Power Nation"), boredom and futility ("Release the Pressure"), and violence ("Definitely Down for Trouble"). On the question of making radio-friendly material, D-Rob said, "Fuck the top-10 hit, man." MC Deff added: "I didn't make no record to play radio. Radio play only makes a person weak, or something like that. Now, if I make a song they like and it gets radio play, then . . ." The group reflected a familiar frustration that local artists felt toward "Black" radio. D-Rob: "Black radio, man, it's a bunch of bullshit." Pook Love added: "The head of it is somebody white, and they sayin no to this. There's a lot of stuff I didn't know about the radio business, the PR men, the promotions, how they lie in your face. It's a dirty business."[88]

Some artists changed their focus over time. High Performance—MC Duce, MC Microphone Ace, DJ Mad Dog, and MC Action—first gained local and regional prominence as dancers by defeating the New York City Breakers at the Tacoma Dome in 1985. By the end of 1990, they made the successful transition to signed recording artists, releasing their debut album, *All Things Considered*. In *The Rocket* writer Greg Barbrick described the record as "a piece of knowledge dropping a little different from the usual angry tone." High Performance's intent was to send a positive message, starting with the name of the album. MC Duce said, "We want people to consider all the possible consequences of their actions, to put themselves in different situations." The group made two videos—"Do You Really Want to Party" and "All Things Considered," which was shot in Washington, DC, and featured footage of Reverend Jesse Jackson speaking against social injustices.[89]

— —

With the arrival of "Rapper's Delight," the first generation of hip hop in Seattle began a journey for which there was no roadmap. While some early participants went after quick credibility with claims of New York ties, most embraced a more local mind-set. The best example of this was the Emerald Street Boys, who incorporated the city's nickname into the group's name. Their combination of electrifying performances, media coverage, and recording Seattle's first rap record made them the popular face of early local hip hop. Breaking and graffiti in Seattle were given boosts in the early 1980s by the release of such seminal films as the independent movie *Wild Style*, the documentary film *Style Wars*, broadcast on PBS, and the Harry Belafonte–produced *Beat Street*. Media like this helped give visual cues about hip-hop style and attitude to young people who couldn't get enough. Soon spaces downtown and at the Seattle Center became gathering points for local breakers, and instances of oversized aerosol art began to appear in strategically visible locations around the city.

Local radio history was made in 1981 when DJ "Nasty" Nes Rodriguez began hosting *FreshTracks* on KFOX, the first rap radio show west of the Mississippi River. His presence on KFOX led to a fateful meeting with Sir Mix-A-Lot one night at the Rotary Boys & Girls Club, and the path of local music was changed forever. With KFOX as a platform to showcase his music, Mix-A-Lot's already rising star built more momentum. An early example of hip hop intersecting with local activism came with the occupation of the abandoned Colman School building by the Citizen's Support Committee for the African American Heritage Museum/Cultural Center. In 1986, Los Angeles hip-hop pioneer Egyptian Lover came to play two benefit shows in support of the occupiers and their cause. However, while groups like the Citizen's Support Committee were fighting for the community, local hip hop and youth culture were hit hard by a series of sociopolitical events in the mid-1980s. One was the Teen Dance Ordinance, first introduced in 1985, which crippled the local youth music scene for nearly two decades, with rap music saddled by perceptions that it caused violence. The spread of crack cocaine and the corresponding arrival of street gangs from Southern California also impacted local hip hop. The explosion in the number of drug users fueled massive amounts of revenue, which brought about competition and gang activity. Before long, the resulting increase in arrests, addiction, and gun violence began to be reflected in local hip hop. Meanwhile, to the south, Tacoma was experiencing growth within its own hip-hop community. The military bases fueled population from other parts of the country, which combined with the local community to support clubs and DJs in a way that allowed Tacoma to hold its own as a hip-hop scene through much of the 1980s.

By the end of the decade, Sir Mix-A-Lot and NastyMix Records had succeeded in placing Seattle firmly in the national hip-hop consciousness. Mix-A-Lot's 1988 debut album *Swass* had gone platinum, the video for "Posse on Broadway" was being played on *Yo! MTV Raps* and BET's *Rap City*, and both programs came to Seattle to interview him. In 1989 he released his second album, *Seminar,* which sold more than one million copies. The seismic nature of an independent, Seattle-based record label releasing back-to-back platinum-selling rap albums by a Seattle-based artist in 1988 and 1989 cannot be overstated. While the rest of hip hop was being seduced by the oncoming rise of West Coast gangsta rap, Mix-A-Lot had answered the question of who would be the first from Seattle to make it by going the opposite way.

The overall depth of activity and growth during the 1980s set the foundations for Seattle hip hop to enter the world stage in the 1990s. This entrance, signaled by Sir Mix-A-Lot's Grammy for his song "Baby Got Back," would soon be overshadowed by the musical tidal wave of grunge rock. As incredibly popular groups like Nirvana and Pearl Jam cast the brightest of lights on the local alternative rock scene, Seattle hip hop worked to further distinguish itself. One way this happened was related to what was sometimes referred to the "fifth" element of hip-hop culture: fashion. Two Seattleites, Tony Shellman and Lando Felix, collaborated to create not one but two iconic hip hop–inspired clothing lines. Another path to growth was increased opportunities in print journalism, radio, community access television, and the rise of the Internet, which created space for Seattle hip hop to define itself in new and different ways.

3

"We got the talent, microphones, turntables, and crates"

SEATTLE HIP HOP IN THE 1990S

I N the early 1990s hip hop merged into the national mainstream. The 1991 beating of Rodney King in South Los Angeles and the subsequent uprising and revolt, fueled by decades of police brutality and neglect, demonstrated the intensity of urban racial and economic tensions. During the late 1980s, "gangsta" rap had articulated feelings of marginality, isolation, and frustration that existed in Los Angeles as well as in other urban communities around the United States. King's videotaped assault illustrated NWA's song "F-ck the Police," while the resulting not-guilty verdicts for the officers involved and subsequent outrage and civil unrest echoed songs like Ice-T's "Squeeze the Trigger" and Ice Cube's "AmeriKKKa's Most Wanted."

Several other US cities, including Seattle, experienced civil unrest in the aftermath of the King verdict, although not close to the destruction in Los Angeles. Over two nights beginning on May 1, 1992, rioters in downtown Seattle and the Capitol Hill neighborhood, mostly young white men along with some young African Americans, threw stones, overturned cars, broke windows, looted stores, and set fires. One young man who identified himself as Khalif said, "What we want is justice. When we kick down doors, windows . . . it's for Rodney King." A total of 150 people were arrested over two nights of disturbances, which mirrored the rioting in Los Angeles. The violence overshadowed the numerous peaceful protests in colleges and high schools around the Puget Sound area.[1]

For some, the Rodney King saga showcased hip hop's social range, as rap music not only drew attention to problems in the community but also essentially predicted the resulting civil unrest if nothing changed. To others, the episode simply represented criminals who had been allowed to run amok, fueled by the rise of crack cocaine and street gangs. In the aftermath emerged a federal initiative through the

United States Department of Justice called "Weed and Seed," ostensibly designed to combat the social and economic deterioration of the
inner city. Seattle was among several cities selected to participate in
the pilot program.[2] Adopted by the Seattle City Council in December
1992, the Weed and Seed initiative was described as an "incubator for
social change to stabilize the conditions in high crime communities
and to promote community restoration." The key components of the
program included enhanced local coordination, concentrated and
enhanced law enforcement efforts (weeding), community policing,
and increased human services (seeding).[3]

Community leaders like Arnette Holloway, president of the
Central Area Neighborhood District Council, and Reverend Harriet
Walden, leader of Mothers Against Police Harassment, immediately
challenged the program. They held press conferences, led demonstrations, and pointed out that two-thirds of Seattle's Weed and Seed
money would be allotted to law enforcement, with only one-third
going to social services. A group called the Seattle Coalition Against
Weed and Seed was organized, and the Puget Sound Coalition for
Police Accountability distributed a list of fifty-five community groups
that were opposed to Weed and Seed. Among other things, leaked
federal Weed and Seed documents included items such as "street
sweeps" where anybody on a public street in an area designated as
"high crime" could be taken into custody and forced to prove their
innocence.[4] Norm Rice, who served as Seattle's first Black mayor from
1990 through 1998, and supported Weed and Seed, faced a tough task,
attempting to sell a program many residents viewed as simply further
license for police to harass and a tool of gentrification.[5]

An additional factor in hip hop's rapid rise in the early 1990s in
California and elsewhere was the massive success of MC Hammer.
Hammer, an Oakland native, became the first hip-hop artist to achieve
"diamond" status, ten million copies sold, following the release of
his 1990 album *Please Hammer, Don't Hurt 'Em*. The popularity of
MC Hammer generated unprecedented mainstream access for a hip-
hop artist, which led to endorsements with Pepsi and Kentucky Fried
Chicken, an action figure carried in toy stores, and a Saturday morning cartoon television series. These and other examples were driving
forces that shifted the traditional center of hip hop away from New
York to the location and sensibilities of the West Coast.[6]

Along with hip hop's higher national profile, new controversies
about the content and context of hip-hop music and culture emerged.

By the end of the 1980s, Miami-based 2 Live Crew had firmly established themselves in the national consciousness with their sexually explicit lyrics. Journalist and editor Alan Light wrote: "If, in 1990, people new to rap gave it any thought at all, they would have concentrated on the crudeness of 2 Live Crew—who may have a constitutional right to be nasty, but there is no way around the ugliness of their lyrics."[7] Several counties in Florida attempted to ban the group's 1989 album *As Nasty as They Wanna Be*, while a record store owner in the state was charged with a felony and an Alabama shopkeeper was fined for selling copies of the record. In the Pacific Northwest controversy about the album prompted State Representative Richard King, a Democrat from Everett, to sponsor HB 2554, or the Erotic Music Law. The bill prohibited minors from purchasing "sexually suggestive" records, tapes, and compact discs. It made record store owners liable for displaying or selling any music that "appeals to the prurient interest of minors in sex"; those who violated the law faced a $500 fine and six months in jail for a first offense, while repeat offenders could get as much as a $5,000 fine and a year in jail. By a vote of 96–2 the Washington State House passed HB 2554, which Governor Booth Gardner eventually signed into law. However, only four months after taking effect, the Erotic Music Law was struck down in the fall of 1992 by a Superior Court judge in Seattle.[8]

During the 1990s the hip-hop scene in Seattle resonated with these nationally profiled issues of racialized urban violence and policing and the critiques of the sexually explicit character of hip-hop lyrics. But the scene also responded to more local and regional influences. The decade was the heyday for grunge music and fashion in Seattle, which claimed a great deal of media attention on the national stage. At the same time, Seattle hip-hop music and culture also garnered national recognition in the form of several Grammy nods as well as the cultural exports of fashion, with the urban clothing brand Mecca, and breaking.

The Closure of NastyMix Records

With two platinum-selling Sir Mix-A-Lot albums, things appeared to be going well at NastyMix Records in the late 1980s and early 90s. However, as was common among hip-hop artists in the early days, Mix-A-Lot was largely unfamiliar with the record business. That changed in late 1989, when he was introduced to the concept of publishing by Public Enemy front man Chuck D during a conversation while touring together. Mix-A-Lot was looking for a new manager, which led him to Ricardo Frazer, a young NastyMix intern known for his knowledge of the music industry and business sense. Mix-A-Lot offered Frazer the job, which began a manager/client relationship that has thrived for some three decades without ever having any formal written contractual agreement.[9]

Mix-A-Lot was unhappy with the promotion of his second album, *Seminar*, which marked the end of his contract with NastyMix Records. One of Frazer's first tasks was to try to sort out the issue of publishing monies owed by NastyMix to Sir Mix-A-Lot, which had grown in excess of $300,000. Mix-A-Lot and Frazer were on the verge of closing a new deal with RCA, which subsequently backed out when NastyMix CEO Ed Locke, claiming tampering, threatened to sue any record company that signed Mix-A-Lot. Unable to resolve their differences, the matter was eventually decided in court. "We spent a lot of money on this case ($1.2 million), more than we won," Mix-A-Lot explained, "but it was worth it to get off that label. We didn't win any money from Ed [Locke], all we got was our old masters. All I wanted was the masters. I realized that my masters would get my 1.2 back." *The Rocket* attempted to get Locke's version of the story, describing him as sounding "hurt and angry." Locke said: "I don't want anything to do with his [Mix-A-Lot's] publicity." A call to Ichiban Records confirmed that the Atlanta-based rap and blues label was now NastyMix's primary stockholder. "In essence," *The Rocket* concluded, "Locke has sold a controlling interest in Seattle's first rap label to out-of-towners."[10]

The eventual closure of NastyMix Records in 1992 represented the end of an era. According to the *Seattle Times*, "NastyMix put Seattle on the rap map and contributed to the city's image as a hotbed of new, young music talent."[11] Both of Sir Mix-A-Lot's NastyMix albums, *Swass* and *Seminar*, were RIAA (Recording Industry Association of America) certified platinum. Despite how it ended, NastyMix helped provide a blueprint of how to build a successful, minority-owned rap label outside New York that put out local music with global reach. Future examples of this dynamic would include Dr. Dre and Suge Knight's Death Row Records in Los Angeles; Master P's No Limit Records in New Orleans; and James Prince's Rap-A-Lot Records in Houston.

Sir Mix-A-Lot's Next Chapter

Attention continued to follow Sir Mix-A-Lot into the 1990s. Controversy erupted in 1991 when Vanilla Ice, rap music's first white male sex symbol, best known for his number one, platinum-selling single "Ice Baby," was accused of plagiarizing lyrics from Sir Mix-A-Lot's 1986 song "I'm a Trip." The issue, discussed in a book written by Vanilla Ice, was addressed by his publicist, who said, "The book never said that he [Ice] actually wrote it—it just said he *had* it." [12]

As a musical free agent, Mix-A-Lot drew immediate interest from several major record companies. He found a partner in Rick Rubin, who cofounded iconic hip-hop label Def Jam Records with Russell Simmons out of his New York University dorm room in 1984. Over the next four years, Rubin helped launch the careers of rap superstars such as LL Cool J, Public Enemy, the Beastie Boys, and Run DMC. In 1988 Rubin left Def Jam, moved to Los Angeles, and started Def American Records. Although he focused primarily on working with rock and heavy metal acts such as Slayer, Danzig, and System of a Down, Rubin also signed rap artists like the Geto Boys out of Houston, Texas. [13]

Rubin offered Mix-A-Lot the chance to operate his own label, Rhyme Cartel Records, under Def American distributed by Warner Brothers. Ricardo Frazer was named president and Mix-A-Lot chief executive officer. The first release on the Rhyme Cartel label was Sir Mix-A-Lot's third album, 1992's *Mack Daddy*. In addition to investing $1 million in his new signing, Rubin had some marketing ideas. The Mix-A-Lot bio distributed by Def American featured a list of his personal gun collection, which included a MAC 11, Glock 19, Mossberg Pump, an HK 91 and 93 with laser sights, and .44 auto mag Desert Eagle. Despite this, Rubin did not see Mix-A-Lot simply as a "[Los Angeles] Raiders baseball hat and jacket" rapper a la NWA. Rubin's vision for Mix-A-Lot was this: "If you're gonna be a gangster, you'd be the boss." The look, complete with fur coats and cigars, was of a pimp who drives a Porsche, a rapper who was "too legit to give a shit." [14]

The initial single from *Mack Daddy*, "One Time's Got No Case," focused on police use of racial profiling in deciding which drivers to pull over. The single sold fifty thousand copies and set the stage for the album's second single "Baby Got Back." When "Baby Got Back" was released in the spring of 1992, the response was immediate and not all enthusiastic. Because of its suggestive nature, MTV banned the video for "Baby Got Back." MTV had done this in the past—for example, refusing to broadcast the NWA video "Straight Outta Compton" in 1988 amid claims that the song promoted violence.[15] MTV eventually agreed to air "Baby Got Back" but only at night.[16] Just as it had in the case of NWA, the controversy simply made "Baby Got Back" more popular. The song spent five weeks at number one on the *Billboard* pop chart, making Mix-A-Lot the first Northwest artist to reach the top spot since Heart's "Alone" in 1987. The song was certified double platinum (two million copies sold).[17]

Writer and editor Charles Mudede argued that Sir Mix-A-Lot's success "caught everyone by surprise because (1) Seattle was completely off the hip-hop radar, and (2) there was nothing in the mainstream that sounded remotely like his music." Sir Mix-A-Lot rapped only like Sir Mix-A-Lot, but, most important, "Sir Mix-A-Lot wasn't so fucking serious." "Baby Got Back," which opened with a conversation between two white girls disgusted by a Black woman's huge butt, "returned laughter to the hip-hop charts and the dance floor. The record felt like a window being opened in a stuffy room." KEXP DJ Riz Rollins added: "This was Seattle's big gift to black America. People remembered it was good to have fun now and then. And it could only happen in Seattle because we were so isolated. We were free to do whatever we wanted."[18]

"Baby Got Back" was based on Mix-A-Lot's critique of traditional Eurocentric beauty standards and body shape. As he told *Entertainment Weekly*, "I'm sorry, but the popular image of a beautiful woman today is a bean pole. A lot of women, white and black, have thanked me for 'Baby Got Back.'" Controversy hovered as the song was labeled racist and sexist, and several Mix-A-Lot shows were picketed by protesters that accused him of exploitation by disparaging one group of women to build up another.[19] When the nominations for the Thirty-fifth Annual Grammy Awards were announced on January 7, 1993, Seattle hip hop had truly arrived on the world stage. In the category for Best Solo Rap Performance, "Baby Got Back" faced superstar competition—"Addam's Groove" by MC Hammer, "Strictly Business" by LL Cool J, "You Gotta Believe" by Mark "Marky Mark" Wahlberg, and "Latifah's Had It Up 2 Here" by Queen Latifah. The announcement of Mix-A-Lot as the winner and presentation of his trophy was not seen on television as the Grammys had not yet made the decision to include the rap awards as part of the regular broadcast.[20]

Since its release, "Baby Got Back" has made numerous appearances in movies such as *Charlie's Angels* (2000), TV shows like *The Simpsons*, and commercials for Burger King.[21] In 2013 the song appeared on the Fox television show *Glee*, and rapper Nicki Minaj sampled the song in her 2014 single "Anaconda." Other items from Mix-A-Lot's catalogue have continued to earn what he called "long money," such as the Pussycat Dolls' sample of his 1988 song "Swass" for their 2005 multiplatinum smash hit "Don't Cha."[22] With the formation of his label Rhyme Cartel Records, Sir Mix-A-Lot had a platform to bring more attention to Seattle artists. The result was a local rap/R&B compilation album titled *Seattle . . . The Darkside* (1993), which featured nine songs, including "Drop Top" by E-Dawg featuring Filthy Rich, "Just da Pimpin' in Me" by Sir Mix-A-Lot, "Menace Crook" by Jay-Skee, "Flava You Can Taste" by Kid Sensation, "12 Gauge" by Jay-Skee, and "Don't Play Me" by 3rd Level. The general theme of this album was more hardcore, as reflected by some of the song titles and parental advisory sticker on its cover. *The Definitive Guide to Rap & Hip-Hop* argued the album "takes an enjoyable look at Seattle hip-hoppers and detours into urban contemporary and spoken word."[23] Meanwhile, *The Rocket* argued that "he [Mix-A-Lot] can't be knocked for ignoring local talent. Kid Sensation and Jazz Lee Alston, just to name a couple, wouldn't have gotten as far as they have without him. Criticism hasn't stopped him from helping other artists."[24] The first single released from *Seattle . . . The Dark Side* was "Drop Top" by E-Dawg featuring Filthy Rich, a feel-good warm-weather anthem. The B side of "Drop Top" was "Little Locs," which music critic Greg Barbrick described in *The Rocket* as "a rap about E-Dawg's days on the streets. It is a story that could have come out of Compton or any other urban war zone, and stands as Seattle's first major entry into the gangsta rap field."[25] *Seattle . . . The Darkside* was an early example of a phenomenon that helped define Seattle hip-hop music during the 1990s: the compilation album.

Meanwhile, Mix-A-Lot kept making regular appearances across popular culture. MTV's controversial 1990s animated series *Beavis and Butt-Head* produced a compilation album, *The Beavis and Butt-Head Experience* in 1993. Artists such as Megadeth, Nirvana, and Cher appeared on the platinum-selling album along with Mix-A-Lot, who contributed his single "Monsta Mack."[26] Mix-A-Lot earned another Grammy nomination in 1994 in the Best Solo Rap Performance category for his song "Just da Pimpin' in Me," and the following year, he made the move to television. By this time, rappers such as Will Smith, Ice-T, and Queen Latifah had begun second careers in movies and TV. Mix-A-Lot joined this trend as the star of the short-lived 1995 drama series *The Watcher* on the fledgling UPN network. Reviews were mixed. According to *Los Angeles Times* writer Chris Willman, Mix-A-Lot "plays jive-talking host to this Las Vegas–set anthology series, tracking all sorts of goings-on from a high-tech, high-rise control room with monitors hooked up to every nook and cranny in the city."[27] This, said the *Chicago Tribune,* allowed Mix-A-Lot to "spy on the lives of high rollers, lowlifes and underwear-clad women.... Almost everybody who shows up on one of his screens is a con artist, a murderer, a model, a junkie or an Elvis impersonator."[28] *The Watcher* filmed only a handful of episodes and was canceled by UPN after one season.

Following the success of his album *Mack Daddy*, Sir Mix-A-Lot remained active musically. When his 1994 album *Chief Boot Knocka* was released, he again pushed the envelope with another risqué music video. In addition to this new album following up on the themes explored on *Mack Daddy*, "like that record it comes with plenty of pre-release controversy. The first single, 'Put 'Em On da Glass,' features an X-rated video that's so explicit even his publicist says she hasn't seen it and doesn't want to," wrote journalist Scott Griggs in *The Rocket*. "Even though the video was produced on Mix's property, don't expect to see it on MTV anytime soon. But exposure on the Playboy Channel will help continue Mix's career, and he admits that he's 'king of the strip clubs.'" Mix-A-Lot's 1996 album *Return of the Bumpasaurus* went essentially unnoticed by the mainstream. *The Rocket* reported Mix-A-Lot's success had created tension with some elements in the Central District: "Without going incognito, the man can't go back in the neighborhood he grew up in without a death threat. Please, he didn't kill anyone so what's the problem?"[29] Two factors potentially contributed to this strained relationship—one was the natural tension that occurs as an artist makes the transition from local to national/global, and the other was the ultra-competitive nature of hip-hop culture, which does not always celebrate the success of others without expecting said success to be spread around the scene.

Hip-Hop Events in Seattle and the Region

Voices that blamed hip hop for violence at live events were fueled nationally in the late 1980s by a stabbing at a Run DMC concert in New

Jersey and locally by a shooting at a hotel in Sea-Tac, where DJ Jazzy Jeff and the Fresh Prince were staying after a show. This image was not improved when three people were shot, one was stabbed, and another hit by a vehicle outside the Paramount Theatre in Seattle after an Ice Cube concert in 1992. City officials blamed the Paramount and the event promoter for not giving police adequate notice that extra security would be needed.[30] Negative publicity around live shows was reaching an all-time high the same year one of the area's longest running annual hip-hop events debuted, followed by a series of local and regional events that continued to breathe life into the scene.

As the biggest radio station playing a Rhythmic Contemporary/ Top 40 format in Seattle, KUBE 93 used its power to hold the first annual Summer Jam at Tacoma's Cheney Stadium in 1992. Performers at the event included Kid Sensation and New York artists Nice and Smooth, Das EFX, and Pete Rock. The following year, Summer Jam moved to the Evergreen State Fairgrounds in Monroe, thirty miles north of Seattle. Summer Jam 2 saw a significant increase in the number of nationally known hip-hop artists with a lineup that featured Tupac Shakur, Run DMC, Pharcyde, Onyx, Immature, Funk Doobiest, Tag Team, and Guru from the group Gangstarr.[31]

At the time, KUBE faced criticism over its failure to give local artists consistent airplay. Although Kid Sensation was a headliner for the first Summer Jam, the lineup for Summer Jam 2 in 1993 featured almost all national artists. Community-based events have traditionally played an important role in providing opportunities to showcase local hip-hop talent. For example, Autumn Jam, was put on by the Central Area Youth Association (CAYA) in fall 1993. Formally established in 1964, CAYA originally focused on organizing football for Central District youth. Over time the organization grew to provide education, social development, and recreation activities for neighborhood young people between the ages of nine and eighteen.[32] Autumn Jam, an obvious play on Summer Jam, showcased more than a dozen teen hip hop, rock, R&B, and gospel artists from CAYA's Multimedia and Performance Program. The event was held at Seattle Central Community College's Broadway Performance Hall.[33]

Community-building events within Seattle's hip-hop scene continued through the 1990s. Several examples included veteran local presence Jace, who organized the inaugural Hip-Hop Forum in 1993. The second annual forum was held at the Seattle Center and included such panelists as Mike Clark, J-Styles, Jonathan "Wordsayer" Moore, B-Self, Mr. Supreme, Blaac, B-Mello, and Soul-One. In 1995 local DJ and promoter Robert Brewer organized the Northwest Hip-Hop Forum. The program at the Showbox downtown included panel discussions on networking strategies and getting media coverage for artists. The music showcase featured local artists E-Dawg, Beyond Reality, 22nd Precinct, DMS, Narcotic, Jace, Infinite, Prose and Concepts, and Portland artist Cool Nutz.[34] Payton Carter noted in *The Rocket* that attendance for the music showcase in the evening was negatively impacted at 10:00 p.m., when the Teen Dance Ordinance went into effect.[35]

Seattle hip hop flexed its regional muscle in 1994 at the CITR 101.9 FM DJ and MC Soundwar Chapter Four held in Vancouver, Canada. The first edition of Soundwar, held in 1990, represented Vancouver's first rap competition and drew talent from up and down the West Coast of the United States.[36] Subsequent Soundwars grew to include more categories, and, at Chapter Four, Seattle dominated as B-Mello won the DJ competition, Blind Council won the group award, and DVS won the dance contest.[37] Events located outside Seattle also helped expand the influence of hip hop in Washington. One instance was Phunky Phat 95, an all-day event held at Evergreen State College, a small, public liberal arts school located in the state capital of Olympia, sixty miles south of Seattle. With opening remarks beginning at noon, nearly twenty primarily local artists were set to perform well into the evening, with the last scheduled to go on at 10:00 p.m. Among them were DJs such as B-Mello, Vitamin D, and Kamikaze; dance acts like DVS Floor Rockers and Preach and Teach; and rappers, including Prose and Concepts, Beyond Reality, Source of Labor, Phat Mob, Sinsemilla, Ghetto Children, Shabazz Coalition, Jace, and Blind Council.

Ishmael Butler and Digable Planets

As the Seattle scene developed, local MCs interacted with scenes in other cities. Growing up in the Central District, Ishmael Butler spent summers in New York with his father and the school year in Seattle. During his junior and senior years at Garfield High School, Butler played on back-to-back state championship basketball teams in 1986 and 1987. He also dabbled in hip hop during high school, including an appearance as one half of a duo called The Cold Crushers at FunFest, the annual Garfield talent show. After graduating, Butler signed to play at the University of Massachusetts. However, balancing basketball and a full college load proved to be a challenge, and he left UMass after a year. Butler found himself in New York City with an internship at Sleeping Bag Records, an independent rap label with artists like Mantronix, Nice and Smooth, and EPMD. He paid dues working in the mail room, running errands, handing out flyers, and absorbing as many aspects of the recording industry as he could. One album from that time, *3 Feet High and Rising* (1989) by De La Soul, caught Butler's attention more than any other. "When that came out," he said, "it sparked something in me. My dad was really into avant-garde jazz, so from a musical standpoint I always knew that you could be original and succeed. Then De La came along, and a lot of stuff I was thinking about started adding up very quickly."[38]

After a few lineup changes, which included fellow Seattleite Michael Gabre-Kidan, Butler, who went by Butterfly, combined with Craig "Doodlebug" Irving and Mary Ann "Lady Bug Mecca" Vieira to form Digable Planets. The group signed with Pendulum Records in 1992 and began recording their debut album, *Reachin' (A New Refutation of Time and Space)*, released the following year. Conceptually, Butler envisioned members of the group as insects who work together for "the good of the colony. It was a socialist, communist thing that I was talking about." Not many rappers in the early 1990s were comparing themselves to insects, pulling their album names from the title of a book by Argentine author Jorge Luis Borges, or taking a genre-defining pro-choice stance while mentioning *Roe v. Wade* in their song "La Femme Fetal." Although nobody in the group was originally from New York, having lived there for several years Digable Planets was described in the press as a "Brooklyn-based trio."[39]

The lead track from *Reachin'* was "Rebirth of Slick (Cool Like Dat)," released in the fall of 1992. Digable Planets was asked to perform the song on the Emmy Award–winning Fox Television comedy-sketch series *In Living Color*. Created by brothers Keenen Ivory and Damon Wayans, *In Living Color* generated massive ratings and stirred controversy in the early 1990s for the way it took on issues of race.[40] Soon after the episode aired in January 1993, both the single and the album were certified gold (500,000 copies sold).[41] In January 1994, "Rebirth of Slick" earned a Grammy Award nomination for Best Rap Performance by a Duo or Group, and Digable Planets was also nominated in the Best New Artist category. Other nominees for

Best New Artist were Belly, Blind Melon, SWV (Sisters With Voices), and Toni Braxton, the eventual winner. The competition for Best Rap Performance by a Duo or Group included "Revolution" by Arrested Development, which appeared on the soundtrack for the 1992 Spike Lee biopic *Malcolm X*. Arrested Development won Grammys for Best New Artist and Best Rap Performance by a Duo or Group for their song "Tennessee" in 1993. Cypress Hill's "Insane in the Brain" was a number one hit for the first Latino hip-hop group to achieve large-scale mainstream success. "Hip-Hop Hooray," with a Spike Lee–directed video, was a number one hit for Naughty By Nature. The legendary Dr. Dre and Snoop Doggy Dogg's "Nuthin But a 'G' Thang" also spent time at number one; Snoop had quickly become one of the brightest stars in all of music without having yet released a solo album of his own.

When Digable Planets won the Grammy over a field that was essentially a who's who of early 1990s hip hop, not everyone was impressed. Pioneering MC KRS-One of the group Boogie Down Productions voiced his opinion that a hardcore group should have won instead. Looking back on their unlikely victory, Butler reflected, "I don't know how those decisions are made and maybe we got it because we were more friendly to the public. I think we had a good record, but for impact it wasn't bigger than Snoop and Dre, and it wasn't better than Cypress Hill either."[42] *Blowout Comb,* the second album of the Digable Planets, was critically well received but did not match the commercial success of *Reachin'.* In a 2013 interview with Butler, *Rolling Stone* magazine noted that fans and critics hailed *Blowout Comb* when it was released in October 1994, but radio seemingly did not quite know what to do with it. "The album just really wasn't selling," Butler said. "But it wasn't really that discouraging to me, because we were still touring—and we didn't really give a shit about the pop world like that, anyway. The album itself we were always happy with."[43]

Blowout Comb was the final album of original music from Digable Planets, who broke up in 1995. The group briefly reunited and toured for a period in 2005; however, subsequent attempts to perform were marked by creative differences between members. Butler returned to Seattle in the aftermath of Digable Planets and remained active, appearing on Bronx hip-hop duo Camp Lo's 1997 song "Swing" as well as in their video "Luchini AKA This Is It." Butler resurfaced in 2003 with Cherrywine, a live hip-hop group, and released the album

Bright Black. He also appeared in a short film called *I Am Ali* (2002), written, produced, and directed by dream hampton, a longtime music and culture writer for *The Source* and *Vibe* magazines. *I Am Ali* featured Butler as a man with schizophrenia who thinks he is legendary boxer and former world heavyweight champion Muhammad Ali. The story follows the daily lives of Butler's character and his girlfriend as they attempt to come to terms with this mental illness. In 2004 Butler made his feature film debut starring in the comedy/drama *Men Without Jobs*, portraying an eccentric slacker/graffiti artist facing the increasing responsibilities of adulthood.[44]

Seattle Hip Hop and Sports

Ishmael Butler's status as a state high school basketball champion who went on to win a Grammy Award was an example of the connection between rap and sports, a dynamic present virtually from the beginning of hip hop. In 1979 "Rapper's Delight" referenced watching the New York Knicks on television, and legendary New York MC Kurtis Blow released the song "Basketball" in 1984. In Seattle the link between hip hop and sports came in 1992 with a collaboration between Kid Sensation and Seattle Mariners superstar outfielder Ken Griffey Jr. That year Griffey and Kid Sensation released the single "The Way I Swing," which Griffey cowrote:

> Ken Griffey is a swinger, not a singer;
> A def rhyme bringer;
> A home-run hitter but I'm not a dope slinger.

The song appeared on Kid Sensation's 1992 album, *The Power of Rhyme*, with a baseball card included in the cassette single for "The Way I Swing."[45]

The relationship between sports and hip hop in Seattle continued during the NBA playoffs in the spring of 1993. With the single "Not in Our House," Sir Mix-A-Lot provided a hip-hop narrative for a young and exciting SuperSonics team making a deep playoff run. The video featured cameos from numerous players and team personnel, including point guard Gary Payton, forward Shawn Kemp, play-by-play broadcaster Kevin Calabro, and the Sonics cheerleaders. The song, produced in association with radio station KUBE 93, enjoyed large amounts of local popularity and airplay.[46] The Sonics lost a tough seven-game series that season to league MVP Charles Barkley and the Phoenix Suns in the Western Conference Finals.

   B-Ball's Best Kept Secret, a compilation album of rap songs featuring several NBA players, was released in 1995. Participants included Jason Kidd, Dana Barros, Dennis Scott, Malik Sealy, Brian Shaw, Chris Mills, and Cedric Ceballos. Because Shaquille O'Neal had released a debut solo album, *Shaq Diesel*, in 1993 that was a platinum record, his participation brought some credibility to the project. Sonics All-Star point guard Gary Payton's contribution to *B-Ball's Best Kept Secret* was the song "Livin' Legal and Large." Although the album was widely panned by critics, *XXL* magazine wrote about Payton: "Best Line: 'And that's real we all know the deal / And for all those that criticize / I'm not trying to be Shaquille.' GP gave us a pretty decent look into his ability to flow, almost-maybe-kinda-sorta sounding like a lesser version of Warren G." The review credited Payton for keeping the song "pretty clean and positive, which is surprising since we're pretty sure the things he said to opponents on the court were not in fact, pretty clean and positive."[47]

Connections to Seattle Music beyond Hip Hop

As the 1990s got under way, new connections between Seattle hip hop and the broader Seattle musical scene took off, including an innovative mixture of jazz and hip hop as well as positive and negative effects from the rise of grunge rock on local rap music. In 1993, five years after he formed Incredi-Crew and self-released the single "High Powered Hip-Hop," Danny "Supreme" Clavesilla met Shane "Sure Shot" Hunt at the record store where Hunt worked. After discovering a shared obsession for vinyl, Supreme and Sure Shot began working together and eventually became the Sharpshooters, which merged traditional, rugged hip-hop beats with a variety of musicians to create a natural fusion between hip hop and jazz. Things moved quickly—less than a month after meeting, they recorded an instrumental titled "Pork Pie Stride."

   After playing the song over the phone for San Francisco–based Luv'n'Haight Records, Sharpshooters received a check and a contract in the mail the next day. As journalist Cynthia Rose wrote in the *Seattle Times*: "'Pork Pie Stride' fit right into a booming trend. This was the ascent of acid jazz music, a sound born in England around 1990. A fusion of hip-hop techniques with dance-floor warmth, it crossed computerized sampling with live players." Sharpshooters followed up this success with the EP *Buck the Saw*, and suddenly "in both Europe and Japan, acid jazz was hot. Sharpshooters found they couldn't export fast enough. Their name started cropping up in charts around the world."[48] Supreme, Sure Shot, and Strath Shepard, whom Supreme had met while writing for Seattle hip-hop magazine *The Flavor*, formed Conception Records in 1995. As their success continued, Sharpshooters was offered a deal with New York–based label Instinct Records, which produced the album *Choked Up* in 1997. Unlike "Pork Pie Stride," *Choked Up* featured vocals from rappers. An article by Payton Carter in *The Rocket* stated, "Although they are commonly labeled as acid jazz, the Sharpshooters more accurately represent an appreciation of the history of jazz, funk, rhythm and blues and hip-hop. In other words, hearing their music is like hearing a little bit of all types of black music over the past 50 years."[49]

Conception Records trailblazed by forming a pressing and distribution agreement with Seattle-based alternative rock label Sub Pop Records. Conception's deal with Sub Pop included a sizable advance, a studio, and an office on Capitol Hill. In 1998 Conception released *Walkman Rotation*, a compilation album featuring all of the label's artists. Later, after Sub Pop terminated its deal with Conception, Supreme used his considerable industry contacts to simply find another deal. Conception's new agreement with New Groove Records in California distributed the 1999 album *Passage Through Time* by a three-man hip-hop production crew from Toronto called Da Grassroots.[50] Sharpshooters and Conception Records represented the expansion of Seattle's influence as an exporter and developer of diverse styles of urban music.

Although Sub Pop dabbled in local hip hop through its relationship with Conception, its rise to prominence was rooted in grunge—the existence of which, along with the Teen Dance Ordinance, contributed to Seattle hip hop living in a semiunderground space during much of the 1990s. Beginning in the mid-1980s, Seattle became the epicenter of this fresh strain of alternative rock. Characterized by distorted electric guitar riffs, lyrics based in angst and apathy, and a scruffy-looking "thrifting" appearance, grunge was initially often referred to as "the Seattle sound."[51] Several Seattle area grunge acts experienced massive amounts of international success in the 1990s. These local bands included Pearl Jam, Alice in Chains, Soundgarden, and Nirvana. Pearl Jam headlined the 1992 Lollapalooza Tour and has had five albums reach number one on the *Billboard* chart.[52] Alice in Chains' album *Dirt* (1992) sold more than three million copies, their release *Jar of Flies* (1994) became the first EP to top the album charts, and the group's 1995 self-titled album debuted at number one on the *Billboard* chart.[53] Soundgarden's 1994 album, *Superunknown*, debuted at number one, sold five million copies, earned a Grammy nomination for Best Rock Album, and featured the Grammy-winning hit singles "Black Hole Sun" and "Spoonman."[54] However, of all the grunge groups to emerge from Seattle in the 1990s, perhaps the most influential was Nirvana.

Originally from Aberdeen, a city of sixteen thousand along Washington's central coast, Nirvana consisted of drummer Aaron Burckhard, bassist Krist Novoselic, and lead singer/guitarist Kurt Cobain when it formed in December 1987. After going through several drummers, Dave Grohl, formerly of the Washington, DC, band Scream, joined Nirvana in 1988. That same year, the group signed with Sub Pop Records to put out a Nirvana single. It wasn't until their album, *Nevermind*, was released in September 1991 that Nirvana truly entered the national consciousness. With the single "Smells Like Teen Spirit" receiving massive airplay on MTV and radio outlets, *Nevermind* sold more than half a million copies in three weeks, and in January 1992 it reached number one on the *Billboard* album chart, displacing Michael Jackson's *Dangerous*. The group's meteoric rise continued with an appearance on the cover of *Rolling Stone* in April 1992, the release of a second album, *In Utero*, on September 21, 1993, the taping of an all-acoustic show on the popular series *MTV Unplugged*, and performances all over the world.[55]

On April 8, 1994, Nirvana lead singer Kurt Cobain was found dead of a self-inflicted shotgun wound in his home in Seattle's Denny-Blaine neighborhood. Cobain's death by suicide sent shockwaves through the music industry, and although it focused even more attention on the genre, the event also signaled an end of sorts. In the 2014 book *Here We Are Now: The Lasting Impact of Kurt Cobain*, writer Charles R. Cross said, "It would, oddly, be in fashion that the word 'grunge' would continue to survive in current culture, a life that the word has not had within music." It was the constant need for trend stories that created grunge in the first place, and following Cobain's death this trend was declared dead by "the same kingmakers who had flown out to Seattle and looked for patterns in every coffeehouse or concert stage. The Grunge movement, just as Kurt had predicted, had 'phase[d] into nothing.'" Cross concluded that "the headlines, at least in music, moved on to further stops, with hip-hop culture and electronica."[56]

As Soundgarden, Alice in Chains, Pearl Jam, and other groups such as Mudhoney, the Presidents of the United States of America, and Screaming Trees continued to receive international attention in the post-Nirvana era, talent scouts in Seattle for the next few years would have a nearly singular focus on finding the next grunge sensation. The sheer volume of success in a relatively short span of time created within many industry writers something akin to "Seattle music fatigue." As a result, many local hip-hop performers, while creating an active and vibrant scene, found it difficult to generate sustained attention outside the region through traditional industry avenues.

Jonathan Moore and Consciousness in Seattle Hip Hop

In the shadow of grunge and under the confines of the Teen Dance Ordinance, a vast and healthy array of different styles and trends in local rap music continued to develop throughout the 1990s. One of these new voices was the husband-and-wife team of Kevin and Monica McAfee, aka Kev the Rap'N Rev and Sister Harmony. With the exception of MC Hammer's 1990 top-five hit single and video "Pray," overtly Christian rap music, or "holy-hop," was generally a tough sell in mainstream culture. However, it has managed to carve out a place for itself within the Black church community. Kev the Rap'N Rev and Sister Harmony's 1995 album *Bible Stories* was self-released on New City Records. With song titles like "Miracle Man," "Holy Trinity," "Highest Praise," and "Rap'N Bout a Bless'N," *Bible Stories* was an example of the gospel tradition, which itself influenced the birth of hip hop, intersecting with local rap music.

The diversity of local hip-hop perspectives was further exemplified by El Mafioso, part of the wave of West Coast Latino hip hop that included California artists Kid Frost, A Lighter Shade of Brown, and Cypress Hill. Song titles like "Aztec Assassin" and "Mafioso Style" were made "to entertain as well as grab the attention of the Chicano youth," El Mafioso explained: "KRS [One] once said that in order to change minds you first have to get the hardcore audience's attention and later on, when they have faith that you're down, they'll listen to you when you're spittin' knowledge."[57]

With the soaring popularity of "gangsta" rap, positive energy and educated perspectives in hip hop seemed increasingly marginalized.

As a student at Roosevelt High School in the 1980s, Jonathan "Word-sayer" Moore rented out spaces at the Seattle Center and threw "Prep" parties. After graduation, he attended Morehouse College in Atlanta but spent large amounts of time during summers in Seattle at Madrona Presbyterian Church, which had an old keyboard and drum machine in the basement. By the time Moore moved back to Seattle in 1992, he, his brother Upendo "Negus 1" Tookas, and Atlanta native DJ Kamikaze had become Source of Labor. If the Rotary Boys & Girls Club was a symbolic Central District home for the first generation of hip-hop kids in Seattle, the Langston Hughes Performing Arts Institute served that purpose for the second. Originally constructed in 1915 as a synagogue, the facility had deep history within the African American community. Funded for years by the Seattle Parks Department, in 2013 the institute came under control of the city's Office of Arts and Cultural Affairs.[58] Not long after Moore's return from Atlanta, he approached Langston Hughes's director Steve Sneed. Soon Moore was coordinating regular open mic and turntable nights in the building's basement as well as formal shows like *African Echoes—A Hip-Hop Continuum*.

By 1993 opportunities at downtown locations for local performers, limited because of fear and ambivalence toward hip hop by some promoters and venue owners, increased as Source of Labor played on an all-Seattle bill at the Crocodile Café that included multiracial crew Six in the Clip and the metal band Metaphysical. Moore leveraged this foot in the door to establish a local hip-hop beachhead downtown. He booked a concert in 1994 with Source of Labor, the Ghetto Children, Blind Council, and Jace and the Fourth Party, and then he set up a regular open mic night at the popular downtown venue RKCNDY.[59] Throughout the mid-1990s, Moore brought national artists such as Ice Cube and The Roots to Seattle. The Sacramento, California–based duo Blackalicious was impressed enough with Moore as a promoter to hire him as their tour manager. Moore's increasing experience with the business end of the music industry led him, his then-wife Erika White of Beyond Reality, and Negus 1, to form Jasiri (Swahili for "courage") Media Group in 1994. The independent recording and publishing company initially handled artists Source of Labor, Beyond Reality, Lisa Loud, and Cecil Young.

It was not just a label, scholar Mickey Hess argued in *Hip-Hop in America: A Regional Guide* that Jasiri also represented a frame of mind. "Moore and the other artists in the Jasiri group wanted to break away from the vision of gangsta rap, which was the main focus of the rap industry at the time, and promote a positive energy and medium for education in the community," Hess wrote. "The artists in Jasiri forced the Seattle hip-hop scene to move from the grandiose, self-aggrandizing rap of Sir Mix-A-Lot to a more educated, meaningful form of musical expression."[60] During the 1990s, Jasiri released several projects, including its debut EP *Sureshot Singles* in 1995 and the compilation album *Word * Sound * Power*, featuring Beyond Reality, Felicia Loud, Theaster Gates, Source of Labor, and Cecil Young. Several of Jasiri's artists made guest appearances on numerous other compilation albums, including *14 Fathoms Deep*.

Erika "Kylea" White, who has been called the "godmother of Seattle hip-hop," combined with vocalists Shelin and Nikki to form the group Beyond Reality.[61] In yet another example of the intersection of local hip hop and sports, she played guard on the state champion Garfield girls' basketball team of 1987. Like others before her, Kylea experienced the pressures of being a woman in the predominantly male field of hip hop. However, from the beginning she held her own. Referring to Jasiri's debut release *Sureshot Singles*, Novocaine wrote in *The Rocket*, "Kylea came just as solid as the fellas, adding vocals to 'Quietly Resurrect' and dropping a fresh flow on 'Come with Me,' proving even back then that she's an MC to reckon with." Describing herself, Kylea said, "I'm just a seed. I'm a seed because I'm just trying to grow."[62] Beyond Reality expanded the relatively small amount of local hip hop created by female artists by releasing the singles "Whatever" and "I Reality" on the Jasiri Media Group label in 1997. Beyond Reality shared the stage with another pioneering female group when they opened for New York–based trio Salt-N-Pepa at the Showbox in 1998. As hip hop in general and the portrayal of female artists in particular became more sexualized in the late 1990s, journalist Steve Stav declared in *The Rocket*: "Kylea's up-front, socially conscious lyrics and keen rhymes are a far cry from the misogynistic, egocentric chatter that a great deal of her male counterparts produce."[63]

In 1998 Source of Labor experienced a lineup change when Vitamin D took over for Kamikaze as DJ and musicians Darrius Willrich, Kevin Hudson, and D'Vonne Lewis also joined. The following year, Source of Labor released its debut album, the nineteen-track *Stolen Lives*, on the Jasiri label in partnership with New York's Subverse Records. Although it was Source of Labor's only full album, the group toured and performed until 2005. The value of artists who did more than just rap had been demonstrated in the 1980s by the likes of the

Emerald Street Boys and Sir Mix-A-Lot and in the 1990s by folks such as Jonathan Moore. Greg "Funk Daddy" Buren started out in the 1980s as part of Masters In Control (M.I.C.) and Ready and Willin. As a DJ, Buren worked with Kid Sensation and won the 1989 Battle for Seattle Supremacy as well as the first Soundwar in Vancouver, BC, in 1990.

In a remarkable show of versatility, Funk Daddy returned to the 1991 Soundwar and took first place in the MC competition. He released his 1994 debut album *Funk You Right on Up* on Shot Records out of the Bay Area and would become one of only two Seattle artists to appear on the cover of *The Flavor*. Two other solo albums followed, *Funk Daddy Is Tha Source* and *I Want All That*, as did a host of production credits with such artists as Sir Mix-A-Lot, Daz, D12, Dru Down, Cool Nutz, B-Legit, Rass Kass, Money B, N2Deep, and Mac Dre. In addition, his music was included in the ABC drama series *Dangerous Minds*, based on the 1995 movie starring Michelle Pfeiffer, as well as in the films *Rhyme and Reason* (1997), *3 Strikes* (2000), and *Street Racing* (2002).[64]

The Bay Area's association with local hip hop expanded in the 1990s as Seattle's production talent attracted the attention of hip hop's best and brightest. One example was E-40's 1995 album *In A Major Way*. Hailing from Vallejo, California, E-40 began in the late 1980s as a member of The Click. One of the early West Coast hip-hop entrepreneurs, he built a national following self-releasing music on Sick Wid It Records. E-40's independently released debut album *Federal* (1993) created enough buzz to attract the attention of Jive Records, leading E-40 to become among a wave of West Coast hip-hop artists to sign with a major label in 1994. *In a Major Way* became E-40's second solo album as well as his debut for Jive.[65]

Two Seattle producers were tapped to contribute to the project. Funk Daddy, whose body of work, including the 1994 album *Funk You Right on Up*, had solidified his reputation as one of the West Coast's hottest producers. He got the call soon after his manager and former University of Washington football player J. D. Hill connected with E-40 at the Gavin Convention, a music industry conference in San Francisco.[66] The other producer, Kevin Gardner, had grown up absorbing the production styles and techniques of early local legends like the Emerald Street Boys and West Coast Funk Brigade. After working locally with legendary producer Robert Redwine and Kid Sensation, Gardner did extensive production during the 1990s, including numerous projects from members of The Click. On *In a*

Major Way, Gardner produced the song "Smoke 'n' Drank" while Funk Daddy was responsible for "Sideways," "It's All Bad," and "Fed." *In a Major Way* proved to be E-40's breakout record, peaking at number thirteen on the *Billboard 200* and number two on the R&B Albums chart. The record was certified gold (five hundred thousand units sold) by the Recording Industry Association of America (RIAA).[67]

The Seattle–Bay Area hip-hop relationship continued to strengthen when local group DMS (Dee.ale, Moe-B, and Sheriff) released their debut EP on Shot Records, owned and operated by D-Shot. He was a member of The Click, along with his brother, E-40. DMS's 1994 six-track release *Takin Ends* featured the song "Sunshine," an ode to the group's love for marijuana. As connections to hip hop in other regions brought more outside attention to the local scene, Seattle artists opened doors for themselves. Since his days as a beatboxer and member of DURACELL Crew in the 1980s, Silver Shadow D pushed grassroots hip hop, making his name as a multitalented artist who rhymed, produced, and scratched all his own material. In the early 1990s he opened for such national acts as E-40 and The Click, Da Lench Mob, and Sinead O'Connor. Silver Shadow became the first rapper to perform at the Bite of Seattle and opened for Naughty By Nature at Bumbershoot (both summertime events held at the Seattle Center). He was written up in *Vibe* magazine and toured with Sir Mix-A-Lot. While appreciative of the opportunity, Silver Shadow D said of Mix-A-Lot: "He's never seen me perform and I talked to him a total of 10 or 15 minutes the whole time we were on tour." Silver Shadow launched his company Lost and Found Productions and self-released his debut album *Sleepless—Tha BricKKKs* in 1994.[68]

Political content in hip hop was swiftly evaporating in the face of gangsta rap of the era, but "Phunky Phat 95" performers Black Anger reclaimed it. Made up of DJ E-Real, Wicked D, Kendo, and Kendo's younger brother Sayeed, Black Anger out of Tacoma exemplified hip hop's connection to the military. E-Real met the other three group members in the early 1990s while living at Fort Lewis Army Base. Not satisfied with the movement of Tacoma hip hop, the group gravitated toward Seattle's independent rap scene. Kendo described Black Anger's music as "a 50/50 fusion of Hip Hop culture and Black Liberation movement."[69] In 1996 Olympia–based K Records released the group's single "Feel What I Feel" (B side "No Commercial"). Critic Dan Johnson wrote in *The Rocket* that the lyrical focus of both tracks was revolution, a subject important to Black Anger. "The lyrics painted a picture of corrupt capitalism and economic slavery while also hinting that maybe a shift in the balance of power is imminent," Johnson explained. "All this without ever actually defining revolution." Kendo said that was the point: "I don't want to tell you what it is. I want to give you something that will make you decide what it is."[70]

The political attitudes of local hip hop were not only expressed in words but in action as well. Even before he was eligible to run for public office, Kwame Wyking Garrett represented the intersection of community activism, politics, and hip hop. Growing up in the Central District, he listened to the latest rap music at the home of his childhood friend Jacob "Jake One" Dutton. Garrett was immersed in activism at a young age when his father, Omari Tahir-Garrett, helped lead the occupation of the Colman School building in 1985. The younger Garrett spent substantial amounts of time in the building, absorbing the Afrocentric ideology and atmosphere of civil disobedience. As soon as he turned twenty-one—the minimum age to run for elected office in Washington State—Garrett officially became a political candidate. In 1998 he ran for state representative Position 1 from Seattle's Thirty-seventh District as a Lincoln Republican, an African American party that patterned itself after abolitionist Frederick Douglass. Garrett said he would work to "pass legislation establishing a Truth and Justice Commission to study racism." He was "neutral on Initiative 200, the statewide ballot measure to end racial and gender preferences in government hiring, contracting, and education, saying it would not bring about economic or institutional change."[71]

Garrett ran again in 2004, and his statements in the *Seattle Times* reflected his community-centric approach: "We have more young people going to prison than we have going to college," he said. Teachers should be better paid, and school curricula need to be culturally relevant to encourage positive self-identity and prepare students to participate "in an increasingly competitive global economy." Gentrification of the Central District and other neighborhoods in the Thirty-seventh District amounted to "'ethnic cleansing' of Seattle's black community," Garrett said. "We see our community plagued by problems," but political leaders have failed to provide opportunities to solve them. "I know my community feels left behind."[72] Garrett also advocated for increased funding to support small businesses to encourage job creation. Losing both races in the general election to Democratic Representative Sharon Tomiko Santos, Garrett received 10 percent of the vote in 1998 and 12 percent in 2004.[73]

Seattle's Underground Rap Producers and Perceptions of Growth

Political candidacies and diverse content were indicators of a healthy and growing hip-hop scene. However, the growth of all local rap music generally relies heavily on a handful of talented producers who are consistently willing to put art first. One such producer was Derrick "Vitamin D" Brown. Vitamin grew up with deep musical roots as the son of Herman Brown, who played guitar with the Motown Records group Ozone. Although Vitamin lived in Los Angeles, he visited Seattle often before he and his family moved to the Central District in the mid-1980s. His cousin was Eddie "Sugar Bear" Wells of the Emerald Street Boys, a connection that led Vitamin to his first set of turntables at age thirteen. Vitamin performed at Garfield High School assemblies under the name $D=MC^2$, where he would emerge from behind his DJ equipment and deliver clever freestyle rhymes that brought the house down. His comfort in front of an audience came at least in part from a junior high experience acting in the Steve Sneed and Reco Bembry–produced play *Peer Pressure*. Over the years Vitamin has maintained this connection by occasionally directing musical theater.[74]

By 1989, with his growing collection of equipment and his developing production skills, Vitamin converted the basement of his Central District home into a full-fledged studio. This recording space came to be known as The Pharmacy, "where Vitamin D became one of the most important hip-hop producers on the Seattle scene."[75] While still in high school, he became known as Vitamin D, a name that was given to him "by Garfield." In 1991 he teamed with another Garfield student, Bill "B-Self" Rider, to form the Ghetto Children. Music critic Vanessa Ho described their style in the *Seattle Times* as jazzy and smooth, paired with strong beats and intelligent lyrics. "'Ghettoriffick vibrations' is how they describe it," Ho wrote. "Both Derrick Brown, 18, and Bill Rider, 20, rap and produce, and they share the same taste in the old school: Ramsey Lewis, John Coltrane, Grandmaster Flash and the Furious Five, and Cold Crush Brothers." Ho noted the duo rapped about poverty, growing up, wanting to be successful. "In 'Odd Ball Sindrome,' they rap about being strong to yourself. And in 'Questions,' they sample De La Soul and a lecture on slavery."[76]

The collective of artists who hung out and recorded at The Pharmacy—Ghetto Children, Sinsemilla (DJ Topspin and H-Bomb),

Union of Opposites (Truth, Black Star, and Native Son), Phat Mob, and Narcotik (C-Note and T-Dog) as well as solo artists Infinite and Sho-Nuph—eventually became known as Tribal Productions. Tribal released the compilation album *Untranslated Prescriptions* in 1995, recorded, produced, and mixed entirely by Vitamin D at The Pharmacy. With sixteen tracks, the record was described by Novocaine in *The Rocket* as "more dope than pharmaceutical, this tape nevertheless represents a medicine for the ailing hip-hop enthusiast, in the form of an intricate, yet inviting puzzle, non-conventional and untranslated." The numerous members of the Tribal collective had maintained an active presence in the local scene. The Ghetto Children won the Black Student Union Talent Show at the University of Washington in 1995, and Sinsemilla's DJ Topspin released *101.1 KTOP FM [Fat Mixtapes]— Broadcast #1*, the first mixtape from his self-created fictional radio station "KTOP." Tribal followed *Untranslated Prescriptions* with *Do the Math* in 1996. The music being produced by Vitamin D prompted *The Rocket* to refer to The Pharmacy as "one of the least prominent but most pre-eminent hip-hop recording studios in the Northwest, where aspiring jewelers can elevate and build through the art of rhyme." As popular as gangsta and hardcore rap music had become during the 1990s, *Do the Math* presented an alternative approach. "The lyrics are not only from the heart but are also vocabulary-oriented toward the more cerebral listener."[77]

Tribal kept pushing with another compilation. *14 Fathoms Deep* was released in 1997 on Pearl Jam guitarist Stone Gossard's label Loosegroove Records. "The project is absolutely monumental in scope and could almost double as a 'who's who' of Seattle's underground hip-hop scene. Among the groups involved are Blind Council, Jace, DMS, Source of Labor, Union of Opposites, Beyond Reality, Mad Fanatic, Narcotik, and many more," wrote Novocaine in *The Rocket*. "There are enough dope tracks here to keep you away from *Yo! MTV Raps* for a month."[78] Loosegroove had multiple local hip-hop connections as it also released the album *Procreations* by the group Prose and Concepts in 1994. Formerly known as Six in the Clip, all six members of Prose and Concepts—DJ Ace, MC Dope, Rawi, Shark E., Beatnik, and Mic Dub—graduated from Garfield High School. However, this multiracial crew experienced some pushback. "Regulars of the Seattle club scene, the band built name recognition and a fan base as Six in the Clip. They got press, and because of it, some resentment from other hip-hop acts. People thought that because some of the band members were white, the press were supportive of the group," wrote Jason Sutherland in *The Rocket*. "That's the vibe I got from people," explained DJ Ace. "It was just that we were playing a lot of shows so our name would get out there."[79]

Prose and Concepts worked on a record deal with Loosegroove, which was distributed nationally by Epic/Sony. Before what turned out to be the group's final album *Everything Is Nice* was released in 1997, however, the label and Prose and Concepts went their separate ways; sadly, Mic Dub died by suicide in December 1996.[80] Despite how it ended, Loosegroove's association with Prose and Concepts furthered the relationship between Seattle hip hop and local grunge-related record labels. Sub Pop Records' initial foray into hip hop through its 1995 production and distribution deal with local label Conception Records helped expand the profile of underground Seattle hip hop, both regionally and nationally. The first hip-hop act to formally sign with the label was The Evil Tambourines in 1998. Formed in the mid-1990s by Andy Poehlman and Tobias Flowers, the group released their debut album *Library Nation* on Sub Pop in 1999.

In a profile in the *Seattle Times*, journalist Tom Scanlon noted that the Tambourines' upcoming show at the Breakroom in support of the album would be "the band's first Seattle concert—and only fourth public performance, anywhere." In terms of the group's sound, he wrote: "They knew they wanted to do something like De La Soul and a Tribe Called Quest, and they knew they had to find skilled musicians to help them." Poehlman, a native of Kent, Washington, admitted: "We're not good musicians. I'm not, and Tobe's not. We're just two guys with ideas on how to make records."[81] With production help from the Sharpshooters, their single "Saturn" was praised by critics. However, *Library Nation* experienced only marginal commercial success, and Sub Pop refocused exclusively on rock for the better part of the next decade.

The connections between Seattle's hip hop and rock communities continued with a brief collaboration between two of the biggest names. In 1998 Sir Mix-A-Lot and the Seattle-based, multi-platinum-selling, Grammy-nominated band the Presidents of the United States of America formed the group Subset. Incorporating local rock into his music was nothing new for Mix-A-Lot. His 1988 debut album *Swass* contained a cover of iconic metal band Black Sabbath's song "Iron Man," featuring local rockers Metal Church, and he also teamed with Seattle group Mudhoney to record "Freak Momma," which appeared on the soundtrack for the 1993 movie *Judgment Night*. Subset recorded several songs and toured briefly in 2000 but parted ways over creative differences and never officially released any material.[82]

Although there was plenty of activity, some opinions painted a dismal picture of the late 1990s local hip-hop scene. In 1997 *The Rocket* published "The Beat Writers: A Seattle Hip-Hop Roundtable," moderated by *Rocket* features editor S. Duda and featuring promoter Robert Brewer, Tribal Music co-owner Damisi Velasquez, Jonathan "Wordsayer" Moore, Erika "Kylea" White, Major Weight Media founder Kriz Beeber, DJ Topspin, Silver Shadow D, and "Nasty" Nes Rodriguez. Asked to rate the current Seattle hip-hop scene on a scale of one (worst) to ten (best), the panelists were brutally honest, giving an average answer of five among them. Silver Shadow D gave it a seven: "As far as the actual scene, it's kind of shaky." Velasquez rated it a three: "Venue owners are scared of hip-hop, period." Brewer estimated the scene at six: "The Teen Dance Ordinance really ruined chances for hip-hop to grow." Kylea said five: "It's tough to do a show here. If you're not opening up for someone, you're not gonna get that large a crowd." DJ Topspin said: "As long as the powers that be are the *only* powers that be, we'll be in the four-five range." Nasty Nes rated the scene at five: "I've been doing this since 1980 and I've seen a lot of groups come and go and the main problem is the lack of good promotion behind the stuff."[83]

In response to that piece, one *Rocket* reader wrote in a letter-to-the-editor: "The Seattle hip-hop scene is so fucking sad. Tiny places like Davis, California, are doing worlds of work to expand the culture, and what do we have?" Strath Shepard, partner in Conception Records, responded with a column in *The Rocket*. He defined "progress" within local hip hop as "having a fair number of artists achieving that coveted balance between creativity and capital—doing enough of what they want and still being able to feed themselves." After defining what it meant, the question still remained: "Is Seattle hip-hop moving forward? It's not. Really. Overall it's not moving forward. Critical acclaim and no sales. Incredible music and no distribution. Ambitious management and wack product." However, Shepard offered a set of solutions and accompanying commentary in what he called "Moving Seattle Hip-Hop Forward: Ten Points of Light." He suggested the following:

1. Quit pretending you're from somewhere else. Why is it no one will admit they're from Seattle?

2. Get off the Balzac. Quit imitating what other cities were doing six months ago.
3. Have a savings account. There are too many wack MCs out there and not enough back-up plans.
4. Pay attention. Try to understand the industry.
5. Make records. Tapes don't count.
6. Ask for help. If you don't know anything about business or other aspects of the game, ask someone who does.
7. No more compilations. People don't buy compilations because they tend to be overwhelming for press and radio and often don't get the attention they deserve.
8. Support local music. Of course you're a DJ; who isn't now? That doesn't mean you should get every new record for free.
9. Quit hating. Stop falsely shifting responsibility for stagnation outside yourself.
10. Stay in the game. To earn a reputation, we have to stay focused and keep putting out good records, just like Toronto, Davis, and other respected outsider cities. Keep the faith and don't stop.[84]

Local Hip-Hop Radio Controversies

Although criticisms about the state of the scene were present, there was also a shared dissatisfaction regarding the inadequacy of Seattle radio as it related to exposure for local hip-hop artists. During the 1990s major changes took place in the landscape of Seattle hip-hop radio. "Shockmaster" Glen Boyd left *Rap Attack* on KCMU for a job with Def American Recordings in Los Angeles in 1992. After a decade "Nasty" Nes Rodriguez also left as host of "Seattle's-Only-All-Rap-Show-in-FM-Stereo," moving to LA in 1997 to take a position with the music industry magazine *Hits*. In a controversial decision, KCMU program director Don Yates hired a Vancouver, BC, DJ named Maximus Clean to take over the show. The response from Seattle's hip-hop community was skepticism. Mr. Supreme stated in *The Rocket*: "It's nothing personal, but I think there is absolutely no way for an outsider—someone from another city—to stay in touch with the local scene." DJ B-Mello added: "I don't think it's impossible for someone from another city to host a good rap show here, but I was surprised they didn't choose a local DJ." The KCMU program director responded: "We want the most qualified person to host *Rap Attack* and Maximus Clean has the most experience." Less than a year later, Maximus Clean resigned as host of *Rap Attack* due to an unresolved immigration issue that forced him to return to Canada. Mr. Supreme and Kutfather took over the show, which was subsequently renamed *Street Sounds* in 1998.[85]

Aside from *Street Sounds*, other options to hear hip hop on the radio in Seattle were few and far between. During most of the 1980s, KFOX was the dominant force for hip hop on local radio. By 1999 hip hop on radio in Seattle was "either diluted on KUBE or concentrated into one Sunday night slot on KCMU." As culture critic Charles Mudede wrote in *The Stranger*, "KCMU's hip-hop show, *Street Sounds* (formerly known as *Rap Attack*), is currently hosted by local superstars Kutfather and Mr. Supreme, with frequent assistance from turntablists like DJ Topspin." Mudede credited both Supreme and Kutfather as talented with great voices and sharp comments about the music they played. "My gripe has nothing to do with the content of the show," Mudede wrote. "My gripe is that there is only one such show to gripe about."

Jonathan "Wordsayer" Moore, quoted in Mudede's piece, added that hip hop has often been marginalized and had its legitimacy questioned while becoming the most dominant music art in this generation. "So, when you have two hours out of the week, not out of a day, you take it as an insult. Sunday from 6:00 to 8:00? Why not have it on Friday from 5:00 to 10:00, at a time when I can remember to listen to it? This is like the stone ages," Moore said. "In fact I think they should have a show just for local hip-hop alone, hip-hop from Tacoma, Bellingham, Vancouver." Ethnomusicologist Joe Schloss, quoted in the article by Mudede, compared the Seattle market to other regions. "There is something like 16 different radio shows for different types of hip-hop in the Bay Area. It doesn't make sense, economically or socially, that we have only one hip-hop show. It doesn't seem to benefit anyone. As popular as hip-hop is, it seems the normal thing is to have a lot of hip-hop on the radio," said Schloss. "Seattle will continue to suck as long as it fails to offer us two competing hip-hop shows on FM stereo, Friday and Saturday nights, from 5:00 p.m. to 5:00 a.m."[86]

Although stations like KCMU and to a much lesser extent KNHC were known for playing local hip hop, they existed on public radio. The king of commercial urban music ratings during the 1990s in Seattle was KUBE 93 FM, part of Ackerley Communications, whose chairman Barry Ackerley also owned the Seattle SuperSonics. For most of the decade the station operated primarily under a rhythmic contemporary hits (RCH) format, playing top-40 rap and R&B hits by national artists. However, the tension that had been growing between KUBE and the local hip-hop community eventually came to a head in the spring of 1997. Picketers holding signs saying BOYCOTT KUBE 93 and DON'T SUPPORT A STATION THAT DOESN'T SUPPORT LOCAL ARTISTS appeared in front of the radio station. Gordon Curvey, creator and host of Seattle's public access television show *Music Inner City*, said: "For 16 years they haven't supported local artists, and KUBE only has *one* black DJ, and they put him on in the middle of the night. Ninety-nine percent of KUBE's playlist consists of black-music artists, but they aren't playing what kids in the inner-city want to hear. KUBE is targeting young, white, suburban teenagers." He continued: "They don't care about inner-city youth, although they are making all their money off black people." Other community members participating in the protest included organizer Silver Shadow D, Curtis Elerson of Just Cash Records, and former Emerald Street Boy and CEO of CD Raised Records James Croone, who added: "We're just asking them to play our artists, to care about the local independent scene."[87]

Mike Tierney, KUBE music program director, responded to the criticism in *The Rocket*: "I don't make music calls—that's not what I do here. There are specific hours and specific personnel [at KUBE] who handle submitted tapes and requests, but that's not my job." Journalist Tina Potterf pressed him on the point: "So just what does a music program director do? According to Tierney, his job is to find and play hits, which is what listeners want." Tierney explained that "KUBE's playlists are compiled from record sales, local Soundscan figures and requests." Potterf noted that Tierney admitted to not listening to much of the music that crosses his desk, including artists represented by labels present at the demonstration. "By *looking* at a tape or the name of the artist, I can usually tell if it's going to be a hit," Tierney said. Potterf asked Tierney why there were no African Americans in various departments at the station and no African American DJ during primetime hours. "I think it'd be great to have more blacks [at KUBE]," he said. KUBE agreed to meet with the protesters and discuss ways that the station and local artists and labels could work together. "It was either KUBE meet with us or they knew we were going straight to their advertisers and promoters," Curtis Elerson remarked. "We're frustrated that local artists cannot get any love in their hometown.

We just want some airplay. It's not like we're asking for a Grammy—I mean we'd take it—but for now, we just want to be heard."[88]

These protests represented the continuation of a long tradition of direct social action within Seattle's African American community. The overlap between hip hop and demonstrations of this type was new, unique, and impressive. It showed the strength of social fabric that supported artists and the local scene, as there were few cities challenging media over exposure for homegrown talent in this way. While it struggled to play local artists consistently, KUBE actually did contribute to more nontraditional hip-hop programming. One example of this expansion on radio was Tony B's show *Street Beat*, broadcast on KUBE, which engaged the community on a broad level. After taking over a doomed AM music station in KFOX and changing the station's call letters to KJAM in the late 1980s, KUBE hired Tony B. *Street Beat*, which premiered in 1990, was a weekend hourlong urban affairs program that discussed such issues as gang violence, HIV/AIDS, and drug abuse prevention. As a veteran of the local scene, Tony B made sure that *Street Beat* served as a forum for music from Seattle.[89]

Television and Seattle Hip Hop

While radio remained a key ingredient, the emergence of cable and alternative/public access television stations created an increased demand for content just as hip hop was poised to invade popular culture. The archetype for the local urban music television series premiered in 1983 with New York City's *Video Music Box*. Hosted by Ralph McDaniels on public station WNYC-TV, *Video Music Box* was the first program to prominently feature hip-hop videos and became an extremely influential outlet in exposing up-and-coming New York area artists to the mainstream. Instead of a studio, the show was shot at various locations around New York City such as parks, schools, and nightclubs.[90]

In Seattle the first locally produced television program to showcase rap videos was *Music Inner City* on Seattle Community Access Network (SCAN). The show, executive produced and hosted by Central District native Gordon Curvey, premiered in December 1990.[91] Curvey's goal for *Music Inner City* was twofold: one was to play videos from local artists that were not being shown on MTV or BET; the other was to include interview segments with various guests—both inside and outside the world of hip hop—that discussed youth-oriented issues such as education, drugs and gangs, and violence prevention. Some of the guests to appear on *Music Inner City* included Michael Jordan, Oprah Winfrey, Stevie Wonder, James Brown, Dionne Warwick, Rick James, Al Green, Chaka Khan, George Duke, George Clinton, Ice Cube, and Seattle native Quincy Jones. Local artists featured on *Music Inner City* included Sir Mix-A-Lot, E-Dawg, DJ B-Mello, Kevin Gardner, KUBE radio personalities Eddie Francis and Tiffany Warner, and Redwine. The show received a nomination for a *Billboard* magazine award for Best Regional Video Show and was named Urban Music Video Show of the Year by *Urban Network* magazine in 1999. In 2005 *Music Inner City* became available on Comcast's On-Demand service, and Curvey himself was honored with the fifth annual Mayor's Award for Excellence in Hip-Hop for media in 2006.[92] First presented in 2000 by Seattle mayor Greg Nickels, the award recognized important contributions of community members to local hip hop.

Within a year, there was another hip-hop video show available on SCAN. *Coolout Network*, started in 1991, was the creation of New York City native Georgio Brown, who moved to Seattle in 1990. Brown had witnessed the birth of hip hop firsthand and had seen the transformative effect of *Video Music Box* on local hip hop. After seeing an episode of *Music Inner City*, he learned that anyone could produce a show on public access television after completing some basic free broadcasting classes at the SCAN offices. Upon completion of a video production class, Brown started his own show—a weekly thirty-minute time slot for thirty-six weeks, called *Coolout Network*—a name based on his past as promoter of a series of parties, "The Coolout Club," while in college in the mid-1980s.

The first episode was broadcast on April 4, 1991. Initially Brown did not intend to be the star of the show, preferring instead to focus on artist interviews and performances. He was largely unaware of the show's impact until the second year of production, when he posted his home phone number at the end of each episode. Almost immediately he received a flood of phone calls from artists, managers, promoters, record companies, and others interested in connecting with *Coolout Network*.[93] The show sought to cover local rap music as well as other elements of hip-hop culture. In addition to nearly every relevant local name, Brown interviewed national artists like Afrika Bambaataa, KRS-One, Naughty by Nature, Mary J. Blige, Public Enemy, Rob Base, MC Serch, and Digable Planets. In 2004 he and *Coolout Network* received the third annual Mayor's Award for Excellence in Hip-Hop. "Our region is home to a flourishing artistic community," said Mayor Nickels, "in fact, a recent study showed that we have more arts businesses per capita than any other metropolitan area." He continued: "Seattle has one of the strongest and most creative music scenes in the country. This genre (hip hop) deserves credit for innovation, creativity, musical excellence and diverse appeal." [94]

The Flavor: Seattle's International Rap Magazine

Television was not the only local emerging media platform for highlighting hip hop–related content. An example of local print media in the early 1990s was *The Flavor* magazine. Founders Alison Pember and Rachel Crick met in junior high while taking an elective radio class, which involved working at KASB, a low-wattage radio station at Bellevue High School. In 1991 the sudden death of Pember's close friend Jennifer Peet inspired Pember to act on her dream of starting a hip-hop magazine. She and Crick used the industry contacts they'd accumulated while working at Tower Records and Sony Music, respectively. With Pember set as publisher and Crick aboard as co-editor-in-chief, the search for a name began.

The decision to name the magazine, initially published as a quarterly, *The Flavor* came at least in part from the hit 1991 song "Flavor of the Month" by New York duo Black Sheep. Coincidentally, beginning in 1993 on the Fox television network sitcom *Living Single*, Queen Latifah played a character who was the editor of a fictional hip-hop magazine called *Flavor*. Planning for *The Flavor* began in fall 1991, and several guiding principles emerged. As a grassroots publication in Seattle, they initially vowed not to cover Sir Mix-A-Lot due to his national popularity. The writers at *The Flavor* would cover the music that they liked. Advertising would not influence editorial content, and the magazine would not require its staff writers to have any formal training. Instead community members from the local scene—such as DJ DV One, DJ B-Mello, and Supreme—would conduct interviews and write stories. *The Flavor*, which was free, specifically targeted rap music's early 1990s demographic: fifteen to thirty-four-year-olds, one-third female and two-thirds male.[95]

Using their own savings, Pember and Crick published the first issue of *The Flavor* from the home of Pember's parents in Shoreline, just north of Seattle, in January 1992. A mission statement on page three announced that *The Flavor* was a "Seattle-based hip-hop music publication focusing on, but not limited to, the Northwest. We are the only print medium devoted exclusively to hip-hop in this region. This area has a sizable underground scene that needs an outlet such as this."[96] Pember's father, a media law professor at the University of Washington, served as a consultant for the fledgling magazine. Pember and Crick threw a launch party, starring their first cover feature, an up-and-coming West Coast group named Cypress Hill. From the very first issue, the magazine's mailing list included numerous record companies. MCA Records called to inquire how they could get legendary DJ/MC duo Eric B. and Rakim on the cover. After the second issue, advertising revenue—the lifeblood of any commercial publication—started flowing.[97] However, it was not all smooth sailing, particularly at the beginning. "There was lots of local resistance," Pember noted. "Lots of 'what are white girls doing with a hip-hop mag?'"[98]

Following its launch in 1992, *The Flavor* had experienced steady growth both as a business and as a credible hip-hop publication. With this growth came various functions and celebrations marking anniversaries and accomplishments, a practice common within hip hop since the beginning. In 1994 the magazine celebrated its second anniversary by bringing to Seattle Ed O.G. and Da Bulldogs from Boston; New York artists Nas, whose debut album *Illmatic* had just received the coveted "5 mic" rating by the iconic hip-hop magazine *The Source*; the Fugees, featuring Wyclef Jean and Lauryn Hill; and Coolio, out of Compton, who would soon release his number-one Grammy-winning single "Gangster's Paradise."[99]

Rather than being a local hip-hop publication, *The Flavor* functioned as an international magazine based in Seattle. Every issue had a local section, but only two Seattle artists, Sir Mix-A-Lot and Funk Daddy, ever appeared on the cover. The world of magazines dictates that covers move copies, and artists who were most widely recognizable served to promote growth. By 1995 the magazine had become a monthly, increased in size, included a hip-hop crossword puzzle, and undergone a change in format to all newsprint paper, which put it in direct competition locally with *The Rocket* and *The Stranger*, another Seattle alternative newspaper established in 1991 by Tim Keck and James Sturm. Launched during the era of flashier, male-founded hip hop and R&B publications such as *The Source* and *Vibe*, *The Flavor* was different: it was free and it primarily courted the record store market in a time when such outlets, in addition to selling music, served as social gathering and listening spots. Housed in an office in the University District, *The Flavor* had a staff of sixty, which included several correspondents in different cities. "Few magazines cover the swaggering world of rap music," the *Seattle Times* explained. "And there is certainly no other run by a team of women—especially women who are white, black and Hawaiian. Yet as a team they are leaders in a global field: making a product appreciated far away." The co-owner of a London record store remarked: "Those guys are on the case. Our shoppers pick up that magazine like they pick up records."[100]

Circulation grew, and at its peak *The Flavor* reached tens of thousands of readers across the United States as well as in countries such as Great Britain, Denmark, and the Netherlands.[101] While raising its international profile, the magazine remained active on a local level. In 1994 *The Flavor* collaborated with Folklife Festival program director Paul de Barros to produce "The Flavor Magazine Showcase" at the annual festival. Performers included Source of Labor, Jace and the Fourth Party, and DJ B-Mello. The following year, *The Flavor* sponsored "Homegrown Hip-Hop II," featuring Tribal Productions, J. Moore, Beyond Reality, and Shabazz Coalition.

The Flavor ceased publication suddenly in the summer of 1996, after De La Soul appeared on the cover of issue number thirty-four. A December column in *The Rocket* by Payton Carter noted: "Six months ago, Seattle's premier hip-hop magazine, *The Flavor*, disappeared off the racks and has been out of circulation ever since. . . . What happened to it?" Strath Shepard of Conception Records and general manager at *The Flavor* explained: "The magazine is on an extended hiatus because everybody is doing their own thing. It's kinda doubtful there will be any more issues of *The Flavor*." The story reported that Pember and Crick had accepted jobs in New York City and Los Angeles, respectively. Carter reminisced: "For as much flak as *The Flavor* sometimes took in this town, it was extremely well received outside the Northwest as an honest, self-respecting, slick-looking, good-old-fashioned hip-hop rag, and dang, I miss it."[102]

Digital Hip-Hop Media Outlets Emerge

With *The Flavor* shut down and the Internet just beginning to take off, new people using fresh technologies began to pick up the slack as the transition was being made from print to digital media. One of the more visible examples of this shift was Chukundi "DJ Kun Luv"

Salisbury and his Seaspot Media Group. A native of Seattle's Central District, Salisbury graduated from Garfield High School in 1987 and attended Elizabeth City State University, a public, historically Black college in North Carolina. During his time on the East Coast, Kun Luv became a well-known DJ in the Elizabeth City community. Upon moving back to Seattle in 1992, however, he was forced to start from scratch in a highly competitive DJ environment. Kun Luv turned to the fertile market of "hood spots" in the Central District, including places like Fabros, The Turning Point, 24 Hour Social Club, and Uncle John's Tavern. He introduced his "Big Fella Blends" line of mixtapes, which he marketed at every opportunity. He was active in the community, receiving the Seattle-King County Generations United Hand in Hand Award for promoting positive intergenerational relationships in 1994. DJ Kun Luv played top clubs around the city by 1997 such as Pier 70 and the biggest parties, including Seattle SuperSonics point guard Gary Payton's annual cruise.[103]

By the late 1990s the Virgo Party, which started in 1992 as a birthday barbeque for Kun Luv at a house in the Central District, had become urban Seattle's biggest gathering of the year. Held each September, the party had grown quickly in popularity and soon was held at major downtown venues. Controversy arose when the 1997 Virgo Party, held that year at the Showbox, was blamed as the source of a riot. The *Seattle Times* reported that police were hoping videotape from a surveillance camera in Sneaker City on Pike Street would lead to arrests after looting that involved nearly seven hundred people took place downtown. "The shoe store was one of several downtown businesses looted or vandalized during the riot," the newspaper reported, "which police said began when a group of young people was turned away from an event at the Showbox on First Avenue near Pike Street." The article noted that some two hundred people were ejected from the event, "billed in entertainment listings as 'DJ Kun Luv's Virgo Birthday Party,' [Seattle Police Lt. J. J.] Jankauskas said yesterday. Those ejected joined more people waiting outside, who had tried to rush the door. The crowd had grown to between 600 and 700 people, Jankauskas said." The story described more looting and arrests at The Bon Marche (Macy's), public urination, and the exchanging of high-fives among the looters. When fifty additional police officers arrived to help deal with the situation, the crowd threw bottles and bricks at them. One downtown resident described the scene: "It was complete and total anarchy." Also mentioned was a 1992 nuisance-control ordinance approved by the Seattle City Council that gave the police sweeping powers over businesses with repeated cases of loud noise, fights, and illegal drinking. In response to the ordinance, at least one club owner sued the city, charging bias against businesses that played hip-hop music and catered to an African American customer base.[104]

Although a follow-up interview in *The Stranger* allowed Kun Luv to put his side of the story out there, the question of direct media access remained. As a computer science major, Kun Luv saw tremendous possibility in the still relatively young Internet. The answer, launched in 1998, was Seaspot Media Group, which Kun Luv branded as "the gateway to Northwest urban culture." Seaspot.com grew to include comprehensive information on Northwest urban nightlife, photo galleries of recent events and happenings, music headlines, news, and a regular op-ed column called "Knowledge Street." In addition to the website, there was a monthly print version of *Seaspot* magazine. At the height of its popularity during the early and mid-2000s, Seaspot was in fact the "gateway" for urban culture in the Pacific Northwest.

Kun Luv was not working alone. Local entrepreneur Keith "Ghetto Prez" Asphy brought a special skill set to Seaspot. As Charles Mudede explained in *The Stranger*: "Be it local artists who are on his record label, or national acts, or designs for CDs or fliers that advertise dance and rap competitions . . . if you need black entertainment services, and are in the Pacific Northwest, 'the Ghetto Prez' will provide it." People like Kun Luv, the Ghetto Prez, Keith "Bear" Anker, and numerous others built Seaspot into the first predominant multimedia urban-culture platform for the Northwest, including Canada. "Of all of Asphy's operations, the one that impresses me the most is *Seaspot*—not so much the magazine, which is glossy and colorful, but the website. Hands down, it's the most comprehensive resource for black entertainment in the Pacific Northwest," Mudede continued. "If you want to find where black people or black music be at, then that's where you go." Asphy said: "That's my business. Those who want to know where it's happening, I let them know. We get 100,000 hits a month on the website. And it's not just to see what's going on, but also the pictures. We send photographers to the shows, and they take pictures and we post them, and a lot of people visit the website to see themselves." Seaspot's headquarters featured a map of America hanging over a number of high-powered computers. The Northwest section of the map contained a cluster of pins marking cities and towns in Idaho, Montana, and British Columbia—all important markets. The extent of Seaspot's reach and influence made it "the center from which black entertainment radiates across the Great Northwest."[105]

Seaspot Media was not the only local company using the new-found power of the Internet. Launched in 1999, Skratchcast.com was an early version of an online hip-hop radio station headquartered in the northeastern Seattle neighborhood of Lake City. The site's founders, Joshua Kusske and Jason Schluter, had been involved in online day trading when they came up with an idea to put hip hop on the Internet. Skratchcast.com had audio and video feeds and ten hours of daily original programming, featuring both local DJs and others from various parts of the country. Within six months Skratchcast .com was drawing more than five thousand visitors every day. The ultimate goal was to create an online portal for hip-hop culture. "A lot of people out there are just getting into hip-hop, and don't really know where it came from. We have some people who can provide education; the older DJs like to talk about what it was like before you could make money in hip-hop. We're a place to bring people together," said Schluter. "Right now our main stream of revenue comes through our record shop. But we're basically a TV station or a radio station, and how do they generate revenues? Through advertising. It's basically the same thing we'll have to do."

Schluter and Kusske's plan was to turn Skratchcast into an independent hip-hop media empire. "We need to increase content: editorial, broadcast, and the graf[fiti] gallery. We need to improve the store. Right now we sell 12", singles, LPs, mix tapes, and we're moving into videotapes, magazines, clothes, and DJ equipment," Kusske explained. "With the Internet you can provide more content, more knowledge, more products, and more service, so we wanna do that." These longer-term plans included developing a variety of online channels for different aspects of hip hop such as interview, mix show, turntablist, and b-girl and b-boy channels. Advertising would become a primary revenue stream, making Kusske and Schluter early adopters of what would become the basic business model for the most popular hip hop–based websites in the twenty-first century.[106]

As the Internet's popularity soared, traditional media platforms still told the story of local hip hop in the late 1990s. One example of this was the MAD Krew's 1998 documentary film *Enter the Madness*. Produced by DJ Scene and directed by King Khazm, the film presented different aspects of the Seattle scene by featuring the breaking crew Massive Monkees, DJs like Kutfather, and rappers like Khingz and Alpha-P. The film presented a regional look by including Swollen Members of Vancouver, British Columbia, and Portland, Oregon-based Lifesavas. *Enter the Madness* experienced moderate success with screenings around the country and provided an insider's view of the happenings in and around Northwest hip hop during the late 1990s.[107]

The do-it-yourself attitude that created hip hop translated well to the world of public access television in both New York during the 1980s and Seattle in the early 1990s. Following in the footsteps of Gordon Curvey's *Music Inner City* and Giorgio Brown's *Coolout Network*, King Khazm, Dirty Dev, and the MAD Krew created *Hip-Hop 101* in 1999 on Seattle public access television. The show served as a destination for local and national hip-hop artists and provided a platform for the greater community to learn about the latest news and trends within hip hop. "Viewers would tune in religiously and even call in and ask questions, often to really learn that hip-hop is not just this image that is perpetuated by mainstream media, that there's a whole range to it," recalled King Khazm. "It's not necessarily all the glitz and glamour, and the misogynistic and materialistic stuff—there is a local community for one. And, two, it's very diverse." Georgio Brown became a part of *Hip-Hop 101* in the early 2000s, contributing content, staff, and overall production, and soon after, 206 Zulu took over the reins. When resources became scarce in the late 2000s as a result of the Great Recession, funding for public access television was cut, and *Hip-Hop 101* came to an end in 2009.[108]

Hip-Hop Fashion

While hip-hop music from Seattle may have struggled at times for recognition in the mid-to-late 1990s, one locally-rooted company's interpretation of hip-hop fashion did not. For many, clothes have been an important source of cultural symbolism within hip hop from the beginning. Tony Shellman and Lando Felix grew up in Seattle's Madrona neighborhood. As a teen in the 1980s, Shellman worked at Nordstrom before moving to the trendy boutique Zebra Club, where Felix joined him. By the early 1990s both had moved to New York City to attend the prestigious Parsons School of Design. Shellman got a job with clothing manufacturer International News, where he met his supervisor and eventual partner, Evan Davis. In 1994 Shellman, Felix, and Davis—with financial backing from International News—launched the urban clothing company Mecca USA. "Mecca started with a revelation," Felix recalled. "Kids were getting their looks from different stores. Shoes from Foot Locker, baggy jeans at Nordstrom, funky tops from some streetwise boutique. We knew we could do an integrated line—and make it logo-driven, with a sporty flair." Felix was proven correct as Mecca USA sold more than $20 million worth of merchandise in three seasons. After the flood of initial success, however, International News pushed for Mecca branding on everything from socks to jewelry to cologne. Shellman, Felix, and Davis disagreed with this approach, and in 1996 the founders of Mecca USA sold it to International News and left the company together.[109]

Shellman, Felix, and Davis were ready to unveil their next concept by 1997—a clothing line that paid homage to New York City, the birthplace of hip hop. The name of the new company—ENYCE— phonetically spelled NYC but was pronounced eh-NEE-chay. The company partnered with Italian athletic sportswear company Fila. "When I first hooked up with Fila," Shellman recalled, "executives from the headquarters in Italy flew in to meet us. I sat in the boardroom wearing cargo shorts and a T-shirt." His new partners didn't recognize Shellman as they walked in to the meeting and asked him to leave. "So I waited outside, and after everyone arrived, I went back in and introduced myself. They all felt terrible and apologized, but it just spoke to my philosophy to be yourself. Wear your own suit."[110]

The official ENYCE spring launch was held in Seattle. "We just had to show ENYCE here. We learned so much growing up in Seattle. We learned all this stuff from local lines. It's been just a major, major influence," Felix explained. "I'm Filipino, Evan's white, Tony's African-American. We have employees who are Ukrainian, who are Chinese/Indian, Japanese/Hawaiian. Everyone is very different." The ENYCE spring line was shown in Nordstrom locations at malls in Tacoma, Bellevue Square, and Southcenter. The launch included a party presented by *The Source* magazine at the Showbox, featuring Los Angeles rap group Tha Alkaholiks, local hip-hop crew Oraclez Creed, and DJ B-Mello.[111] ENYCE became a top urban fashion label specializing in outerwear, graphic tees, denim, and knits for men and boys; a line for women and girls; and a "big and tall" line for men. The company's wide appeal was affirmed when Liz Claiborne Inc.

purchased ENYCE for $114 million in February 2004. The recession of 2007, combined with Liz Claiborne's relative inexperience with urban fashion, devalued the company significantly, and in 2008 current owner Sean "Diddy" Combs acquired ENYCE for $20 million.[112]

In 2006 Shellman, Davis, and several former ENYCE executives launched yet another clothing line, this one called Parish Nation. Unlike his other previous two ventures—Mecca USA and ENYCE—Shellman started Parish Nation without any outside financial backing. The creative inspiration for Parish Nation came from "comics/TV/hip-hop iconography, politics, religion, basically anything we talk about on a daily basis. Things we've grown up on are what inspires the brand." Shellman explained that he and his partners left ENYCE, wanting to start "a brand that would inspire creativity and would be about the talent, the designers. Everything in life is a risk, some are willing to take it, others just stay reserved and wish they had. We're about action."[113]

Hip-Hop Community Action and the Birth of Massive Monkees

The community-centric focus of some hip-hop media at the end of the 1990s was mirrored by events and organizations that placed equal amounts of focus on serving young people. Ten years after Seattle's Teen Dance Ordinance, all-age resources in the city had become increasingly vital and scarce. One effort to give all-age access to hip hop was Sure Shot Sundays at the Sit & Spin, on Fourth Avenue in downtown Seattle across from the historic Cinerama movie theater. Beginning in 1999, Sure Shot Sundays was a family-friendly, alcohol-free, smoke-free event that ran from 12:00 noon to 6:00 p.m. every Sunday and featured local dancers, DJs, and MCs. Organized by Jonathan "Wordsayer" Moore and Jasiri Media Group, the venue itself was actually a Laundromat with a café and a performance space that included a stage, sound system, and lighting with a capacity of nearly 150. Sure Shot Sundays enjoyed a successful five-year run until the building, which housed Sit & Spin, was sold to a developer in 2004.[114]

In the 1980s hip-hop programs on college radio stations around the country helped grow underground aspects of the culture. In the 1990s campus-based student clubs organized and provided outlets and opportunities for the hip-hop community. One local example was the Student Hip-Hop Organization of Washington (SHOW) at the University of Washington. Meli Darby, a UW student who would create Obese Productions, recalled: "I was at a meeting at the mayor's office regarding the TDO [Teen Dance Ordinance], and met [then-UW student and future *Stranger* hip-hop columnist] Sam Chesneau. Sam was saying he felt the hip-hop scene was being unfairly targeted— and that hit me very hard." Along with Chesneau and Darby, several other students formed the original nucleus of SHOW. They included George "Geologic" Quibuyen and Saba "Sabzi" Mohajerjabzi of Blue Scholars, Jason "J-Promo" Norcross, and Marc Matsui. Among other things, Darby was in charge of designing the majority of the group's promotional materials. During SHOW's existence the organization was a key agent for underground hip hop and an advocate for the under-drinking-age hip-hop crowd. In its five-year tenure, SHOW never put on a twenty-one-and-over event, including a performance by New York rapper and actor Mos Def at the Husky Union Building (HUB) in 2000.[115]

While specific events and groups like Sure Shot Sundays and SHOW served a vital purpose, the decision by individuals to reach out and make themselves available to youth has always been at the heart of service. One case of this during the 1990s was DVS. Fever One and Jeff "Soul One" Higashi began b-boying together as junior high class-mates in 1982. Initially a graffiti crew, their name DVS originally stood for "Da Vandals Succeed." Over time it also came to mean "Droppin Vicious Styles" and "Dissin Various Suckas" among other things and in 1992 members Sneke and Rey joined. The crew's reputation grew as they entered and won local and regional competitions such as the Soundwar in Vancouver, British Columbia.[116] DVS actively promoted the local scene, as in 1993 when they teamed up with Mr. Supreme, Kutfather, DJ B-Bello, and Source of Labor to launch The Foundation, a weekly hip-hop night at the Art Bar.

As much as DVS became known for their dancing, by the late 1990s, with Fever also now a member of Rock Steady Crew, their repu-tations as premier graffiti artists were equally widespread. The group eventually expanded to include honorary members in Miami, Paris, Switzerland, Germany, and Vancouver, British Columbia. DVS's busi-ness interests were represented by their company Kuthroat Designs, specializing in custom clothing, logos, business cards, live shows, and video production.[117] As global as DVS's reach was, the continued work of its members in schools and community centers around Seattle and the Northwest during the 1990s helped lay groundwork for future generations of local b-girls and b-boys.

In the later part of the decade, DVS used hip hop as a means of grassroots youth outreach at Mercer Middle School and Jefferson Community Center on Beacon Hill. Fever, Soul, and other local artists built various programs using different aspects of the culture, including breaking. Their work turned Jefferson into a destination for aspiring local b-girls and b-boys, and the sessions there served as an incubator for up-and-coming dancers who wanted to show and prove themselves against the best. During his time at Jefferson Community Center, Fever noticed a young Filipino dancer named Jerome Aparis. "Jeromeskee," as he would become known, had gotten hooked watching *Beat Street* and VHS tapes of local crews like DVS and Boss Crew. In his early teens Aparis wasn't always the best dancer, but his willingness to learn and ability to focus made him stand out.[118]

Jefferson Community Center's popularity among the breakdance community meant two things: First, it was common to have enough dancers or crews present for pickup or practice battles to take place on a regular basis. Second, individuals from these different crews got to know each other in ways that segregated separate practice sites would not have permitted. This type of interaction brought members of two Beacon Hill groups, Massive Crew and Untouchable Style Monkees, together in 1999. The cofounding members of Massive Monkees were Terry "Dancing Domes" Guillermo, Brysen "Just Be" Angeles, Marcus "Juse Boogie" Garrison, and Jeromeskee. After working their way through the community center competition circuit, Massive's first major title came in 2000 at the B-Boy Summit in Los Angeles, when group members Juse and Twixx won the two-man category.[119] This initial triumph laid the foundation as a new generation of Seattle b-girls and b-boys competed and won national events as well as those on the world stage.

— —

The conclusion of the 1990s marked the end of a historic, Grammy-winning yet seemingly mixed decade in local hip hop. Fever One became the first Seattle dancer to join the world-famous Rock Steady Crew. Not content to simply leave town and relocate to New York, he returned frequently and set about creating spaces for younger, up-and-coming breakers to test their skills under his watchful eye.

His affiliation with the Jefferson Community Center on Beacon Hill helped turn Jefferson into an oasis for b-girls and b-boys, which would eventually spawn individuals like Jeromeskee and groups like Massive Monkees. Although there were increased levels of activity and success, *The Rocket* published an article in the late 1990s that indicated local attitudes about the current state and future of Seattle hip hop seemed uncertain at best. On a scale of one to ten, the average score given to the local scene by several of Seattle hip hop's movers and shakers was a five. Despite this, the turn of the century held promise for the possibilities of local hip hop, as there was less focus on New York and Los Angeles as the "capitals" of rap music. The twenty-first century would see a blossoming of hip hop from Seattle as different elements of the culture prepared to take the world by storm.

This continued growth in various areas benefited from a maturing hip-hop infrastructure. Experience was teaching best practices for local people and organizations involved in the culture on nearly every level. The results would speak for themselves in terms of mainstream recognition and success, from future award nominations to breaking victory on the world stage. Aside from the glamour of such achievements, the spirit of community drove the heart of local hip hop. Whether it was standing up to politicians in the name of hip hop or collaborating with a mayor in recognition, the soil from which grassroots hip hop in Seattle grew remained rich and fertile.

Photos

(*opposite, top*) In the early 1980s DJs and MCs such as the Emerald Street Boys, Jam Delight, West Coast Funk Brigade, 3D, Duke and Double Rock, Silver Chain Gang, and the Emerald Street Girls helped lay the foundation for a dynamic local scene. (*left to right*) Emerald Street Boys' Edward "Sugar Bear" Wells, James "Captain Crunch" Croone, and Robert "Sweet J" Jamerson. Courtesy of Kristine Larsen.

—

(*opposite, bottom*) "Nasty" Nes Rodriguez (*right*), DJ at radio station KKFX (KFOX), meets Anthony "Sir-Mix-A-Lot" Ray (*left*) at the Boys and Girls Club in the Central District, and the Seattle rap scene grows. They founded NastyMix Records in 1985 with partners Ed Locke and Greg Jones. Courtesy of Sheila Locke.

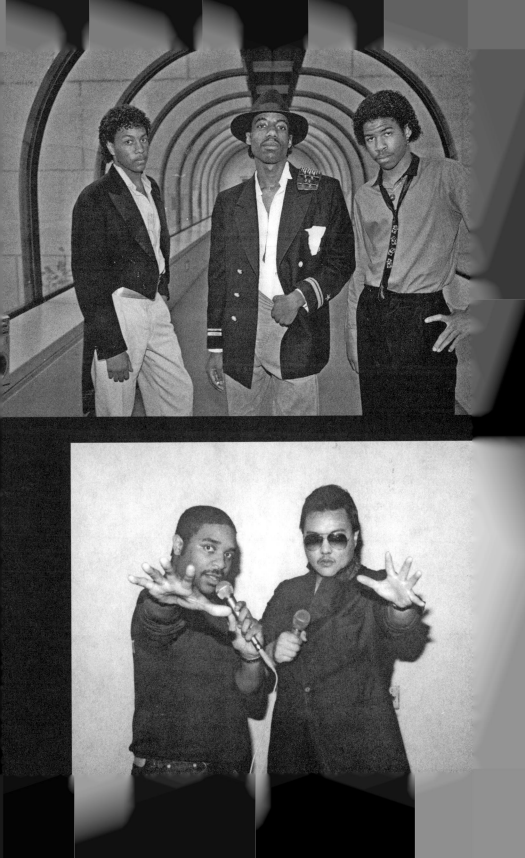

HIP, HOP DANCE CONTEST

Sunday, August 26, 1984

Featuring: Breaking, Bopping, Popping

Demonstrated by Seattle Circuit Breakers
1:30 to 1:45 p.m.

The Seattle Breakers, the #1 group in Seattle, was founded by Dan "Glide" Claverilla and Judge "Kid Loose" Garvey. The eight member group has climbed to dominance in the Seattle area and has staged exhibitions and performances not only in Washington, but Oregon, California and Canada. The Circuit crew, sponsored by Adidas*, has strong feelings about positive attitude and to always do its best. The crew currently teaches classes in five different studios.

Contest starts at 1:45 p.m. with no intermissions!

So, come on down to the Seattle Center Flag Plaza and show us your bop, pop, and break style!

Prizes for the best hip hoppers!

Lots of fun!

Free to carriers!

HIP, HOP DANCE CONTEST RULES

1. Must be a contracted carrier.
2. May not be affiliated with any professional dance group.
3. Must provide own music and dancing surface.
4. Contestant has a maximum of one (1) minute to execute routine.
5. Contestant may enter only one time regardless of number of routes contracted.
6. Contestant must sign liability release to participate. It must be completed and brought to the competition. See your district adviser/suburban representative for extra forms.
7. Decision of judges is final.

PRIZES PRIZES PRIZES

Each contestant receives a rhinestone studded white glove!

1st Place —$25 gift certificate, The Athlete's Foot*

2nd Place —$15 gift certificate, Tapetown

3rd Place —The Jackson's "Victory" album

(*opposite*) Hip, Hop Dance Contest, 1984. Hip-hop dance contests and gatherings like the one advertised in this 1984 poster served as sites of community and creativity for local talent. Courtesy of Supreme.

—

(*below*) Posing in front of local graffiti, 1988. (*left to right*) Stash, Supreme La Rock, and CMT. (*front*) Icey Ice. Danny "Supreme" Clavesilla's contributions as a DJ, producer, label founder and owner, and overall industry connector have spanned decades. Courtesy of Supreme.

(*opposite, top*) Jonathan "Wordsayer" Moore of Jasiri Media Group (*left*) with Damisi Velasquez of Tribal Music (*right*). Both operated independent record labels in the 1990s, further expanding participation expectations in local hip hop beyond simply performing. Courtesy of Kelly O Photography.

—

(*opposite, bottom*) After graduating from Garfield High School and moving to New York, Ishmael Butler, aka Butterfly (*right*), joined with Craig "Doodlebug" Irving (*center*) and Mary Ann "Lady Bug Mecca" Vieira (*left*) to form Digable Planets. The group's debut album was titled *Reachin (A New Refutation of Time and Space)*, and its lead single, "Rebirth of Slick (Cool Like Dat)," won Best Rap Performance by a Duo or Group at the Grammys in 1994. Photo by Barry King, Alamy Stock Photos.

(*above*) Record producer, DJ, MC, musician, audio engineer, and creator of the 1990s basement recording studio "The Pharmacy," Derrick Brown, aka Vitamin D, is widely known as one of the most important contributors to the Seattle hip-hop scene. Courtesy of Kelly O Photography.

HIP-HOP GUIDE FOR SEATTLE AND BEYOND

free december 1992 no. 4

the FLAVOR

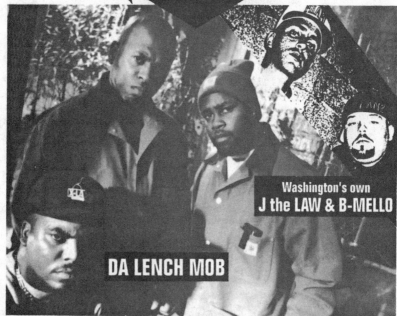

Washington's own
J the LAW & B-MELLO

DA LENCH MOB

**INSIDE: DA LENCH MOB DIGABLE PLANETS J THE LAW & B-MELLO MC SERCH
ZHIGGE DIAMOND (D) KOOL G RAP & DJ POLO YZ REVIEWS MORE**

(*opposite*) Seattle-based monthly hip-hop magazine *The Flavor*, founded by Allison Pember and Rachel Crick, focused on the music scene in the Pacific Northwest and beyond, opening a space for local and nationally renowned artists while being distributed at record stores across the United States and in several European countries. The cover of the December 1992 issue featured Da Lench Mob. Courtesy of Allison Pember.

—

(*below*) Sir Mix-A-Lot poses with his signature Lamborghini Diablo. One of three Seattle-bred artists to win a Rap Grammy, Sir Mix-A-Lot and his song "Baby Got Back" brought unprecedented global attention to local hip hop in 1993 by beating out the likes of MC Hammer, LL Cool J, Mark "Marky Mark" Wahlberg, and Queen Latifah in the Best Solo Rap Performance category. Courtesy of Ricardo Frazer.

(*opposite, top*) Erika "Kylea" White (*left*) and Jonathan "Wordsayer" Moore of Jasiri Media Group perform a DJ set at the opening of a clothing boutique on Broadway in 1999. White has been called the "Godmother" of Seattle hip hop, while Moore performed, managed artists, and in the 1990s fought to bring local hip hop to downtown venues that were hesitant to embrace live rap shows. Courtesy of Erika White.

—

(*opposite, bottom*) (*clockwise from bottom left*) Sneke, Hews, Jeromeskee, Fever One, and Soul One, photographed on the stairs of Soul One's North Beacon Hill house. Fever One, who grew up in the local scene before joining the world-famous Rock Steady Crew in New York City, returned to Seattle in the late 1990s to mentor youth with Soul One and others at what would become the mecca of breaking in Seattle, Jefferson Community Center on Beacon Hill. Courtesy of Matthew Chernicoff.

(*above*) Hip-hop artist, organizer, activist, educator, community leader, and founder of 206 Zulu, Daniel "King Khazm" Kogita. Courtesy of the artist.

—

(*overleaf*) 206 Zulu is a Seattle-based non-profit established in 2004 that uses hip-hop culture and arts as a path to community empowerment, education, and social change. Pictured here is the 206 Zulu family inside historic Washington Hall. Courtesy of King Khazm.

(*above*) Sportn' Life Records' (*left to right*) Spac3man (artist), Jennifer Petersen (staff), Fatal Lucciauno (artist), Nissim Black (artist, formerly D. Black), and DeVon Manier (owner), following a performance by Nissim Black at the 2010 Capitol Hill Block Party. Established in 2002, Sportn' Life's goal was to produce authentic, street-based Seattle hip hop. Courtesy of Sportn' Life Music Group.

(*opposite, top*) A native of Seattle's Central District, in 1998 Chukundi "DJ Kun Luv" Salisbury launched Seaspot, a multimedia platform that included a community-focused glossy, full-color magazine and an expansive website billed as "The Gateway to Northwest Urban Culture." Courtesy of Chukundi "DJ Kun Luv" Salisbury, Seaspot Media Group.

—

(*opposite, bottom*) Alexei Saba "DJ Sabzi" Mohajerjasbi (*left*) and George "MC Geologic/ Prometheus Brown" Quibuyen (*with hat*) met as students at the University of Washington and formed Blue Scholars in 2002. Based out of southeast Seattle, their music touches on issues of social justice, class struggle, and youth empowerment. Courtesy of Tone Photography.

(*opposite, top*) Raised in the Central District, Jake One became part of 50 Cent's G-Unit production team, the Money Management Group, in the early 2000s. The multiple Grammy Award–nominee has produced music for the likes of De La Soul, E-40, Tupac Shakur, 50 Cent, Rakim, Cypress Hill, T.I., Pitbull, Ghostface Killah, Snoop Dogg, Rick Ross, Drake, and Fun. Courtesy of Kelly O Photography.

—

(*opposite, bottom*) A third-generation Central District community builder, mayoral candidate, and founder of the local chapter of the Hip Hop Summit Action Network, Wyking Garrett, is president and CEO of Africatown Community Land Trust and a founding director of Seattle's African American Heritage Museum and Cultural Center at Colman School. Courtesy of Geekwire.

(*above*) Beginning in 2004, Larry Mizell Jr. had a long-running weekly column in local alternative newspaper *The Stranger* and later a show on KEXP. Through his extensive work in print and radio, Mizell was a key observer and critic of Seattle's varied and vibrant hip-hop community. Courtesy of Larry Mizell Jr.

(*opposite*) Hip-hop and breaking crew Massive Monkees was formed at Jefferson Community Center in 1999. Massive would go on to win the 2004 World B-Boy Championships in London, England, and the 2012 R16 World B-Boy Masters Championship in Seoul, South Korea. Courtesy of Jeromeskee.

—

(*right*) Jerome "Jeromeskee" Aparis started b-boying at Jefferson Community Center in the late 1990s as Fever One and Soul One were mentoring young dancers there. Jeromeskee is a founding member of two-time world champions Massive Monkees and their studio, the Beacon. Photographer unknown.

—

(*below*) Fides "Anna Banana Freeze" Mabanta is a Filipina American b-girl and teaching artist from Seattle's Beacon Hill neighborhood. She is the founder and instructor of classes such as "Way of the B-Girl" and programs like Mini BREAKS dance, and is the only active b-girl in the world-renowned Massive Monkees crew. Courtesy Vivian Hsu Photography.

(*opposite*) Ishmael Butler, aka Palaceer Lazaro (*left*, formerly Butterfly of Digable Planets), and Tendai "Baba" Maraire (*right*), son of mbira master Dumisani Maraire, make up hip-hop duo Shabazz Palaces. Initially shrouded in mystery, this duo has engaged in genre-defying creations such as "boho-gangster," which covered "gun talk and atmospheric rain sticks," according to the *Seattle Times*. Courtesy of SUBPOP.

—

(*below*) Stasia "Stas" Irons (*left*) and Catherine "Cat" Harris-White (*right*) came together as THEESatisfaction in 2008 and continued Seattle's practice of going against traditional hip-hop norms as LGBTQ-identifying artists on a major label. Courtesy of SUBPOP.

(*opposite, top*) Blogger, event producer, and content creator Miss Casey Carter is the host of KUBE 93.3's *The Come Up*, home to new and local music in the Pacific Northwest. Courtesy of Ivan Mrsic Photography.

—

(*opposite, bottom*) Macklemore and Ryan Lewis's 2012 hit single "Same Love" was the first song explicitly embracing and promoting same-sex marriage to make it into the Top 40 nationally. Here Macklemore poses in front of the Green Room in support of marriage equality for the August 1, 2012, cover of *The Stranger*. Courtesy of Kelly O Photography and *The Stranger*.

(*above*) Local MC "Gifted" Gab Kadushin commands the stage while performing at the 2014 Sasquatch! Music Festival. Courtesy of Connor Jalbert.

—

(*overleaf*) *The Legacy of Seattle Hip-Hop* exhibit (Museum of History and Industry, September 2015 to May 2016), curated by Jazmyn Scott and Aaron Walker-Loud, featured items such as custom-made Massive Monkees graffiti jackets, a local hip-hop timeline, a hands-on production workstation featuring music from Vitamin D and Jake One, and the fur coat worn by Macklemore in the "Thrift Shop" video. Courtesy of Museum of History and Industry (MOHAI).

4

"Solo Doe is my idol man, Cherry is the Street"

206/2K

THE debate about the connection between hip hop and violence in Seattle resurfaced in the fall of 2000. Early on the morning of Saturday, September 23, five people were shot outside the Bohemian Backstage nightclub, located in downtown Seattle's Pioneer Square neighborhood. The club had recently begun playing hip-hop music on weekends, and Police Chief Gil Kerlikowski said his officers had responded to numerous incidents over the previous few months. "The issue is, quite frankly, hip-hop," one neighborhood resident complained. "It has to do with the pathetic lack of emotional maturity of many hip-hop patrons." The rhetoric escalated at a joint press conference with Chief Kerlikowski and Seattle Mayor Paul Schell. Although the police described the shootings as an isolated gang-related incident, Schell said hip hop "can make audiences excitable" and claimed: "It has to do with a recipe of alcohol, guns and the wrong kind of music."[1]

The hip-hop community swiftly rallied to counter the mayor's position. By the following weekend, local companies Darkside Productions, Jasiri Media Group, L Brothers Entertainment, and Pak Pros organized a peaceful protest at Westlake Park in downtown Seattle. "I'm not here to defend hip-hop," said Jonathan "Wordsayer" Moore of Jasiri Media Group. "It speaks for itself. This is not about seeking any justification or to portray ourselves as being good or civilized. We already are those things." Aware of the anger Schell's comments caused, the protest organizers sought to cultivate connections among artists as well as promote discussion and relationships between the hip-hop community and local government.[2]

Schell's handling of the World Trade Organization (WTO) protests that rocked Seattle in 1999 had already doomed his chances at reelection, and in November 2001, Greg Nickels replaced Schell as mayor. Nickels and his administration brought an attitude toward hip hop that seemed to be the opposite of Schell's, as reflected in the creation of the Mayor's Award for Excellence in Hip-Hop. Originally proposed to Nickels's office by Tony B's MUSICA organization, the award acknowledged and honored innovative performance, community service, and entrepreneurial achievement by local members of the hip-hop community whose work had significant impact in Seattle. The institution of this award in the early 2000s signaled the city administration's newfound interest in embracing the cultural contributions of hip hop and more acceptance of hip-hop culture within the Seattle mainstream.[3]

Expanding the Variety of Seattle's Hip-Hop Music

The first recipient of the Mayor's Award for Excellence in Hip-Hop in October 2002 was Benjamin "Mr. Benjamin" Smith for the breadth of his community service. As an artist Mr. Benjamin, who started Deuce 8 Records in 1997, called his regional hip-hop dialect "Northern Flow." He said: "You know how everybody categorized their raps, Nelly had 'Country Grammar,' Master P had a down-South flow, Tupac had the East Coast–West Coast sound. My style I like to call the 'Northern Flow.'" In addition to releasing music, Mr. Benjamin spent years in area schools and youth centers, giving pro-education and anti-drug speeches.[4]

Mr. Benjamin and Deuce 8 Records were part of a larger group of local, independent record labels founded during the 1990s, which helped power Seattle hip hop into the new millennium. Among them were Seasick Records, which started off in 1990 as KL One Productions with Keek Loc and DJ DV One, and Dark Diamond Records, formed by Cedric Prim and Steven Johnson. Dark Diamond featured Step One Mobb, 2-Tyght, and Hustlers For Life, who combined to form the collective Mobb Tyght Hustlers and released a self-titled compilation album in 1997. Also that year, Edward Dumas launched Wet City Records; Street Level Records, founded by David "D-Sane" Severance III in 1996, which would produce such local artists as Full Time Soldiers and Byrdie; former Emerald Street Boy James Croone's CD Raised Records, which released the 1994 single "Krakerbashin" by the group Darkset; and Just Cash Records led by Curtis Elerson. Leading into the 2000s, the diversity of styles and approaches within Seattle hip hop kept the scene from being defined strictly by the more "hardcore" standards of rap that had come to dominate the charts nationally. This variety included pushback against post-9/11 "patriotism," a collaboration with funk legend Rick James, a local record company with an ear to the street, the rise of blue-collar rap and an accompanying record label, an out-of-town record company making a major play for local talent, the emergence of an independent white hip-hop culture, a spoken-word appearance on HBO, and a strong female influence.

Like others in the United States, hip-hop artists responded to the terrorist attacks that bought down the World Trade Center towers on September 11, 2001, as well as the subsequent run-up to the US wars in Afghanistan and Iraq with critical artistic responses. One of these came from Seattle in the form of *911 Amerika*, a fifteen-track compilation released in 2002 that critiqued post-9/11 government policy, executive-produced by King Khazm and Gabriel Teodros. The album featured production by Vitamin D and vocalists including Teodros, E-Real Asim of Black Anger, Erika "Kylea" White, and Silas Blak. Thematically, two things stood out in *The Stranger*'s review of *911 Amerika*. The first was that the events of September 11 were destined to happen "because of the U.S.'s ruthless political and economic policies toward foreign countries, especially Afghanistan," wrote music critic Brian Goedde. The second theme was that these artists refused to go to war for America "because they do not pledge allegiance to what they see as a corrupt, racist, morally reproachful government." The liner notes for the CD included "anti-military opinions and statistics" as well as contact information for groups like the Committee for Conscientious Objectors.[5]

The variety of rap music coming from Seattle during this period spanned the political to the popular, and the work of local hip-hop artists caught the attention of some larger-than-life musical figures. Following the release of their 2002 self-titled debut album, Seattle group Nocturnal Rage—made up of Caligula, PyroManiak, and Fo'Feva—scored a hit with their debut single "Miss Mary Jane." After performing and promoting the track around the country, the group got the opportunity to record a remix of the song, based on legendary funk musician Rick James's 1978 smash hit "Mary Jane" with James himself. Caligula said, "For Rick James to join us on our debut project is the total validation of our skills."[6] The timing of the collaboration coincided with a resurgence in James's popularity following his appearance in the skit "Charlie Murphy's True Hollywood Stories" on the Comedy Central network series *Chappelle's Show* with Dave Chappelle.

Diversity of Sportn' Life and Mass Line Records

The legacy of independent local record labels continued to inspire new generations of Seattle hip hop. DeVon Manier was a Southern California native and cousin of DJ Yella from NWA, who moved to the Northwest in junior high school. In the 1990s Manier was a part of Last Men Standing, along with Jamal Henderson, Emery "Slim" Buford, Bean One, and Jonathan "Fleeta" Partee, which Manier described as "a crew of friends that used to hustle together." From this group Manier formed Sportn' Life Records in 2002. "At the time, it seemed like nothing was coming out of the hood that was really worthy. We wanted to take off where Tribal [Productions and Vitamin D] took off," Manier explained. "We wanted to produce quality Seattle shit, not the generic Bay Area–style shit that was goin' on then. We wanted to be an independent force like so many black labels were becoming."

The debut release on Sportn' Life was a vinyl single by fourteen-year-old D. Black, who was known as Danger at the time, with "Last Men Standing" on the B side. As the son of both an Emerald Street Boy (Captain Crunch) and an Emerald Street Girl (Mia Black), D. Black was literally a product of the beginnings of hip hop in Seattle. Sportn' Life followed this with a compilation album, *The Sportn' Life Compilation Vol. 1*, released in 2003. The twenty-one track collection featured local artists D. Black, Fatal Lucciauno, Vitamin D, Calvin "Bean One" Stocker, Silent Lambs Project, and Big Partee. Over the next several years through acts such as Dyme Def, Spac3man, Larry Hawkins, and J.Pinder, Sportn' Life Records "put its stamp on the town and put out some landmark Seattle hip-hop albums. Not only that, it has curated and exposed some of the best artists from here."[7]

The growing diversity of the local scene was illustrated by the artists themselves as well as by style and subject matter. Born in Long Beach, California, George "Geologic" Quibuyen spent his early years in Hawaii before moving to Bremerton, Washington, in 1991. Geo listened to fellow Filipino hip-hop lover "Nasty" Nes Rodriguez, host of *Rap Attack* on KCMU and fell into informal rhyming sessions with his friends in parties at Silverdale Community Center, the Bangor Lighthouse, and the basements of the Masonic Temple and Star of the Sea Church. Outside of Seattle city limits and the grips of the Teen Dance Ordinance, a thriving all-ages hip-hop scene in Bremerton grew from these smaller venues to much larger ones such as the Kitsap Pavilion and the ballroom at the Bay View Inn.[8]

After Geo graduated from Bremerton High School, he moved to Seattle, enrolled at the University of Washington, and immersed himself in the local hip-hop scene, going to shows at venues like RCKNDY and Sit & Spin. As a member of the Student Hip-Hop Organization of Washington (SHOW) at the University of Washington, Geo met Alexei Saba "Sabzi" Mohajerjasbi, an Iranian American with a background in music. Sabzi and Geo found common social and political ground and clicked artistically, forming Blue Scholars in 2002. The name was a play on the term "blue collar," and *Billboard* described them as a "politically minded duo, marked by Geologic's working-class calls for action and Sabzi's jazzy backdrops." In 2004 they independently released their self-titled debut, which was named Album of the Year by the *Seattle Weekly*, received airplay on radio station KEXP, and earned them a second-stage appearance at the 2005 Sasquatch! Festival.[9]

Blue Scholars approach of hands-on do-it-yourself activism led them to form Mass Line Records in 2006 with manager Dave Meinert, RA Scion of Common Market, and the duo Abyssinian Creole made up of Gabriel Teodros and Khingz. Journalist Charles Mudede compared changing regional demographics to the Mass Line collective. "Like Mass Line's members," Mudede wrote, "Seattle is becoming increasingly culturally mixed. In 1990, white Americans made up 75 percent of the population; now that figure is close to (or has even passed below) 65 percent." From Everett to Tacoma, cities north and south of Seattle respectively, the numbers of East Africans and Latinos increased sharply, and the number of Asian Americans, African Americans, and Eastern Europeans in the region also continued to grow. "The metropolis's cultural mix is mirrored by the ethnicities of the collective, whose DJs and MCs (Iranian American, East-African American, Asian American, white American) will soon begin piping hip-hop through Mass Line."[10] In addition to *Sexy Beast* (2005) by Abyssinian Creole and Blue Scholars' and Common Market's self-titled debut albums from the Mass Line group were others such as *This What I Do* (2005) by Ballard rapper Grynch, records from Grayskul and Boom Bap Project, and *Hello World* (2005) by Framework. Of the material being produced, music critic

Larry Mizell Jr. was cautious. "True, 206 rap fanatics have been treated to a series of dope albums from their own backyard," he wrote; "let's hope our scene and our city's notoriously low self-esteem will improve accordingly."[11]

Rhymesayers Entertainment and Jake One

The development of local talent can be gauged by the level of attention it draws from out-of-town interests. Like Seattle, Minneapolis has had a long and active underground hip-hop scene dating back to the 1980s. In the early 1990s a group of local DJs, MCs, b-boys and b-girls, graffiti artists, producers, entrepreneurs, and promoters formed a crew called Headshots. Although Headshots would eventually dissolve for a variety of reasons, that collective gave birth to Rhymesayers Entertainment in 1995. The independent record company was founded by Sean "Slug" Daley, Anthony "Ant" Davis, Musab (formerly "Beyond") Saad, and Brent "Siddiq" Sayers and was soon the largest hip-hop label in Minnesota. Rhymesayers became known for its in-house retail outlet Fifth Element, which sold music, clothing, art supplies, DVDs, and specialty items.[12]

Rhymesayers signed several artists in 2004 from Seattle, including the groups Boom Bap Project and Greyskul, who released the albums *Reprogram* and *Deadlivers*, respectively, in 2005. Rhymesayers brought on Grieves, Vitamin D, and Jake One. A native of the Central District, Jacob "Jake One" Dutton made his name as a producer in the 1990s working with Conception Records. A disciple of Vitamin D, by the early 2000s Jake worked with some of the biggest names in hip hop, including De La Soul, Busta Rhymes, Gift of Gab, Mos Def, and many others. The trend continued in 2007, when Curtis "50 Cent" Jackson recruited Jake to produce for his third studio album *Curtis*. Jake's contribution was the song "All of Me," featuring the "queen of hip-hop soul" Mary J. Blige. The song and album became involved in the drama of 50 Cent's publicity stunt declaration that since the two albums shared a release date, if Kanye West's *Graduation* outsold *Curtis* in the first week, 50 Cent would retire from music. Though the publicity helped both albums post impressive sales numbers, Kanye West came out on top.[13] Jake One released his debut solo album in 2008, and Grieves's label debut *Together/Apart* came out on Rhymesayers in 2011.

Macklemore's Beginnings

Almost from the beginning, hip hop displayed multiracial character-
istics. However, around the turn of the millennium, a trend emerged
in the Seattle hip-hop scene—shows at predominantly white venues
where the promoter, producer, crowd, and artist were all white. This
active subculture of white hip hop in Seattle went through a lengthy
incubation process. About this time, fifteen-year-old Ben "Macklemore"
Haggerty made his live stage debut in 1999 at the Jonathan Moore-
produced Sure Shot Sundays in the Sit & Spin as a member of a group
called Elevated Elements. Macklemore eventually self-released a solo
EP, *Open Your Eyes*, in 2000 and his debut full-length album, *The Lan-
guage of My World*, in 2005. "My inspiration was honesty," Macklemore
said of his early work. "I wanted to capture every element of my life
regardless of how I'd be perceived. Hip-hop—and just music in general—seems to be in a state where artists are afraid of being human . . .
whether it's fear, insecurity, ego, struggles, or happiness, I wanted to put
it all out on the line. All of it. From addiction, to penis size, to white privilege, I chose subject matter that I feel people overlook in general."[14]

Macklemore met his musical partner, Ryan Lewis, in 2006 and
grew his name by performing at local community events and music
festivals such as Bumbershoot and the Sasquatch! Music Festival.
Appearances like these gave Macklemore the opportunity to play
larger national events like the Outside Lands Music Festival in San
Francisco, Lollapalooza, Rock the Bells, Soundset, and the Bonaroo
Music and Arts Festival in Manchester, Tennessee. "Dude is one of
my favorite cats in town with his sharp observations and keen sense
of humor," wrote *Stranger* journalist Larry Mizell Jr. "He never takes
himself too seriously and is a master at the fine art of self-deprecation.
My joint right now, 'Claiming the City' (which sports a choice appearance from Abyssinian Creole), is an insightful snapshot of Seattle's
quickly changing landscape. It cites racial politics and exponential
growth as reasons you might not recognize Seattle in a few short
years. Get up on this one, I'm telling you."[15]

As a descendent of the legacy of privilege, power, and oppres-
sion that helped lead to the creation of hip hop in the first place, the
white MC has traditionally occupied a complex space in the culture.
Journalist Charles Aaron described this complexity as coming from
Black people's suspicion of "whites who identify too closely with

African-American culture, primarily because those same whites often want to boost the culture wholesale."[16] Macklemore's association with figures like Abyssinian Creole, Blue Scholars, Suntonio Bandanaz, and other credible musicians indicated his navigation not only of the preexisting Black network of local hip hop but a newer multicultural one as well. Within this context potential resistance against Macklemore was relatively minimal.

Expanding Gender Diversity in the Seattle Hip-Hop Scene

Differences in perspective and approach continued to drive Seattle hip hop forward. The group Beyond Reality remained active with the release of their 2007 album *A Soul's Journey*. The bulk of production work was handled by well-known Seattle producer Bean One. "Kylea's staccato lines are devoid of any verbosity," music critic Rowald Pruyn wrote, "and her window to the world on *A Souls Journey* is strictly focused on the culture she has devoted so much time to. Songs like 'Clap Your Hands,' 'The 1-2,' and 'B-Girls' leave little to the imagination."[17] In addition to recorded material, female-centric events were an important aspect of building a diverse local hip-hop community. One example was a 2005 installment of Power Bill, a monthly series presented by Vitamin D and The Pharmacy at the War Room, which featured several standout Seattle artists, including Kylea of Beyond Reality who Larry Mizell Jr. said possessed "deft lyricism" and "certified b-girl pedigree"; Felicia Loud whose "superb soul is as filthy as it comes"; Laura "Piece" Kelley, "jazzy, intelligent, and insightful, she delivers the goods every time"; and soul singer Choklate, a rising talent and veteran of numerous hip-hop appearances.[18]

In 2004 Kelley continued the trend of local artists appearing on national platforms to display their talent as she was on the HBO program *Russell Simmons Presents Def Poetry Jam,* which aired between 2002 and 2007. The show, hosted by New York rapper and actor Mos Def, primarily featured performances by both up-and-coming and well-known spoken-word poets. The program was hailed by some as groundbreaking and labeled exploitive of poetry by others. Kelley appeared in season four, episode six, and in her poem "Central District," she dropped references to local history:

> For me it started with block parties
> And all night long gatherings

The standard greeting was
"Man, what's happening?"
Back when Empire Way became MLK

Even after Kelley's appearance on *Def Poetry Jam*, she continued to serve the local community. Among other things, Kelley taught poetry at Rainier Beach Community Center and was a program director for Powerful Voices, a Seattle nonprofit serving adolescent girls. She also presented a poem on stage at Key Arena in 2008 for the Dalai Lama, who was so impressed he requested a copy to take home.[19]

Kelley was an active part of Seattle's spoken-word community, performing with national artists such as Gil Scott-Heron, the Last Poets, Saul Williams, Gwendolyn Brooks, Angela Davis, and Bobby Seale. However, Seattle's spoken-word/hip-hop connection dated back to poetess and songstress Jazz Lee Alston, who released her self-titled debut EP on Sir Mix-A-Lot's Rhyme Cartel Records and appeared on the 1993 compilation album *Seattle . . . The Dark Side*. Poet Melissa Noelle Green was awarded the Mayor's Award for Excellence in Hip-Hop in the Spoken Word category in 2005. As for Kelley, in 2004 and 2005 she was named Seattle's Grand Slam Poetry Champion and became the youngest member of the Seattle Arts Commission. She continued her work with a one-woman show called *Street Smarts: The Story of a True School B-Girl*.[20] In addition to starring, Kelley produced the show, which had a two-week run at the Rainier Valley Cultural Center. The show positioned Piece as a "seeker of truth, keeper of peace and student of the street" who "performs her life work and calls for one people from her stage of life. As a poet, actor, and flow specialist, 'Piece' takes you running through her hood on a quest for urban enlightenment." Each act was poetically performed, and each song was a "northwest coast hip-hop original." Kelley's message was designed to unshackle minds "out of the mainstream ghetto, as she unites the power of the pen with the power of one in this theatrical breakthrough. Her lyrics are freshly woven into northwest coast beats, composed and produced from this Seattle native of the grid-block."[21]

Seattle Breaking Takes on the World

In addition to rap and spoken word, Seattle's breaking scene remained active, vibrant, and diverse around the turn of the century. One key example of this was the Lords of the Floor competition, first held in 2001. Sponsored by energy drink Red Bull, the competition was created by Bob "The Balance" of Circle of Fire. The Seattle-based crew earned international acclaim in 2000 by representing the United States in Germany at the Battle of the Year, the world's premier competition. Lords of the Floor was held at the Sand Point Naval Station, now Magnuson Park, in northeast Seattle. In addition to several invited teams from different parts of the country, more than $5,500 in prize money lured entrants from around the world.

Sixty-four crews began NCAA basketball tournament bracket-style two-on-two battles, with local products Massive Monkees and Circle of Fire among the invitees receiving automatic bids to the "Sweet 16" out of respect for their track record. The judges included Ken Swift, a founding member of New York City's legendary Rock Steady Crew. The following year, Circle of Fire was named producers for Lords of the Floor 2002, again sponsored by Red Bull. The event was described as "light years ahead of its time with its event setup, competition format, design and even graphics." It predated and served as a template for Red Bull BC One, which has become the energy drink maker's signature breaking competition.[22]

The level of breaking in Seattle helped push Circle of Fire to international heights with their appearance at the Battle of the Year, but the question became whether any of the local talent could bring home a trophy. That answer came in 2004, when the World B-Boy Championships were held at famed Wembley Arena in London. Thirty-two teams from numerous countries—Germany, France, Korea, New Zealand, Spain, Canada, and Japan—participated. Massive Monkees was one of several teams representing the United States. In what was "basically the World Cup of Break Dancing," Massive's lineup of Jeromeskee, Just Be, Juse Boogie, and J.D. Rainey took first place in the prestigious four-person battle category. "We were representing our crew at home, knowing that any of them could be in our position," Jeromeskee said after the victory. "When we first won, I couldn't comprehend it. It was different, it was unbelievable."[23]

The accomplishments of Massive Monkees did not go unnoticed in their hometown. Mayor Nickels said, "Massive Monkees have shown that they're the best in the world and they're sharing it with their community," and he declared April 26th as annual "Massive Monkees Day." In 2007 the Seattle Arts Commission presented Massive with the Mayor's Arts Award in honor of the group's continued contributions to the local arts.[24] Massive continued strengthening community connections when crew members began dancing at Seattle Super-Sonics home games in 2004. For numerous dates at Seattle Center's Key Arena, Massive members performed as part of the Sonics' "Boom Squad" during time-outs and at halftime. The Boom Squad was a regular presence at Sonics games until the franchise moved to Oklahoma City in 2008.[25]

Massive Monkees kept the spotlight on Seattle with high-profile events such as their eighth anniversary celebration in 2007. In addition to individual b-girl and popping battles, crews came from California, England, France, New York, and Texas to compete for the grand prize—a free trip to Freestyle Session '07 in Seoul.[26] After the passing of "the Godfather of Soul," Massive collaborated with Aaron Walker-Loud and Big World Breaks to host "4 the Love—A Tribute to James Brown" in 2007.[27] In 2008 the group sponsored Crash Test at the Paramount Theatre, which featured crews competing from Brazil, California, Finland, Florida, Korea, the Netherlands, and New York, along with Massive Monkees and fellow Seattle breakers Circle of Fire.[28]

The dizzying heights of achievement by local breaking crews in the twenty-first century inspired a new generation of dancers, crews, and events not only in Seattle but also around the Northwest. Emerging groups included Fraggle Rock Crew, Dance Broomz, Misguided Steps, Art of Movement (AOM), and Beacon Hill–based b-girls Vivid Vixens. There were also events such as Invasion of the B-Girls sponsored by the nonprofit House of Dames, "The Rec" battles in the Seattle suburb Shoreline, and breaking contests at Pacific Lutheran University in Tacoma. Another example was the Battle of Burien, a breaking competition held just south of Seattle. The event was originally conceived in 2007 by Burien Parks recreation leader Luke Cruise and volunteer Samuel Pasana. Over time the competition expanded to include more than fifty performers participating in one-on-one and two-on-two categories. These events served as breeding grounds for younger dancers. For example, the Vicious Puppies Crew (VPC), which formed at Denny Middle School in West Seattle and has had members compete in several Battles of Burien, was mentored by local legend and Burien native Jeromeskee of Massive Monkees who regularly came out to support the up-and-comers.[29] Local breakers continued to make their presence felt on multiple platforms. Colleen "B-Girl Bean" Ross won the 2008 "Mighty 4 International B-Girl Battle" held in France. Fever One and Jeromeskee were featured in the 2008 documentary film *Way of the B-Boy*. Fraggle Rock Crew took first place at the "Just for Laughs" competition in Montreal in 2013, and Fraggle Rock member Tim Chips won the Blaze Masters Championship one-on-one title in Greece.

Brainstorm Battle and Controversy

An impressive amount and variety of local hip-hop programming, both community and corporate in nature, functioned as a key ingredient in a vibrant scene. One grassroots effort was the first Brainstorm Battle in 2001, presented by the Student Hip-Hop Organization of Washington (SHOW) and MADK Productions (Khazma and Kazuo Oki). Brainstorm Battle was a freestyle rap competition that included some forty MCs from around the United States. The preliminary rounds were held at Sit & Spin in front of two hundred spectators. The top sixteen competitors advanced to the finals, which took place at the Paradox Theater, where an audience of nearly five hundred witnessed Bishop from the local group Old Dominion fall to local MC Khingz, who walked away with the $500 first prize.

The second annual Brainstorm Battle in 2002, presented by SHOW and MAD Krew, ended with controversy. Preliminary rounds took place at the club I-Spy with approximately sixty total entrants and a crowd of three hundred. The top sixteen advanced to the finals at the Ballroom in the University of Washington's Husky Union Building (HUB), where more than a thousand people watched Presence, a contestant from Chicago, take first place and the $2,500 prize. However, throughout the competition eyebrows were raised by the heavy use of homophobic and misogynistic language by numerous contestants during freestyle battles. Presence, who is white, created a stir by repeatedly using racial lines against Asian American and Pacific Islander opponents. In a post on Bay Area journalist and historian Davey D's website, Blue Scholars MC George "Geologic" Quibuyen, a Filipino contestant in the Brainstorm Battle who reached the final eight, recalled that against LDubble, a Chinese American MC, Presence said:

> The only thing missing from your outfit is a camera
> Cook me some Mongolian beef
> You can't hold the mic right, let me get you some chopsticks
> You're a chink with a little dick
> Your chances are slimmer than your eyes

And against Surge, a Puerto Rican American MC who Presence apparently thought was Filipino, he said:

> Go back to the Philippines
> Three lookalike references: you look like a Filipino [fill in
>   the blank]

Quibuyen acknowledged that there are not necessarily rules, written or otherwise, regarding what can or can't be said on onstage. However, "I've seen people get booed off stage for anti-black and anti-women remarks," he said. "Presence's lines did not surprise me. What deeply bothered me was the nearly 1,000 people who cheered on this overt racism, using hip-hop and the color-blind utopian all-about-the-skills-not-the-color mentality to justify it."[30]

In 2003 more than fifty contestants participated in the preliminary rounds of Brainstorm Battle 3 that were held at the club Chop Suey on Capitol Hill before a crowd of three hundred. This time, the winner was an MC named Bo-Rat from the Bay Area. For many, the highlight of the contest came in the round of sixteen when the bracket had yielded a matchup between Geologic and the defending champion, Presence. With the previous year's events in the air, Geologic eliminated Presence, and in the process he dropped several references to the racist lines Presence had used against Asian and Pacific Islander competitors. The fourth Brainstorm Battle in 2004 expanded beyond Seattle as regional preliminary rounds took place in Chicago, New York, Portland, Seattle, Los Angeles, and Ann Arbor, Michigan. All the regional winners received complimentary round-trip tickets to Seattle over Labor Day weekend to compete in the finals at the Bumbershoot Festival, where New York MC Iron Solomon won first prize.[31]

Local Events Large and Small Shape the Scene

The tenth anniversary of radio station KUBE 93's Summer Jam, a milestone corporate hip-hop event, took place in 2002 at the twenty-seven-thousand-seat Gorge Amphitheater in George, Washington, roughly 150 miles east of Seattle. The lineup included LL Cool J, Nelly, Jermaine Dupree, and Da Brat. Due to the distance of the venue in relation to Seattle and western Washington, large numbers of people stayed overnight at an adjacent campground operated by the amphitheater. It was there that Seattle entrepreneur Leonard Smaldino, who was selling food to hungry concert-goers returning to the campground, was shot and killed in the early morning hours.[32] After the incident officials in Grant County, Washington, were intent on shutting down the festival altogether, but the economic viability of the event brought about a compromise that only closed the nearby campgrounds.[33]

Another contribution to the variety of local, organic, underground performance venues in Seattle was Yo, Son!, a weekly Sunday night hip-hop event held at Chop Suey, started by entrepreneur Marcus Lalario in 2003. Yo, Son! was an attempt to combine rock and hip-hop sensibilities, which mainly drew neighborhood b-boys and b-girls without many similar alternatives. Another draw was that Yo, Son! "was clearly not going to be a corporate rap night, but an event affiliated with Seattle's underground hip-hop collective Stuck Under the Needle," Charles Mudede observed in *The Stranger*. "A press release that SUTN e-mailed out last year drew the line in the sand: Yo, Son!'s DJs would not play that 'horrible mainstream, crossover shit with the blingy eight-bar rap and the R&B diva on the hook.'"[34]

The overlapping nature of the musical and cultural infrastructure of the local scene was laid out by connecting the dots between venues and opportunity. "As Jonathan Moore of Big Tune and Jasiri Media Group often points out," Mudede wrote, "before Chop Suey and other Capitol Hill venues began regularly booking local rap shows in 2004, there was almost no place for local rappers to perform in this town. And this shortage not only meant no visibility but also no income. The community had little or no access to the financial infrastructure that's needed to sustain a scene and its artists and businessmen." Access to more and larger mainstream venues around Seattle opened the door to a new generation of local hip-hop performers, providing support that would help facilitate future opportunities. Following the success of Yo, Son!, Mudede concluded, came a series of important hip-hop shows such as Common Market at Neumos, Dyme Def at the Vera Project, and Blue Scholars at the Showbox that eventually "collapsed the wall between indie hip-hop and indie rock venues."[35]

As demonstrated in Tacoma in the early 1980s, the overall health and vitality of the local hip-hop scene did not rely on Seattle-based activities alone. Consistent events in surrounding suburban cities played an important role in growing the culture. One example of these alternative locations took place during the mid-2000s in the Seattle suburb Redmond, the home of Microsoft's main campus and headquarters. The regular hip-hop showcase 425-Get-Live, started in 2005 and named after the city's area code, was held at a venue called the Old Firehouse and the monthly program featured various artists from around the region.[36]

If diversity of location was important in expanding the reach of hip hop regionally, then so was recognizing the range of its participants. The multicultural nature of this environment was further underscored in an exhibit titled *It's Like That: APAs [Asian Pacific Americans] and the Seattle Hip-Hop Scene* at the Wing Luke Museum of the Asian Pacific American Experience in 2003, curated by George "Geologic" Quibuyen. Among other things highlighted were the contributions of local Asian Pacific Americans (APAs) such as "Nasty" Nes Rodriguez, MC Karim Panni, King Khazm, DJs Kamikaze and E-Rok, and the Emerald City Breakers. Quibuyen pointed out that local Asians "have made a name for themselves, especially in the b-boy and DJ sectors. A lot of them relate to hip-hop, having experienced similar oppressive conditions as the working-class black and Latino communities which the culture was born out of."[37]

The perspectives of APAs interviewed by Quibuyen helped illustrate the diversity of the hip-hop experience in Seattle. One example was local MC Paul "Eskatado" Javier of the group MSC. Javier grew up primarily in the West Seattle neighborhood of White Center, which he described as "mostly a Latino type community . . . a lot of black folks in there too . . . with more Southeast Asians that are middle class, lower class and blue collar workers," including "some projects up in there also in the Highland area." Aside from central sources of hip hop from radio programs like *FreshTracks* on KFOX, Javier recalled the action at neighborhood proving grounds such as Southgate Roller Rink in White Center, which regularly hosted breaking and rap battles.[38] Events such as the *It's Like That* exhibit helped set the stage for the eventual arrival of the Asian Hip-Hop Summit Tour, which made its debut in Seattle at the University of Washington's Ethnic Cultural Center in 2007. Initially formed in Los Angeles in 2002, the summit eventually visited twenty-seven cities across North America with the goal of using hip hop to fight prejudices and stereotypes of Asians and Pacific Islanders. While several artists from Southern California traveled with the tour, at each stop local talent was represented. For the second Seattle installment in August 2008, DJ B-Girl,

DJ Soul One, Sonny Bonoho, and Orbitron filled the Northwest Coast portion of the bill.[39]

Local hip-hop programming was a useful tool of expansion, having been present in Seattle nearly from the start. A variety of spaces created by and through the culture allowed individuals and organizations to engage the public and in many ways encouraged a hip-hop style of civic duty. The legacy of local artists engaging in community-driven events powered the Seattle hip-hop scene throughout the 2000s. One case was Hip-Hop Appreciation Week in 2005, sponsored by locally based SCIONtific Records and New York MC KRS-One's Temple of Hip-Hop. Beginning with a kickoff event hosted by Laura "Piece" Kelley at the Vera Project, a variety of performers included DJ B-Girl, Silent Lambs Project, dREDi, Nocturnal Rage, Cancer Rising, RA Scion, and Gabriel Teodros. In addition, the first Temple of Hip-Hop Festival for Kids was held at Rainier Beach Community Center with the purpose of allowing children to see "each element of hip-hop and how it can benefit their lives in a positive way." The four-hour program included a variety of seminars and workshops on such topics as writing and marketing.[40]

Another instance was Dope Emporium, founded in 2006 by tireless Seattle advocate Jamal "Jace ECAJ" Farr. Dope Emporium began as an all-age festival showcasing local MCs, poets, graffiti art, b-girls and b-boys, music video showcase, and producer battle. Educators, activists, artists, and independent media were included as participants. The result was a variety of free family-friendly exhibits and programs that showcased local talent while strengthening community ties. A community vendor marketplace showcased products and information from numerous local businesses.[41]

Big Tunes from Local to National

Occasionally a community-based event would develop into a corporate-sponsored affair. One example of this in Seattle was the inaugural Big Tunes challenge in 2005, a production/beat-making competition created and hosted by Vitamin D at the War Room. Vitamin theorized: "I figure, man, if I can just showcase the talent and bring the rappers and the producers in the same room, the scene's gotta flourish from there. There's gonna be relationships being made, and more shit's gonna build up."[42] Contestants included Specs One, DJ Topspin, the Track-headz, and eventual winner Kuddie Mac. The spirit of Big Tunes and its ability to attract beat makers and MCs from around the region resonated enough for journalist Charles Mudede to call it "one of the most refreshing events to hit the scene in some time."

Mudede linked the success of Big Tunes to four core spatial principles of hip hop. First was that hip hop needed a space, a place to happen such as a club, a house, or a warehouse. Second was the space in which hip hop happened must be "utopian in nature; it is a space of joy, or, as Tricia Rose once put it, a space of 'black pleasure.' This pleasure is not simply pleasure for pleasure's sake, but a form of resistance. It is a happiness that goes against the imposed miseries of poverty, police corruption, and official and unofficial forms of exploitation. In short, hip-hop is a celebration." Third was that this space was open to experimentation. "New ideas, new beats, new raps are welcomed into this celebration." Lastly, the space of hip hop was democratic. The new sounds and ideas were not judged by one or a few but by all in this space. "Big Tune is faithful to these principles," Mudede wrote. "It presents a space of pleasure, creativity, and popular participation. To win a Big Tune battle, a producer's beats must generate the loudest approval from the audience."[43]

Vitamin D combined with Jonathan Moore to grow Big Tunes enough to attract energy drink maker Red Bull as title sponsor. By 2009 the event was touring nationwide, eventually making appearances on television networks such as Black Entertainment Television (BET) and the music network Fuse. Events like Big Tunes, Dope Emporium, and the exhibit *It's Like That* all served their purposes well. The willingness of numerous historians, artists, producers, and others to engage the community on a variety of levels had become the norm. This dynamic was an important aspect of strengthening local hip-hop infrastructure as it supported, and was supported by, its surroundings.

Expansion of Graffiti

As various local media grew and evolved around the music, another aspect of hip-hop culture, graffiti, continued to develop as well. An example of formal graffiti showings occurred in 2000 with *Evidence*, an exhibit at the gallery Consolidated Works in downtown Seattle. Curated by Meg Shiffler and local graffiti artist Cause B, *Evidence* featured work by Barry "Twist" McGee, whose work Charles Mudede described as a mixture of "tags, bottles with weary faces on them, pictures of streets, alleys, walls—things that float in and out of the urban mindset. The work is both funny and sad, lazy and rigorous, delicate and rough, simple and complex." Also featured was San Francisco artist Amaze and local graffiti crews MAD Krew and By Any Means. Mudede noted the excitement around the exhibit and the work of these artists. "It is more fluid, more lyrical, more colorful than the graffiti writing of old," he wrote. "This 'late' gallery is now exhibiting an art that is not only a product of late capitalism, but has reached its final stages as well."[44]

An important part of graffiti, as in all forms of art, is access to materials. By the early 2000s a few retail outlets opened around the country that specifically carried graffiti-related supplies. Art Primo, established in 2003 by a group of friends who shared a passion for graffiti art, was originally launched by an all-volunteer staff as a website. It grew to hire several full-time employees and open a retail location in Capitol Hill. Aside from simply selling materials, Art Primo developed some of its own products. Staff worked in graphic design, organized community mural projects, and curated "open wall" spaces around the city. Art Primo's retail location hosted a variety of monthly shows, ranging from fine art to graffiti.[45]

While exhibitions like *Evidence* and stores such as Art Primo reflected legal aspects of street-inspired art, the shadow of illegal painting remained. Because of its blatant appropriation of public spaces, graffiti has always had an adversarial relationship with the general public, particularly when those painting openly embrace an outlaw identity. One example of this was local graffiti crew Big Time Mob (BTM)/American Aerosol Artists or All Against Authority (3A), formed by brothers Jesse "SEED" and Travis "TRED" Edwards.[46] BTM has long had members active in numerous cities around the world, and the crew commands respect with their attitude and global presence. Organizationally, BTM/3A operated under a constitution "loosely based" on the Mexican Mafia code of conduct: (1) never let the BTM/3A army down; (2) when disrespected by a stranger or group, all BTM/3As must unite to destroy the other person or group immediately; (3) always maintain a high level of integrity; (4) every member has the right to wear the tattoo of the 3 Aces or the BTM; (5) one must always do whatever one can to help a BTM/3A brother who has come on hard times; (6) every member has the right to express ideas, opinions, contradictions, and constructive criticisms; and (7) one must stay as physically fit as possible and continually strengthen their self-defense skills.[47]

It was not until the mid-1990s that Seattle officials made an organized attempt to combat graffiti on city property. Seattle Public Utilities formed a six-member Graffiti Ranger team in 1994 to remove graffiti all over the city. Over time the Rangers painted, buffed, and blasted thousands of illegal markings at a cost of more than $1 million per year. This amount covered only city-owned property as private businesses by law were forced to clean up their own graffiti or face fines of $100 per day. The dance between graffiti writers and city crews like the Rangers was ongoing and repeated around the world. In Seattle the Rangers responded to roughly two hundred complaints each month, and the prevention versus perpetuation discussion was a constant. The argument that the "fresh coat of paint" solution of the Rangers simply offered a fresh canvas that invited more graffiti was frequently proven.

According to Seattle Public Utilities, 90 percent of complaints came from the University District, Capitol Hill, and Ballard neighborhoods, and less than 10 percent of overall graffiti was gang-related. Anthony Matlock, head of the Seattle Graffiti Rangers, said the majority of taggers were middle-class white kids between fourteen and twenty-five years old. He noted that graffiti was almost nowhere to be found in the Central District until it gentrified in the 1980s and 1990s. "When it was a minority community, it was never a problem," Matlock said. "People like to say [graffiti] is a minority thing, but it's not."[48] Indeed, police data from 2005 indicated that fully half the people arrested for graffiti offenses in Seattle actually lived in outlying areas such as Mercer Island, Kirkland, Bellevue, and Tacoma.[49] Meanwhile, the persistent use of graffiti as a subject of formal art showings continued. The exhibit *The Visual Art of SPECSONE*, featuring the work of the veteran local MC, producer, and street artist SPECSONE, was held in 2010 at the Throwbacks NW gallery on Capitol Hill.[50]

Exit *The Rocket*, Enter *The Stranger* and Controversy

The 2000s brought significant shifts in the local media landscape of hip hop. *The Rocket*, which had premiered as a monthly in 1979, published its final issue in 2000. In its most widely read form as a bi-weekly in the mid-1990s, *The Rocket*'s distribution stretched north to Vancouver, BC; east to Missoula, Montana; and south to Eugene, Oregon. After multiple ownership changes beginning in 1995, *The Rocket* abruptly ceased publication without a farewell issue in 2000 amid rumors of shady dealings by the new owner and bounced pay-checks. The importance of *The Rocket* to local hip hop in the 1980s cannot be overstated. Beginning in 1980, it was virtually the only local publication that devoted regular space to hip hop, both local and national. The story of Seattle hip hop in the 1980s would be largely oral in nature were it not for *The Rocket*. *The Stranger* would not be around until 1991, and the city's two biggest newspapers—*Seattle Times* and *Seattle Post-Intelligencer*—barely gave local hip hop the time of day until well into the 1990s. Journalist Brian Goedde wrote in *The Stranger*: "As for local hip-hop, *The Rocket* was much more of a rock rag than a rap one, but it sported Sir Mix-a-Lot on the cover years before 'Baby Got Back,' and put Source of Labor on the cover last summer in response to their years-and-years-long anticipated first LP." Jace of the Silent Lambs Project added: "The city of S.E.A. has a chance to be the 'new spot,' and we'll see if anybody else picks up the peel and runs with it, since now *The Rocket* has left the court."[51]

The demise of *The Rocket* left *The Stranger* as the predominant alternative/arts newspaper in Seattle. While *The Stranger* had cov-ered hip hop sporadically since its launch in 1991, the paper did not carry a regular hip-hop column until 2003. After writing on hip hop for both the University of Washington student newspaper and the fledgling local arts and music magazine *The Tablet*, SHOW cofounder Sam Chesneau wrote about local and national hip hop for *The Stranger*. He named the weekly five-hundred-word column "The Truth." Controversy erupted in 2004 when, after failing to meet a deadline, Chesneau was fired. *Stranger* editor Dan Savage, the well-known queer white writer of the syndicated "Savage Love" column, caused uproar with a tongue-in-cheek but incendiary piece that demonstrated his ignorance of hip hop under the guise of seeking a more qualified columnist. Savage's reference to fellow *Stranger* col-umnist Charles Mudede, who is Black, as "scholar nigger" further alienated and offended many, both locally and nationally, given the racially charged implications of using the term in mixed racial com-pany and public discourse.

The term "scholar nigger" had originally been directed at Mudede before Savage's column by local artist and producer Samson S, who also wrote about hip hop for *The Tablet*. Samson, who is Black, felt Mudede overintellectualized his analysis of hip hop. However, Sav-age's use of the term drew attention from the national hip-hop com-munity including Oakland writer and historian Davey D, who wrote:

"Because now when folks start to object and point out how offended they are, the person using the term—in this case *Stranger* editor Dan Savage can smugly refer back to his colleague Charles Mudede who likes to call himself that." After discussing the distinctions between the hip hop spelling of "N-I-G-G-A" and the slur "N-I-G-G-E-R," Davey D concluded: "This guy Mudede refers to himself as NIGGER and the editor Dan Savage references him with that particular spelling. Hence no matter how you slice it and no matter how many mind games we play with using this word as a term of endearment and pointing out its dual meanings—Savage and *The Stranger* crossed the line. Shame on this Mudede cat who allows himself to be referred to as a 'Scholar Nigger.'"[52]

In the aftermath of the column Mudede met with the local branch of the NAACP to discuss the situation. Another outcome was that in 2004 *The Stranger* hired as its new hip-hop columnist Larry Mizell Jr., who continued in this role until 2016. A native of Los Angeles who moved to Seattle in junior high school, Mizell came from musical roots. His father Larry Sr. and uncle Alphonso "Fonce" Mizell (1943–2011) were the Mizell Brothers, legendary jazz/funk/disco producers who worked with Blue Note and Motown Records in the 1970s. Mizell Jr. was also a distant cousin of Run DMC's legendary DJ Jason "Jam Master Jay" Mizell, who died in 2002. Mizell renamed the column "My Philosophy," a nod to the 1988 Boogie Down Productions song of the same name. In addition to his weekly contribution, Mizell wrote feature articles for *The Stranger* on different artists and events outside of hip hop.[53]

Changes in Local Hip-Hop Radio and X104

While the circle of print-based publications in Seattle was shifting, hip hop's original media vehicle seemed stagnant. By 2001 one small thing about Seattle radio had changed—KCMU 90.3 FM switched its call letters to KEXP. What had not changed was frustration with hip hop's perceived lack of a meaningful relationship with local radio. "I have nothing new to say in this article," vented Charles Mudede. "Indeed, I wrote one exactly like it just over a year ago, but because there has been no change or improvement at all in the matter, because we still don't have a serious hip-hop show on the radio in this city, I must revive my frustration and re-bang my head against the same fucking wall. KUBE still plays the worst hip-hop ever made." The two-hour *Street Sounds* program on KCMU represented Seattle's only regular, dedicated hip-hop radio show. However, the fact that it aired on Sunday evenings put it at a competitive disadvantage. KCMU program director Don Yates cited this as one of the reasons the show was not doing well, admitting that it was on a bad night. "Sunday is just generally the lowest point for listenership," he said. "That is a radio fact. I mean, even Monday night from 6:00 to 8:00 is better. So the point is that hip-hop is not being given the respect it deserves. Maybe that is a cultural thing; maybe it is an insensitivity thing. I don't know."[54]

Local startup Skratchkast.com was an early model of a hip-hop Internet radio station. By the early 2000s more Internet radio options were available, but many lacked a crucial local element. Mudede, although encouraged by opportunities for Seattle hip hop on the World Wide Web, noted that even if one was able to catch online hip-hop stations at home or in the office, they were usually streamed from other cities or unknown sources. "This not only means that local hip-hop is neglected, but the excitement of hearing a DJ mix and cut within the realm of your urban sphere is lost," he explained. "Like rappers, hip-hop DJs are hyper-present; they are aware of their moment in space and time, and that intensity is lost in the zero-geography of cyberspace. In a word, nothing can replace hip-hop radio, and this city, this bizarre city, has brazenly, inexplicably deprived me of one of the greatest pleasures known to urban-kind."[55]

For the most part, commercial stations like KUBE and public, nonprofit stations like KCMU/KEXP were the main sources for rap music over the FM airwaves. High school radio had played a smaller role in Seattle hip-hop since Nathan Hale High School station KNHC 89.5 FM (C-89) began to play rap music in 1981. However, an interesting marriage formed as Mercer Island High School station KMIH 104.5 FM, or X104, adopted a hip-hop and rhythm and blues format in 2002. Before this, KMIH had little to no reputation outside the Mercer Island community, primarily using the pop-music playlists of other local stations and broadcasting the school's football and basketball games. Although only a couple of miles from the Central District, Mercer Island in many respects seemed worlds away. Geographically, Mercer Island is physically separated from Seattle by Lake Washington with the Lacey V. Murrow Memorial Bridge, a 6,600-foot floating span of I-90, serving as the only direct connection between the two cities. Census data from 2010 indicated that Mercer Island had a total population of twenty-three thousand, with more than 70 percent of these people eighteen and older and a median household income of $120,000.[56]

After coming on as a volunteer at X104 in 2002, radio veteran Patrick Lagreid soon was in charge of the station's music, programming, and image. Relying heavily on student volunteers and community fundraising, X104 became a presence at local nightclubs and community events, in mixtapes, and online. Lagreid brought well-known local DJs such as Funk Daddy, DV One, Dilemma, and Krazy in studio to mix live on-air, strengthening the station's grassroots connection with the hip-hop community. X104's contributions were recognized in 2005 when the station received the Mayor's Award for Excellence in Hip-Hop for Broadcast Innovation. A press release from the City of Seattle Office of Arts and Culture highlighted several accomplishments: "For nearly three years X104, located at Mercer Island High School, has been dedicated to exposing Seattle to the hottest new Hip Hop and R&B. X104 is staffed mostly by student volunteers and those who sign up for the Media Broadcast Technology class receive high school credit. X104 has seen amazing growth and penetration into both the Seattle market and the global Hip Hop community." The station was also highlighted in the May 2004 issue of *VIBE* magazine as the "Daily Choice" for radio in Seattle. "Since it began Web casting in January 2005," the release said, "X104 has gained listeners across the country and all over the world. X104 has given the Puget Sound region a new outlet for Hip Hop and a fresh sound for their dynamic music and lifestyle."[57]

Lagreid took a full-time position at another Seattle radio station in 2006, and X104's programming moved away from hip hop. The same year, a larger commercial station from Oregon that wanted 104.5's spot on the local dial took advantage of Federal Communications Commission rules and petitioned to displace X104, a "Class D" station, meaning it broadcast limited hours daily at lower power. After some legal wrangling, a settlement was reached, and KMIH relocated to 88.9 FM. While a relatively young station like X104 was able to make connections with the local community, longtime ratings king KUBE 93 was still struggling. That began to change in 2005 when KUBE asked Jonathan "Wordsayer" Moore to join its on-air staff. Moore's extensive work with Source of Labor, Jasiri Media Group, and numerous other community entities had earned him the Mayor's Award for Excellence in Hip-Hop in 2003. Mayor Greg Nickels said:

"Jonathan Moore and Jasiri Media Group demonstrated a remarkable track record of giving back to the community along with entrepreneurial achievement and business acumen."[58]

The historically rocky relationship between KUBE and Seattle's hip-hop scene reached a peak with protests in front of KUBE's building by members of the the local hip-hop community in 1997. Although station owner Barry Ackerley had since sold KUBE to national media conglomerate Clear Channel, little had changed. For Moore, a non-negotiable condition of his acceptance was control over the songs he played, which included local music. Larry Mizell Jr. noticed: "They showcase local talent on the regular, along with the straight-up hip-hop that you may not be used to hearing from Clear Channel radio."[59]

Along with cohost DJ Hyphen, *Sunday Night Sound Session* made a point to play a minimum of three local artists on each show, helping boost awareness of the scene. The outlook seemed hopeful yet uncertain about the changes in local radio. "The scene in the town is a little tainted. There's way less avenues for getting the real hip-hop out there. Back in the day, you had [radio stations] KFOX and KRIZ—they were putting together the showcases, Nasty Nes was on there playin' local music, you had your Sir Mix-A-Lot and your Emerald Street Boys on the radio," explained local veteran Vitamin D. "Jon [Jonathan Moore of Jasiri Management Group] is trying to bring it back, and play local stuff on the radio—but it's not quite the same. Don't nobody even wanna hear it. But back then we were excited to hear it. Like, 'Man, we wanna hear what's goin on, that's ours!'"[60]

The Rise of Hip-Hop Blogs

The jockeying for media exposure and radio play between local and national hip-hop artists continued through the decade. New generations of performers and promoters hoped to ride the wave of mainstream perception that the Seattle scene was full of potential break-out artists. Charles Mudede theorized in *The Stranger* that within the local scene, a distinction would have to be made between the crews that continued the mainstream approach to hip hop from its national level to a local one. "These groups tend to be black and receive almost no press in this and other publications unless, of course, someone is shot at their shows or parties. The recent explosion of press about the local scene does not include artists and promoters like Ghetto Prez, Gameboy, Funk Daddy, and Skuntdunanna," Mudede noted. "They have their own network of venues (like Vito's—where a man was recently shot) and publicity nodes (Seaspot.com). They want nothing to do with KEXP and have placed their eggs all in one basket, KUBE. These commercially oriented crews exist alongside but very much apart from Seattle's currently successful second wave."[61]

Meanwhile Larry Mizell Jr. weighed in on the potentially harmful effects of so many local artists trying to be the next "king." "It's long been a consensus that the drive to be 'that guy'—the next rapper to blow up Seattle—has held us back as a community, and I'd tend to agree. Deeper than that, I say that hip-hop's 'king' mentality—ever since Biggie was crowned King of NY—has been a straight cancer to hip-hop's creativity," Mizell argued. "Instead of coming up with original concepts, individuals are only out to be the HNIC by following formulas, always to the detriment of the art form."[62] Traditionally, artists striving to become the next "king" had limited channels within which to operate. However, the creation of opportunities for artists to get valuable publicity and exposure soon had another platform to work with. The growth of twenty-first-century technology represented an increasing challenge to print media and record companies. The spread of digital music, mp3 files, and Napster (the free peer-to-peer online file-sharing service) shook the record industry in the early 2000s.

Another Internet-related trend reflected the ways in which music journalism could achieve independence from the box of traditional publications like newspapers and magazines. In 2006 *Raindrop Hustla* became the first blog dedicated to Seattle hip hop. Launched by *Stranger* columnist Larry Mizell Jr. and *Seattle Times* music writer Andrew Matson, the blog vastly expanded opportunities to post new material about Seattle and beyond. "Really though: It's great to see this kind of knowledgeable and playful coverage of hip-hop local and national. These guys are working on several levels at once, which is what makes *Raindrop Hustla* more fun and more entertaining than your average blog," wrote music journalist Jonathan Zwickel. "It's hard to have a scene without someone talking about it, and thoughtful commentary can be both validation and inspiration to any active creative community."[63]

Local blogs served a dual purpose: they helped provide translation for outsiders while also acting as a resource for insiders. However, once local insider conversations made the jump to social media, the external dialogue seemed to become less of a priority.[64] As the technology became more popular, the number of regional blogs, websites, discussion forums, and message boards increased. Some of these included *Tha Northwest, Blogs Is Watching, Seattle Hip-Hop, We Out Here Magazine, The Audacity of Dope, 253rd Street Tacoma, The Sermon's Domain, Hip-Hop Vancouver (BC)*, and *Hip-Hop Heads Northwest*. The rise of the Internet made it possible for a blog to cover a scene even if the blog author didn't live locally. Chul Gugich grew up in Seattle on local hip hop before moving in 2007 to take a job in New York City. After publishing several music critique pieces online, he started the Seattle hip-hop blog *206UP* in 2009. The site offered audio, video, features, interviews, album reviews, and coverage of live shows. With *206UP*, Gugich became a local insider who lived thousands of miles away.[65] Already active in the local music and entertainment scene, Casey Carter launched MissCaseyCarter.com as a one-woman operation in 2011, which focused on local independent artists and events. The site hired staff the following year while developing such content as cooking lessons and street style pieces as well as the "What's in your purse?" and "My date with" interview series.[66]

Local Hip Hop on the Rise

The online presence of local hip-hop media reflected the growth and development of places like Seattle while increasing exposure for artists and shows. The use of social networks such as Facebook, Twitter, Instagram, and others allowed customized content to be accessed and shared on tablets and smartphones. The Internet had increased opportunities not only for artists but for various media members who discussed them. Whether online or in print, while local hip-hop columnists and observers generally served as supporters of the scene they cover, they rarely agreed on much. However, the general consensus among Seattle music journalists who covered hip hop seemed to indicate big things were on the horizon. It all had to begin, wrote Charles Mudede, with local people believing in their scene. "Sooner or later, Seattle has to realize that it doesn't have to look elsewhere for quality hip-hop. If you live in this city," he wrote, "you can relegate the rest of the nation to secondary status. All the hip-hop you need is right here, right now."[67]

Seattle Times music writer Andrew Matson, in a column titled "Right Now, Seattle Is Making Hip-Hop History," agreed. "Seattle's current hip-hop renaissance is deeper than any one blog post, article, concept, or list of artists. Signs abound. Improved stage shows, a heightened sense of community, and unprecedented stylistic variety are the healthiest ones right now is a special time." Matson noted the temptation to assign a singular, tidy cause to the effect of all this "excellent, wildly diverse hip-hop." In reality, it was a result of "something deeper than, say, Marxist aesthetics—'This recession is Darwinism for art'—and deeper than a host of post-prefixes—'the new hip-hop is post-rap, post-race, post-tradition.' It's a whole lot deeper than more people using the Internet more effectively. But the sum of those parts points to a central truth: All possible worlds—economic, values-based, online—are radically different for today's artists than yesterday's, and the artists are adapting."[68] Larry Mizell Jr., who added host of *Street Sounds* on KEXP FM to his local hip-hop media resume in 2009, agreed. "Now I don't doubt that there are plenty of other pockets of brilliance in the U.S. just seething under the radar," he wrote, "but if you can't recognize the gravity and—I'm gonna quote the Chef right here—*mad styles and crazy dangerous, I mean, bust ya shit open beats* native to our region ... well, you're just another hapless victim of that classic Seattle Self-Esteem Syndrome."[69]

Untangling Hip Hop from Violence

The consensus seemed to indicate an optimism that something significant was on the horizon. Journalistic opinion encouraged local people to trust and believe in local hip hop, perhaps in ways they had not before. Yet despite all the positive vibes surrounding Seattle hip hop, the specter of violence cast a shadow. The January 2009 shooting at a show at Chop Suey revived this long-standing discussion. Three people were shot and one person, local artist Joseph "29-E" Ryan, was killed. The incident drew a column from Charles Mudede arguing that Chop Suey should not blackball hip-hop shows. Citing a 2008 fatal shooting at Vito's Madison Grill, a popular venue for rap and R&B nights, Mudede noted that the incident at Vito's was not only part of a recent wave of gang-related shootings but also the long history of violent disruptions inside or outside local clubs that regularly hosted hip-hop or R&B nights. "There was the shooting at Sugar nightclub in November 2007," he wrote, "the shooting outside of Tabella Restaurant & Lounge in July 2007, the shooting outside of Tommy's on the Ave in June 2007, the stabbings and shootings inside and outside of Larry's Nightclub in December 2005, the shooting outside Mr. Lucky's in April 2004, the shootings outside of I-Spy in 2002, and so on and so on."[70]

A distinction was made between clubs that featured hip-hop nights and live hip-hop shows. "Because the shooting at Chop Suey happened during a hip-hop show, it will be impossible for the public to separate the music from the murder. But hip-hop is still just music; a rapper does not go onstage and start shooting people. He may rap about smoking a nigga, but that is not the same as doing it," Mudede lamented. "In fact, the last thing a gangster rapper wants is a real gangster disrupting his show, his career, his mic dreams. The gangster rapper wants none of it. Indeed, the incident at Chop Suey is extraordinary in the sense that—unlike rap/R&B club nights (which feature only DJs)—rap shows (which feature live performers) rarely end in bullets." Because the show at Chop Suey that night featured so-called gangsta rappers, including Fatal Lucciauno, Mudede pointed out that it was a matter of what type of crowd a "particular type of hip-hop attracts. Mass Line's Gabriel Teodros, for example, is scheduled to perform at Chop Suey this Friday. Because Teodros's hip-hop is all about love, unity, the socialization of health care, and the empowerment of women," there was an expectation that the type of crowd attracted to a more hardcore bill would not be present.

"Thugs go where thug life is celebrated," Mudede wrote. His position was specific to Chop Suey but generalizable to all Seattle-area venues that attempted to support local talent. "This is why it is important not to close Chop Suey. Chop Suey is a venue for different types of music, and, specifically, different types of hip-hop." He argued that hip hop is about diversity—it has its "dusty philosophers, dirty jokers, dreamy lovers, mad riddlers, sensitive hippies, and even intelligent hoodlums. When all is going well," Mudede explained, "hip-hop is one big and lively family, and a venue that can one weekend host Fatal Lucciauno and the next Gabriel Teodros captures the spirit of this diversity—a spirit, furthermore, that has been displaced from hip-hop by a commercial monster resulting from the cancerous growth of thug hop (rap) and the diminution of all other forms." Mudede concluded: "In fact, on February 1, 2008, Sportn' Life [Records] had a show at Chop Suey that featured D. Black, Grayskul, the Physics, Action Buddie, and Bean One (street hop, geek hop, gothic hop, and black rock). Any space that supports that kind of diversity should keep its doors wide open."[71] Moving forward, Chop Suey continued to host some live hip-hop shows.

Seattle Police and the Trial of DV One

Fueled by racism and incidents of violence, the tension between hip hop and law enforcement was also present locally. In September 2006 prominent local DJ and Rock Steady Crew member Toby "DV One" Campbell was at the Seattle Center to pick up his teenage daughter after a high school football game. After witnessing and attempting to intervene in an altercation between his daughter and a Seattle police officer, Campbell was arrested and charged with third-degree assault on an officer. Campbell claimed the police used excessive force by tasing him repeatedly and made racist remarks as they arrested him. Campbell's charge was reviewed by the Office of Professional Accountability (OPA), which investigated citizen complaints against the Seattle Police Department, and four officers were subsequently cleared of any improper conduct in Campbell's arrest.

Like other urban communities around the country, this situation was informed by a long legacy of previous allegations of excessive force by Seattle police against unarmed African Americans. Back in 1938, twenty-seven-year-old waiter Berry Lawson was killed at a downtown hotel by three officers who were fired, indicted, tried, convicted on manslaughter charges, and sentenced to twenty years each before all three were pardoned by the governor.[72] In 1998 thirty-five-year-old Michael Ealy Sr. died after being pepper-sprayed and restrained by police and paramedics downtown.[73] In 2001 police fatally shot Aaron Roberts during a traffic stop at Twenty-third Avenue and Union Street in the Central District. The two officers on the scene claimed they feared for their lives when Roberts attempted to flee in his car after being pulled over. In assessing whether charges would be brought against the officer who shot Roberts, the *Seattle Weekly* noted: "The cops have little reason to believe they'll be proved wrong. In 33 police-related shootings since the early 1980s, coroner's inquest juries found every killing justified. That includes shooting a black man with a toy squirt gun, killing a black man as he was surrendering, and shooting another black man in his home as he held a TV remote. Five of the last eight police shootings in Seattle involved black victims."[74]

The trend of the police version of the story being recognized continued with the case of DV One. He was eventually found guilty of assaulting an officer and sentenced to 240 hours of community service, thirty-two days in jail (suspended), and a $500 fine. DV One received strong support from numerous community members who attended the trial as well as unexpected backing from the jurors that rendered the verdict—ten of them were present for the sentencing. Matt Roach, a juror present at the sentencing, spoke on Campbell's behalf saying that the jury had issues with the definition they were given for assault. "Legally they were obligated to convict [Campbell] based on the conditions they gave us," Roach said. "But I did not feel justice has been served." Campbell was just happy for the case to be over. "It's like having to pay for something you didn't actually get," he said. Campbell's attorney announced plans to appeal the case.[75]

dead prez and the Valentine's Day Riot

The debate around hip hop, violence, and law enforcement continued in 2008, following what became known as the "Valentine's Day Riot" at Evergreen State College in Olympia. Evergreen had hosted the incident-free Phunky Phat '95. The evening of February 14 began with a show at Evergreen by New York–based dead prez, made up of stic.man and M-1. The critically acclaimed duo, known for their confrontational style and commitment to social justice, described their music as "Revolutionary Hip-Hop with a Gangsta Lean." The show attracted some nine hundred people, roughly half of whom were Evergreen students, and was going well until just after midnight when organizers attempted to eject a man for smoking marijuana and groping women. In the process punches were thrown and a fight broke out. Campus security was called, but the lone officer on duty that night did not arrive until after the original suspect had already left.

Once on the scene, the officer handcuffed a suspect that witnesses had identified as having been involved in the fight. When word reached the stage about what was happening outside, a report in the *Seattle Times* stated dead prez initially said, "Oh yeah? . . . Say '[Expletive] the police! [Expletive] the police!'" This drew a chanted response from the crowd. However, the group changed its tone, saying, "Hold up, hold up, it's not just '[Expletive] the police.' That's great. But now you've got to organize behind this here. Make sure you find out that man's name and after we organize and have some justice, right?" As the handcuffed suspect was being led to the car, a growing crowd followed the officer, claiming racial bias because the man was African American. As she tried to drive away, a crowd of nearly two hundred blocked the road. Although several Thurston County sheriff deputies arrived on the scene, officers felt overwhelmed and let the suspect go. Despite this, the situation escalated, and police retreated from a hail of rocks, bottles, trash cans, and tree branches. A police cruiser was overturned and looted. Although there were only a few minor injuries, several arrests were made and more than $50,000 in damage was reported in a situation that the responding officer called "Lord of the Flies-esque."[76] Though different circumstances, both the DV One trial and the disturbance at Evergreen State College highlighted the complexities in the relationship between hip hop and law enforcement.

Community-Based Hip Hop and 206 Zulu

Because hip hop began as youth culture in underserved urban neighborhoods, an important aspect has been community outreach. Over time the methodology of this outreach grew as hip hop expanded and matured. Career expos, additional designated physical spaces for hip hop, the rise of hip hop in college classrooms, and an active promotional infrastructure all emerged alongside traditional nonprofit organizations. One of these organizations was the Hip-Hop Summit Action Network (HHSAN), cofounded in 2001 by hip-hop pioneer and mogul Russell Simmons and civil rights veteran Dr. Benjamin Chavis in New York City. Targeting youth, young adults, and urban professionals roughly ages eighteen to forty-five, HHSAN functioned as a nonprofit 501c(4), nonpartisan collective of hip-hop artists and industry executives that convened more than seventy town hall–style meetings around the United States, Canada, and South Africa on topics such as voting rights, sound financial practices, and the home foreclosure crisis.[77]

Community builder Wyking Garrett led the effort to establish a local HHSAN chapter, and in 2002 the Seattle Hip-Hop Summit Action Network (SHHSAN) was born. Serving as a vehicle for leadership development and youth empowerment, SHHSAN worked to engage the hip-hop community and build coalitions with others in the search for social, political, and economic justice. Another important aspect of SHHSAN was the Hip-Hop CommUniversity, housed at the UmojaFest

PEACE Center in the Central District. The project was created by a group of youth and supporters and used technology and digital media as primary teaching tools. CommUniversity offerings included "Seattle Hip-Hop Youth Council," "Young Stars Studio," "DJ 101," "Audio Production 101," "Music Biz & Artist/Label Development," "Graphic Design," "Digital Media 101," "Fashion Design & Merchandising 101," "Boxing & Fitness Club," and "Open Studio 101."[78]

The use of hip hop as a tool of teaching and learning for young people was catching on in other places around the city as well. One example was "Community Through Communication," a class at the Garfield Teen Life Center next door to Garfield High School. The class was sponsored by Arts Corps, a nonprofit, independent education program, which funded numerous after-school programs around the city. The class featured writing workshops, recitations of rap and spoken word pieces, and critical discussions about mainstream rap music.[79] Another well-known hip-hop community group established local roots. Kevin "Afrika Bambaataa" Donovan grew up in the Bronx River Projects and joined the Black Spades, New York City's largest Black street gang, in 1969. After a trip to Africa in 1973, he took the title Bambaataa from a nineteenth-century Zulu leader whose name translated to "Chief Affection." The name of his organization, the Mighty Zulu Nation (later Universal Zulu Nation, or UZN), came after seeing Zulu warriors defend their land against the British Army in the 1964 film *Zulu*.

As his DJ reputation grew, Bambaataa leveraged his popularity and influence to build the ranks of the Zulu Nation, purposefully redirecting the energy of young people from gang life to hip hop. Although the organization's credo was "Peace, Unity, Love & Having Fun," there was an activist component to the Zulu Nation as members led mediations between gangs, sponsored mentorship programs, and held benefits. With the release of his iconic song "Planet Rock" in 1982 and his eclectic sampling habits from nearly every genre of music, Bambaataa led the first international hip-hop tours across Europe in 1983. In 1984 he visited Seattle to play the Gorilla Gardens. His lasting influence and tireless devotion to the culture earned Afrika Bambaataa the title "Godfather of Hip-Hop." This legacy grew as Zulu Nation chapters appeared not only in different cities throughout the United States but also in more than twenty countries around the world.[80]

The Seattle chapter of the Universal Zulu Nation, known as 206 Zulu, was formed in 2004 by King Khazm. From the start 206 Zulu focused on working with and empowering local communities, specifically youth, low income, and people of color "through creative and innovative means, including but not limited to programs and projects involving music, art and culture." A mission statement explained that 206 Zulu was "an independent, nonprofit corporation" that utilized culture, arts, and entertainment "to inspire youth involvement in social action, civic service, cultural creativity, and self-education." It ran youth programs, projects, and resources "to provide necessary tools to pursue future careers." The group sought out financial support "through private foundation and government grants, individual and corporate donations, corporations and contracts with public or nonprofit entities" and empowered "underrepresented, low-income members of the community as a means of building relationships, resources and activities that yield sustainable community empowerment and action."[81] 206 Zulu employed a multilayered approach in its work, focusing on four primary themes. A media justice component offered alternatives to corporate programming and platforms for emerging artists and activists. The youth outreach element collaborated with local schools and nonprofits to provide various youth-centered activities. Informational forums and workshops that covered relevant topics provided the foundation for 206 Zulu's education and leadership development, and the research and documentation of local hip hop continued with "Our Story," an ongoing comprehensive project on the history of hip hop in the Pacific Northwest.

The grassroots, community-based work of 206 Zulu led to the group being recognized locally, nationally, and internationally. Afrika Bambaataa, along with the UZN Supreme World Council, presented Khazm with the Zulu Kingship Award in 2005. When the fifth annual Awards for Excellence in Hip-Hop were presented in 2006, Khazm was recognized by Seattle Mayor Greg Nickels as "Unsung Hero (Community Leadership/Activism)." Seattle Mayor Mike McGinn endorsed the 206 Zulu–led efforts to officially proclaim November as Hip-Hop History Month in 2010. Bremerton Mayor Patty Lent also recognized 206 Zulu with a Hip-Hop History Month Proclamation in 2012 as well as honoring the group's ten-year anniversary in 2014. Massive Monkees presented 206 Zulu with an appreciation award in 2012, and the UZN Supreme World Council honored 206 Zulu codirector Kitty Wu with the Zulu Queenship Award in 2014.[82] *Zulu Radio*, a weekly show hosted by King Khazm, Gabriel Teodros, and WD4D, premiered on community radio station KBCS 91.3 FM in

2005. The playlist included independent, local, and international artists. Initially placed in a timeslot on Thursday mornings from 3:00 to 5:00, *Zulu Radio* received enough positive feedback that the show was eventually moved to Saturday nights from 10:00 to 12:00 midnight.[83]

Building on the work of other earlier local grassroots organizers such as DVS and DJ DV One, newer generations of Seattle hip hop continued the tradition of making community work a part of their art. D. Black of Sportn' Life Records was involved with middle school and high school after-school programs at local nonprofit Union Gospel Mission. Mass Line Records artist Gabriel Teodros mentored teen artists in schools and through such programs as Youth Speaks, while Blue Scholars MC Geologic was active in Bayan USA, a collective of socially progressive Filipino organizations. Members of Massive Monkees taught classes at the Vera Project, Velocity Dance Center, and Mercer and Denny Middle Schools and celebrated the mayor-declared Massive Monkees Day with a citywide b-girl and b-boy event that was also a benefit and canned-food drive in support of nonprofit food assistance program Northwest Harvest.[84]

Events such as the first annual Northwest Hip-Hop Leadership Conference in 2009 served as community forums for critical discussion of relevant issues. Oganized by Wyking Garrett and held at Seattle Central Community College, the conference had panel discussions that included "Hip-Hop 101," "The N-Word," "Women in Hip-Hop," "Hip-Hop Politics and Community," "Hip-Hop and the Green Economy," "Youth Activism and Social Entrepreneurship," "Getting Your Business Tight," "Fashion Biz 101," and "From the Hood to the Club: Violence in Hip-Hop and the Black Community."[85] Teodoros remarked: "There're *so* many active artist-teachers out here. I would say Seattle probably has to be number two at least with all the hip-hop cats here that are involved in teaching and community building."[86]

In 2010 the Seattle Hip-Hop Career and Business Expo was held at the Seattle Center. With events beginning at 10:00 a.m. and culminating with a concert at 8:00 p.m., activities included performances, workshops, and panel discussions covering such topics as "Music and the Media Landscape" and "Start and Grow Your Business."[87] The expo was hosted by the all-ages Vera Project located on the Seattle Center campus. The Teen Dance Ordinance of 1985 had essentially put a chokehold on all-age music events and venues for nearly twenty years. In response to this, James Keblas, Shannon Stewart, and Kate

Becker created the nonprofit Vera Project in 2001 as an all-age music and arts organization. Initially, Vera was staffed by volunteers and funded by the music industry, the City of Seattle, and local foundations. Vera's early years were dedicated primarily to throwing all-age shows and events in rented venues until 2007, when it moved into its full-time home at the Seattle Center. This new space allowed the Vera Project to expand from simply putting on shows to offering audio engineering training, visual art exhibits, live and studio recording, silkscreen printing and classes, event production and leadership training, youth-driven governance, and internships.[88]

Specific non-nightclub hip-hop locations were rare in Seattle, but this trend was reversed somewhat when sisters Asmeret and Rahwa Habte purchased Hidmo restaurant from its founder Amanuel Yohannes in 2007. Hidmo specialized in Eritrean food and décor, served primarily the local East African community, and featured live African music on Sunday nights. It also became a center for underground hip hop in Seattle when Hidmo expanded its offerings such as the free Friday summer concert series called "Live @ Hidmo" which featured local artists Laura "Piece" Kelley, J.Pinder, and Orbitron. Although national artists also performed at Hidmo, the focus on Seattle was intentional, as co-owner Rahwa Habte stated: "We want to make local talent accessible to the local community." In addition to hip hop, "Live @ Hidmo" spotlighted soul, funk, rock, pop, and spoken word. Hidmo also hosted events such as the Hip-Hop Congress National Convention, a meeting of grassroots hip-hop artists and entrepreneurs from around the world.[89] This wide range of hip hop–related activities at Hidmo was similar to the Mecca International, a coffee shop/gathering place opened in the mid-1990s by Mansa and Nebra Square Musa on the corner of Twenty-third and Union. The community-centric presence of such venues, in addition to conferences and expositions, increased valuable opportunities for multiple age groups to experience and participate in local hip hop.

Hip-Hop Education

Grassroots organizations and events often operated within an educational context when framing goals and outcomes. This connection was furthered by events that took place on campuses as well as skill development opportunities at venues like the Vera Project. Because of hip hop's multidisciplinary nature, it has long occupied various formal and informal spaces in education. Community organizations like SHHSAN, 206 Zulu, and the Vera Project regularly presented various examples of hip hop–related classes and workshops. By the turn of the century, hip hop had made its way into the curricula of course offerings at colleges and universities across the United States. Students have taken hip hop–based classes at schools like Stanford, Northeastern University, Ithaca College, Ohio State, UCLA, Syracuse, and the Berklee College of Music in Boston.[90] Seattle reflected this trend with new classes at the University of Washington, Seattle Central College, and Bellevue College, where the power of these classes to attract students was on display early with full classes and lengthy waitlists.

Seattle-area college students and campus clubs played a role in the development of local hip hop in the twenty-first century. Following in the footsteps of the Student Hip-Hop Organization of Washington (SHOW) in 1999, the University of Washington Hip-Hop Student Association (UWHHSA) was formed in 2007. Founding members included Alex Chauhan, Jack Leonard, Gordon Tsai, Chris Lam, and Michael Huang, the group's first president. The UW Hip-Hop Student Association sponsored weekly dance sessions at the Ethnic Cultural Center on campus and special events such as its Fresh Fit Fashion Show, which featured up-and-coming local brands and designers exhibiting live on a runway.[91]

Ante Up was the name of the hip-hop dance club at Seattle Pacific University, organized by students Chris Jellum, Connor Pierce, and Carolyn Lara.[92] The club created its own constitution, and the preamble explained the club's name:

> ANTE UP (HIP HOP CLUB) CONSTITUTION
> *Preamble*
>
> In the game of poker, the phrase "ante up" is the increased "stake" that each player must put into the pool before receiving new cards. We named our club after this phrase because we want to incorporate the idea of putting things on the line. In other words, with whatever cards you are dealt with, you will pull through and do your best. That's the atmosphere and mentality we hope to spread amongst our members.

ARTICLE I. Purpose

Dance is built on inspiration, movement, and blessings from God. Dance is more than just a performance, applause from an audience or an expression of admiration from a side liner. Dance is a journey. Spiritual, mental, and physical growth is met through the many different genres of dance. We hope that this club will provide our student body with place for inspiration, creativity, and release. We hope for every member, officer and bystander to gain some form of inspiration from the art and praise that will take place in our meetings.

We seek to provide free hip-hop dance classes from volunteer dance teachers in the Seattle community. Student members who are interested in teaching will be encouraged as well. We are providing a safe place for dancers of all levels to grow and connect with other students who have the passion for dance. We also hope to help students stay updated on dance events going on in Seattle, including, performances, workshops and auditions.[93]

Management and Promotions

Individuals and companies that focused on promoting and presenting shows and activities played an important, and necessary, part in growing Seattle hip hop during the 2000s. One example was Soul Gorilla, founded by Josh Berman, BBoy, 'Preme, Benito, and Chern in 2004.[94] Soul Gorilla worked on various levels within the industry, from managing artists such as Sportn' Life Records trio Dyme Def to copresenting the Seattle Hip-Hop Career and Business Expo with the SHHSAN.

Melissa "Meli" Darby was one of several former members of the Student Hip-Hop Organization of Washington who remained active in the local scene after college. In 2004 she launched Obese Productions (the company became ReignCity in 2008), which booked shows and formed a partnership with the Vera Project. While promoting shows with national artists, she focused on developing hometown talent by producing such events as the Make It or Break It series, quarterly exhibitions of local artists who were selected on the basis of word-of-mouth promotion and ticket presales. The goal of these competitive methods was to spur an attitude shift. "There are a number of very lazy artists in this town that feel entitled to shows and privileges, and that bothers me when there are so many talented artists *starving* for the same opportunities," Darby explained. "I want to help train artists to be self-sufficient, show them how to hustle like I do. I want Obese and its resources to be a kind of focal point for artist support. We have a very big responsibility in Seattle to make sure that the music is available to our youth, to strengthen our community."[95] The promotional/managerial groundwork that developed served both to support and challenge local artists. This combined with events and physical spaces to form the vital fabric of infrastructure necessary to nurture the still maturing hip-hop scene in Seattle.

Multitude of Styles

An eclectic variety of artists was creating more and new buzz around Seattle's hip-hop scene. An incredible stylistic range included street, blue collar, abstract, a celebration of home, and other approaches all combined to inform this resurgence. Still, due to a variety of factors, some found the going harder than others. The five-year anniversary of Sportn' Life Records in 2007 illustrated some of the complexities that lay in marketing different types of local rap music. Sportn' Life emerged from the Central District and represented the Black experience in America, Charles Mudede argued. "In fact, the very reason for Sportn' Life's existence was to rebuild and recenter hip hop in a neighborhood that was devastated by crack, gangs, and violent crime."[96]

Sportn' Life had a reputation for aggressive promotion, developing relationships with venues, and cultivating contacts with local media. However, "despite Sportn' Life's strong work ethic and commitment to high standards, the label still struggles to obtain the brilliant recognition that [Blue Scholars label] Mass Line basks in. Why?" Mudede concluded, "Because many of its acts are from the streets, they rap about thug life and gang realities." Sportn' Life founder Devon Manier agreed. "The Seattle market is harder for us than the national market. When you do a gangsta record that's about shit happening in your own backyard, the buyers here tend to freak out and stay away from it. But a gangsta record from out of town, like G-Unit or Jay-Z, they'll buy it. Seattle wants a safe distance from hardcore rap. But we do not only do gangsta shit," Manier said. "We also have

J.Pinder, who is much more in the Common/Kanye West school of hip-hop. So our label is really about the diversity of the streets."[97]

D. Black, who served as CEO of Sportn' Life Records, released his debut album *The Cause & Effect* in 2006. His second album, *Ali'Yah*, released in 2009, was well received, and he performed at music festivals around the country. But D. Black gradually withdrew from the scene. His initial refusal to perform shows on Fridays eventually grew into a two-year hiatus and a conversion to Orthodox Judaism. He subsequently changed his name to Nissim and continued to steadily release music.

Controversy came in 2007 when Sportn' Life artist Fatal Lucciauno was arrested after a shooting outside the Tabella nightclub. Lucciauno was convicted on firearms charges and served an eighteen-month prison term. With his album *The Only Forgotten Son* released on Sportn' Life Records the same year, the line between art and life within hip hop seemed to blur. Was it possible to differentiate the two? "Indeed, the theme that dominates Fatal's hip-hop is not the worship of the gangsta lifestyle but the documentation of the poverty that leads a man into that way of life," Mudede contended. "Track after track, he describes the grim realities of being dirt-poor in one of the richest cities of the world. And when he performs, the most powerful moments are when he is expressing these harsh realities directly. He wants you to feel and see it."[98]

The variety of styles being put out by local record companies was significant. Blue Scholars' second full studio album, *Bayani* (2007), was released on their own label, Mass Line Media, in association with New York hip-hop label Rawkus Records. Loosely translated, "bayani" in Tagalog means "hero" or "person who offers free service in a cooperative endeavor." The song and video "Joe Metro" offered a unique take on the Seattle experience. The Emerald City has had a long relationship with its rap MCs making reference to their hometown. Since Sir Mix-A-Lot's song and video "Posse on Broadway," successive generations have expressed their local perspective through the lens of hip hop. In this case, the song's title was a reference to a nickname for King County Metro, the public transit authority that operates bus service in the greater Seattle area. In contrast to Sir Mix-A-Lot riding through town in a Mercedes Benz limousine, Geologic's narrative centered on riding the Route 48 bus, which connected the South End to the University District and the northern part of the city via the Central District. The video focused on the diversity of characters that exit and enter the bus throughout the city, from college kids to a Native American elder.

Following their subsequent tour in support of *Bayani*, Blue Scholars organized an event to further build community. What emerged was a five-night extravaganza celebrating the best of local hip hop. In planning a homecoming after the completion of their tour, Sabzi and Geologic borrowed an idea from the Mighty Bosstones. In the late 1990s that band, from Boston, put on a series of five-night stands they called the Hometown Throwdown, where they headlined each night and had their favorite groups from the scene perform. "The Program is the Northwest hip-hop version of the Hometown Throwdown cooked up by Steven Severin, owner and promoter at Neumo's," wrote Charles Mudede. "The Blue Scholars' five-night run has turned into a NW hip-hop festival that brings in many elements from the scene and puts them back out to the world. It's less a show about the Blue Scholars and more about the present, past, and future of regional hip-hop."[99]

Although "The Program" may not have been solely about them, Blue Scholars continued to gain momentum when *Playboy* magazine named the group among its "Ten to Watch in 2008," adding that "Seattle is slowly becoming a hip-hop epicenter." This comment by *Playboy* was an indication of how Seattle hip hop had over time built a reputation outside of the immediate region. It was an especially relevant point, given the fact that *Billboard* magazine two decades before had openly mocked Seattle as a "hip-hop hotbed."[100]

Maturation and Expansion of the Local Scene and New Business Models

While national publications were just beginning to recognize developments within Seattle hip hop, local writers had sensed a change. "Seattle hip-hop is blossoming. Blue Scholars, after teaming up with Seattle rappers Common Market and Gabriel Teodros to form the Mass Line collective, got picked up by a nationally recognized New York label, Rawkus Records. Unheralded rapper Unexpected Arrival last month revealed he had sold 10,000 CDs and promptly got signed by Koch Records for a distribution deal," wrote Andrew Matson in the *Seattle Times*. "D. Black, 20-year-old co-CEO of Sportn' Life Records, sold more than 4,000 copies of his album hand-to-hand," he continued. "Local jokers the Saturday Knights just signed with Seattle-based national tastemaker Light in the Attic Records. And Dyme Def, according to its manager, is being courted by major labels." The change, Matson theorized, came from a combination of time and experience: "Over the years, Seattle's rap scene has grown from a disorganized, grass-roots endeavor to a navigable marketplace. Now, artists are behaving like businesses, outsourcing labor to managerial teams, and club and concert promoters are savvier too, building formidable street teams."[101]

Jake One noted that ten years ago "the guys behind the scenes were the same age as the artists. They had no experience. No real connections. There weren't any elders to help us." Marcus Lalario, owner of the hip-hop club the War Room on Capitol Hill, agreed that one hip-hop generation later, things had changed: "Now, the roads have been paved and the business side is catching."[102] Blue Scholars embodied this as they found innovative ways to market themselves. In 2009 they ended their distribution deal with Rawkus and re-released their album *Bayani* by instead partnering with iconic New York hip-hop label Duck Down Records as well as local coffee roaster Cafe Vita. A press release by the group spoke to this trend of artist empowerment. "With the record industry in flux, conditions are ripe for an alternative. One where the artist, rather than becoming an employee of a label or sponsor, contracts the label and sponsors to do work for them. Everybody still gets a check. But it's a relationship where the artists (and their handpicked 'team') not only have creative freedom but economic power. Or we can keep chasing the big record-deal unicorn."[103]

Larry Mizell Jr. agreed with the new business model. "Now pay attention, kids, 'cause I know a whole lot of y'all are still out there in full force with your nets and horn guards, hoping to land a big-bank deal like [New Orleans–based label] Cash Money did with Universal [Records] 10 years ago," he wrote. "If you don't recognize that those old ways don't work anymore (in any sense), then as the poet laureate E-40 once said, you're 'playin' football with basketball rules.' Quit grindin' backward."[104]

Local love for Blue Scholars was at an all-time high in 2010 when Geo and Sabzi headlined three consecutive nights of sold-out shows at the 1,100-seat Showbox in downtown Seattle. With opening acts that included Vitamin D and Macklemore, lines of people stretching around the corner and up the next block formed outside the venue hours before the doors opened. A review of the show in the *Seattle Post-Intelligencer* by Humberto Martinez remarked about Blue

Scholars: "The crowd was almost literally at their command, drawing outreached hands that seemed to be tireless." The rise of Blue Scholars continued a few months later when they became the first local rap act to headline a bill at the Paramount Theatre.[105] The multiethnic nature of a show featuring a Filipino and Iranian American duo, along with African American and white performers, highlighted the variety found in local hip hop.

The multiple perspectives of life in the Pacific Northwest continued to make themselves heard. One voice was Komplex Kai, performer at the 2008 Folklife Festival at the Seattle Center, who hailed from the Tulalip Tribe whose reservation is roughly thirty miles north of Seattle. While expressing pride in being a Tulalip, Kai's music addressed very real issues that Native Americans face on a daily basis: drug use, chronic alcoholism, poverty, suicide, teen pregnancy, and "the support/negligence/harm that comes from a fractured, chronically underestimated people." Komplex Kai provided important social depth from a perspective not often heard in contemporary hip hop.[106]

Veterans of the Scene Continue

As newer, lesser known contributors added to the growing pool of local hip hop, an older, more well-known voice remained visible. Although no longer regularly recording music, Sir Mix-A-Lot attracted attention in 2005 when he was awarded the Mayor's Award for Excellence in Hip-Hop and in 2007 when he collaborated with New York hip-hop icon Nas. As one of the premier rap artists in the world, Nasir "Nas" Jones provoked controversy and discussion when he named his 2006 album *Hip-Hop Is Dead*. Nas's reflections on the state of hip hop included the song "Where Are They Now," a tribute to his favorite rappers from his younger days. Subsequent remixes included 1980s and 1990s versions featuring popular artists from each decade. For a 2007 West Coast remix of the song, Nas invited Los Angeles artists Ice-T, Breeze, Candyman, Deadly Threat, King Tee, and Kam as well as the Bay Area–based Conscious Daughters. The only non-California participant was Sir Mix-A-Lot, who discussed his publishing library, the continued use of his material on television and in movies, "seven figure years," the fountain in his yard, and the cars in his garage.[107]

This discussion of financial security represented the business evolution of Sir Mix-A-Lot, who left NastyMix Records in 1990 under a cloud of unpaid publishing monies owed him. The expression of affection for one's hometown, a part of the culture from the beginning, helped establish Sir Mix-A-Lot's early reputation. It continued to play an important role in Seattle hip hop with the 2009 single and video "Home" off of Jake One's debut album *White Van Music* (2008). The album was described by Andrew Matson in the *Seattle Times* as "Jake One doing vignettes. He's a producer, a scene-setter, a director of movies for rappers to act on. 'Home' is the 'I love Seattle' vignette."[108] The song featured verses from Vitamin D, C-Note, Maineak B, and Ishmael Butler, each reflecting on various aspects of life in Seattle. Larry Mizell Jr. added: "'Home' was already the gorgeous Seattle-pride anthem off of *White Van Music*, and now it's the single greatest 206 rap video to date. That gorgeous tone, that muted color, is Seattle to a perfect T; the landmarks and lyrical references resonate like tuning forks in visual form."[109]

Speaking specifically of Butler's participation in a Seattle-centric production, Mizell added: "But it really had to be some kind of cathartic for Seattle native Ishmael Butler, to close the track out with his Central District–heavy verse—rapwise, it was no less than a homecoming for an MC who most heads for years thought was from Brooklyn."[110] As well-known as Butler had become nationally, and internationally, for people who did not know the backstory, his affiliation with Seattle may have seemed almost nonexistent. Charles Mudede went in search of a local opinion on this issue from Merciful of the group dRedi. "I got to give the brother a break," Merciful said. "He had the same dilemma that many rappers have when they start here: They can't get their kick off, so they go somewhere else and claim they are from there. Even Jimi Hendrix had to do that. But me, I'm going to claim S.E.A., the 206, until the wheels fall off."[111]

"Home" was directed by Zia Mohajerjasbi, brother of Sabzi of Blue Scholars. Matson labeled it as "best Seattle hip-hop video ever," complimenting its depth and texture and noting that the video introduces another character: Seattle itself. "Sir Mix-A-Lot's there, still hanging out in front of Dick's on Capitol Hill after all these years—but the 'Posse on Broadway' car is now an orange Lamborghini—and a few Central District spots make appearances. There's just something special about elevating Catfish Corner on MLK [Boulevard] & Cherry [Street] and especially the Grocery Outlet on MLK & Union [Street] to landmark status."[112]

In addition to producing locally, Jake One attracted the attention of some of music's biggest names, including hip-hop legend Rakim, for whom Jake produced the song "Won't Be Long" in 2009 on the album *The Seventh Seal*, released on Rakim's Ra Records and distributed through Universal Music Group. As part of a New York–based duo with his DJ Eric B., Rakim released classic music in the mid-1980s and had since assumed status as one of the greatest MCs of all time.

Macklemore Rising and Shabazz Palaces Mystery

Jake One wasn't the only local artist praising Seattle. After Macklemore's parents checked him into a substance rehab facility in 2008, he emerged ready to produce his own illustration of civic pride. In "The Town" (2009), Macklemore made numerous local references to KFOX, *Rap Attack*, and Sportn' Life Records among others while displaying the diverse nature of the Seattle scene. "Just peep Macklemore's sentimental ode to the Seattle hip-hop experience, 'The Town,' off of *The Unplanned Mixtape*, which shouts-out this very column," Larry Mizell Jr. remarked in *The Stranger*. "The song definitely captures a perspective that's damn familiar to anybody who's been loving this shit for 10 years plus (you know, Sit & Spin, RKCNDY, and so forth), which I guess just means 'old people' to all you New Boyz fans."[113] In 2010 Macklemore and Ryan Lewis released *The VS. Redux EP*, which contained the hit single "Otherside." Macklemore solidified his local status with the 2010 single "My Oh My," a tribute to beloved Seattle Mariners baseball broadcaster Dave Niehaus, who had announced games since the team's inception in 1977 until he passed away in November 2010. Macklemore performed the song in front of a sold-out opening day crowd for the Mariners at Safeco Field in 2011.

In the midst of such activity, there was yet another unique approach that expanded the local scene. Straying off the beaten hip-hop path was something that helped push Digable Planets to the top of the rap world in 1994. In 2009, Ishmael "Palaceer Lazaro" Butler and Tendai "Baba" Maraire of Shabazz Palaces announced their presence with two EPs. The group, described by the *New York Times* as an "eccentric experimental hip-hop act," anonymously released *Shabazz Palaces* and *Of Light*.[114] Although the initial anonymity added an air of mystery to the music, eventually the identity of the group was revealed, and they were hailed by critics as among the most creative artists of the year. After receiving Shabazz Palaces' debut in his mailbox, Larry Mizell Jr. wrote: "Surrounded by mystery, this project is short

on frills (like writing/production credits) but very long on *the boom.*
Egyptology, dancehall, future-beats, patois, slick talk—this is simply
some of the heaviest shit out that could arguably be called Seattle hip-
hop."[115] Andrew Matson agreed, offering commentary about the song
"Capital 5." "It quickly turns into dead-serious raps about gunplay in
the Central District," he wrote. "One unshakable image has the narrator and a buddy driving through town 'like ghosts,' high on cocaine,
possibly possessing a weapon. Let it be known 'boho-gangster' is not
an established hip-hop genre. Shabazz Palaces is in new territory
with its gun talk and atmospheric rain sticks."[116]

The number of artists releasing music increased as the 2000s
came to a close. These included the Saturday Knights, Mad Rad,
Helladope, Fresh Espresso, Black Stax (MCs Jace ECAJ and Silas
Blak, and vocalist Felicia Loud), OCnotes, Yuk, 10.4 Rog, Saba Seven,
Kung Foo Grip, They Live!, Champagne Champagne, and Grynch.
Known as the "King of Ballard," Grynch was interviewed by *Billboard*
magazine in 2009 about the release of his album *Chemistry 1.5.* Among
other things, Grynch discussed attending Pacific Lutheran University
in Tacoma, releasing his music independently, playing traditionally
rock-centric local venues, and the strength of the hip-hop scene in
Seattle.[117] The journey of *Billboard*, which had mocked Seattle hip
hop in the 1980s, showing up to interview Grynch a couple of decades
later, spoke to the long and slow process of local hip hop earning
national respect.

— —

Variety and the continued willingness to try new things and go
against the grain was a recipe that had already proven successful for
Seattle hip hop. Moving forward, the theory of the Pacific Northwest's
geographic isolation being linked to creative freedom stood front
and center in the face of mainstream norms and expectations. Taking
artistic risk would pay off in the form of even more Grammy Awards,
another world title for breaking, and diverse styles and approaches
that ensured Seattle's uniqueness. In addition to outside recognition,
hip hop in Seattle would finally receive some long overdue credit and
acknowledgment from established local mainstream cultural events
and institutions.

5

"The hood ain't the same"

TRADITIONS CHANGE AND CONTINUE

BY 2010, Seattle's well-established cultural and economic hip-hop infrastructure provided multiple platforms that served as jumping-off points for public exposure and industry connections. On the national scene Seattle artists increased their impact. One national stage took place in Austin, against a backdrop of the eclectic scene that includes country, blues folk, rock, punk, and jazz. Every March, more than fifty thousand participants gather in Austin for the South by Southwest Music Conference and Festival (SXSW), which journalist Larry Mizell Jr. described as an assembly of "tastemakers, journalists, bloggers, fans, industry types, and uncategorizable movers and shakers." First held in 1987, SXSW attracted national and international recognition.[1] In 2010 the festival featured an unprecedented number of Seattle hip-hop performers receiving unprecedented buzz. "Seems like half the town-that-is-Sea is all heading down to rock various showcases," Mizell wrote, "including such 206-heavy affairs as the Red Bull Big Tune event and the SXSeattle Party." Seattle participants included Dyme Def, Grynch, Macklemore, Mash Hall, Sportn' Life Records (D. Black, Fatal Lucciauno, Spac3man, SK), THEESatisfaction, JFK, Grayskul, Dark Time Sunshine, J.Pinder, Jake One, adopted Seattleite One Be Lo, and Shabazz Palaces, "all rocking in the storied land of barbecue and bourbon."[2]

The scene in Seattle continued in full swing as well. The well-documented sense of artistic collaboration, which ostensibly helped elevate the scene to national stages such as SXSW, asserted itself. In hip-hop terms that translated into long-form showcases, genre crossover, regular collective gatherings that were about more than rehearsed raps, a specifically female space, and further recognition from the mayor's office. For the first time, hip hop experienced unprecedented acceptance from local mainstream cultural institutions. The

practice of local talent bringing together and supporting local talent—the spirit that had helped inform so many compilation albums—
continued with Go! Machine, a two-day showcase in 2009 at the
Crocodile Café, featuring twelve local acts. Booked by Terry Radjaw
of the group Mad Rad, one of Go! Machine's headliners, the lineup
included Fresh Espresso, They Live!, Macklemore, Helladope, THEE-
Satisfaction, and Champagne Champagne.[3] This collaborative spirit
extended beyond hip hop, creating artistic overlap between multiple
genres. The "high concept concert" known as Kevin Collabo, held
in 2010, was put on by local instrumental electronic group Truckasaurus. The title of the show was based on the name of former beloved
Seattle SuperSonics television and radio broadcaster Kevin Calabro.
The event featured Truckasaurus, sharing the stage with more than
thirty local rappers, including Geologic, Spac3man, Ra Scion, Asun
aka Suntonio Bandanaz, Sol, SK, Mash Hall, Neema, Gathigi, Khingz,
Grynch, Champagne Champagne, and many more.[4]

Seattle hip hop was characterized by various regular hip hop–
themed nights at venues around town. Sometimes these gatherings
turned into something more, as was the case for the weekly event
known as Stop Biting. Beginning in 2004 at the venue Lo-Fi, on the
northwestern edge of downtown, the name came from hip-hop slang
meaning "create your own material/stop copying someone else." The
actual scene included break-dance and freestyle rap sessions and DJs
competing to see who could come up with the best original beat. Stop
Biting became a multimedia experience in 2012 when it produced
yet another compilation album featuring OCnotes, WD4D, and Specs
Wizard as well as a mini-documentary film providing insight into the
creative process of the artists.[5]

Another regular event was the monthly Grand Groove, hosted by
a collective of local rappers, DJs, and producers, including Shabazz
Palaces, THEESatisfaction, Metal Chocolates, Mash Hall, and Black
Book. "They all make hip-hop and music related to it, though each
is at risk to record a song or do a DJ set that does not include rap,"
wrote music critic Andrew Matson. "In general, 'Grand Groove' looks
like a good chunk of the city's most forward-thinking musical minds
of any genre, assembled for a free monthly chillout event. It should
be excellent."[6] The Ladies Night series in 2010 held at Neumos on
Capitol Hill occupied another important space in the local scene. Presented by Lisa Dank, these showcases boasted an impressive range of
local talent, including Luxury A.K., Anomie Bell, Katie Kate, Marissa,

Life with Blythe, Sap'N, Prisilla, Queerbait, DJ Colby B, Seattle Peach, THEESatisfaction, Canary Sing, Blush Photo, Choklate, and Tawnya "Dice" Cunningham. "Hip-hop breaking out of the goddamned hip-hop scene," Mizell called it. "Women in the audience, women onstage—I do so love seeing where it's all at these days."[7]

Seattle Cultural Institutions Embrace Local Hip Hop

In terms of cultural presence, hip hop in Seattle was experiencing a high volume of sustained activity. The regular inclusion of breaking and DJing alongside MCing at long-running events like Stop Biting and Ladies Night provided depth and personality within the scene. The cultural expansion of hip hop within Seattle went beyond performances and into established local mainstream cultural events and institutions. This included politics, as mayoral recognition continued during this period. In 2010 Mayor Mike McGinn pronounced November as Hip-Hop History Month in Seattle, the result of a petition effort led by 206 Zulu and King Khazm. "206 Zulu is excited that Mayor McGinn recognizes the many contributions made by hip-hop artists in the Seattle community," the document stated. "Being able to celebrate Hip-Hop History Month in Seattle is a celebration of all of the hard work, sacrifice, innovation and dedication of local artists whether famous or nameless. Moving forward, this annual occasion will facilitate additional education programs to celebrate the culture in a positive manner."[8] In 2014 mayors of several other Washington cities followed suit: Marilyn Strickland (Tacoma), Stephen Buxbaum (Olympia), Andy Ryder (Lacey), Patty Lent (Bremerton). Washington governor Jay Inslee declared November Hip-Hop History Month across the entire state.[9]

As hip hop received political endorsements from around the Puget Sound region, its presence and history was documented on various levels. In 2012 a wide array of cultural programming accompanied the commemoration of the fiftieth anniversary of Seattle hosting the 1962 World's Fair, which produced the iconic Space Needle and the Seattle Center. One of these projects was "The Next Fifty," a collaborative partnership between businesses, organizations, and community members, coordinated by Steve Sneed, Jazmyn Scott, Avi Loud, and Zachary Self. Out of this project came *50 Next: Seattle Hip-Hop Worldwide*, a short film by Avi Loud, presented by The Town Entertainment, Seattle Center Cultural Programs, and Festal (which worked to preserve community cultural traditions), and scored by Big World Breaks. More than a film, *50 Next: Seattle Hip-Hop World-wide* was also an online interactive experience, featuring some seventy songs from various Northwest artists, including a new single by the Emerald Street Boys called "When Folks Was Real (Back in the Dayz)."[10]

Over time the vast majority of local hip hop–related events had generally operated independent of the mainstream Seattle art/museum/festival circuit. Slowly, however, instances of community programming recognized and hosted outside traditional hip-hop circles started to become part of the scene. An example of this was Seattle's Museum of History and Industry (MOHAI)–sponsored February 2014 event on the legacy of Seattle hip hop.[11] The program included a panel discussion titled "The Hood Ain't the Same: A Conversation about Gentrification in Seattle." In addition to listening stations and interactive demonstrations by visual artists, performances by local MCs and breaking crews were highlighted as well as a screening of Loud's short film *50 Next: Seattle Hip-Hop Worldwide.*[12] MOHAI's *The Legacy of Seattle Hip-Hop* exhibit ran from September 2015 to May 2016, curated by Jazmyn Scott and Aaron Walker-Loud. Featured items included custom-made Massive Monkees graffiti jackets, a local hip-hop timeline, a hands-on production workstation featuring music from Vitamin D and Jake One, and the fur coat worn by Macklemore in the "Thrift Shop" video. A media partner of this landmark exhibit was local radio station KHTP "Hot 103.7" FM. In 2014 the station made Seattle radio history by becoming the first in the market to feature a rap and R&B "all throwback" format. That same year the station introduced "Classic Hip-Hop Sundays," an unprecedented entire day of programming dedicated to old-school rap music.

The phenomenon of hip hop as the focus of prestigious local events and institutions continued through 2015. Since 1972, the Northwest Folklife Festival held annually at the Seattle Center has celebrated local culture through music and dance. The Library of Congress named Northwest Folklife a Local Legacy in 1999. Held over four days during Memorial Day weekend, the festival has become a massive event, with more than six thousand volunteer local performers, eight hundred volunteers, and attendance totals of 250,000 from all over the world. For more than four decades, diverse artists such as bluegrass fiddlers, Middle Eastern dancers, Irish cloggers, West African drummers, ska bands, and more have performed at Folklife.[13]

Since 2000, each festival has included a cultural focus, which functions as a "festival within the festival." In 2015 hip hop was featured as the festival's cultural focus for the first time. Numerous figures from the Northwest hip-hop community, both past and present, contributed their time and expertise. The program included a number of panel discussions, several local and national hip hop–based film screenings, and a variety of music and dance performances, spoken word recitals, visual art displays, and workshops.[14]

The recognition of hip hop by local mainstream institutions had been a long time coming. The 206 Zulu–led mayor's proclamation of November as Hip-Hop History Month continued a partnership between hip hop and City Hall. However, the first-of-its-kind *Legacy of Seattle Hip-Hop* exhibit at MOHAI as well as the cultural focus at the 2015 Folklife Festival made clear that the culture had turned a corner in its relationships with entities outside the traditional local hip-hop framework.

Break-dancing Heritage and Another World Title

Although it may not have been the case in a national sense, breaking and graffiti maintained a strong presence in the region, reflected by several events and achievements. Reunions bringing together generations of dancers existed alongside new campus organizations that put on their own competitions. The blueprint of Massive Monkees claiming a world title and leveraging that success into community service would repeat itself. In 2011 the thirty-year anniversary reunion of the Seattle City Breakers became an occasion to celebrate three decades of local hip hop. Organized by Seattle b-boy veterans David Toledo and Carlos "Sir Slam-A-Lot" Barrientes, the event was held in the performance hall at West Seattle Christian Church. Hosted by DJs Supreme and B-Mello, the reunion featured numerous local breaking pioneers.[15] These included such crews as Emerald City Breakers, Fresh Force, DeRoxy Crew, and 1st Degree Breakers, and individuals like "Seattle's first break dancer" Jonathan "Junior" Alefaio, Ziggy "Zig Zag" Puaa, Rafael Contreras, Danny Molino, Spencer Reed, and Dave "Pablo D" Narvaez with his multigenerational crew North City Rockers. On hand to pay respects were current-day dancers Vicious Puppies Crew and Massive Monkees. The event drew a capacity crowd of nearly six hundred who also heard from featured guest speaker "Nasty" Nes Rodriguez.[16]

Massive maintained a presence at local events despite having won a world title. Even after Massive Monkees Day was declared in Seattle by Mayor Greg Nickels on April 26, 2004, the high-profile movements continued as the Beacon Hill crew was selected to participate in the MTV competitive dance reality program *America's Best Dance Crew*.[17] The show premiered in 2008 and was presented by executive producer Randy Jackson, best known as one of the three original judges on the Fox reality music program *American Idol*. Massive participated in the show's fourth season, competing for a $100,000 first prize and the Golden ABDC Trophy. They ultimately finished in third place behind Cuban-Puerto Rican dancers AfroBorike and eventual champions We Are Heroes, the first all-female group to win the title.[18]

As the landscape of international breaking evolved in the 2000s, Southeast Asia became a center for worldwide competition. By 2012, South Korea in particular was a focal point as the site of the R16 World B-Boy Masters Championship, held in Seoul. Since its inception in 2007, R16 had emerged as one of the world's premier breaking events, thanks to unprecedented support from the South Korean government, specifically the Ministry of Culture, Sports and Tourism, which was a primary sponsor. It had been eight years since Massive won the World B-Boy Championships in London, and in the five-year history of R16, first place had been dominated by South Korea and Japan. In fact, no American crew had ever even made it to the finals at R16. After coming together for another improbable run of qualifying at the US nationals, Massive Monkees made their way through round after round of competition before defeating Simple System, from Kazakhstan, in the finals.

After two world titles, Massive Monkees continued to transform their success as a breaking crew into community service. In 2013 the group opened its own dance studio in Seattle's International District called The Beacon, named in honor of the Beacon Hill neighborhood where the crew was born. Massive took advantage of a program called Storefronts Seattle, which offered grants to fill empty storefronts with art exhibits and creative enterprises in various areas of downtown. Of some four hundred applicants, the crew's proposal for The Beacon was one of eighty applications accepted.[19] The Beacon provided a variety of offerings for dancers, nondancers, and all skill levels in between. There was endurance training or advanced classes taught by the likes of Jeromeskee and Fever One. In addition to paid classes, there was a free after-school program. "This isn't just a working studio for one of the planet's most celebrated break dance crews and their friends," said Storefront Seattle program manager Matthew Richter. "It's a means of engaging the whole neighborhood, the whole city, in making the art that makes the Monkees so successful. They're telling passers-byers to join them inside and help them create this vibrant, exuberant urban art form."[20]

While Massive reached out to the community in general, there were specific efforts aimed at women and girls. One example of this was a class titled "Way of the B-Girl," first offered in 2013. Held at The Beacon, it was taught by Massive member Fides "Anna Banana Freeze" Mabanta. Offered free for newcomers to The Beacon, the class consisted of five one-hour meetings on select Thursdays during July and August. A description of the class asked: "Do you or any other ladies you know want to LEARN TO BREAK and practice WITH OTHER FEMALES? Then CHECK OUT this introductory B-GIRL dance class taught by Massive Monkees' own, b-girl Anna Banana Freeze, for a LIMITED TIME only!" The course promised: "YOU will become empowered, be stronger and feel good as well as; (1) Learn basic moves (toprocks, drops, footwork, freezes); (2) Explore breakin' concepts such as originality, style, character, battling, etc.; (3) Build strength and stamina as we continuously drill moves and sweat out stress during class!; (4) Discover truly awesome music; (5) Learn about b-girl history and discover b-girl role models from around the world; (6) Engage in discussion topics such as 'how to ignore males' and 'you are a b-girl and an individual'; (7) Have FUN!"[21]

This diversity of local dance activity, including grassroots events and competitions, showed no signs of slowing down. Mike "Mikeskee" Huang, founder of the University of Washington Hip-Hop Student Association (UWHHSA), organized the 2012 breaking competition Reign Supreme in partnership with Red Bull, the Associated Students of UW, and Massive Monkees. Contestants came from as far away as Brazil, Japan, and Taiwan to compete for a $2,500 first prize. Relationships with sponsors like Red Bull allowed Reign Supreme to include well-known judges such as Neguin, a Brazilian b-boy who also went by Fabiano Carvalho, who had won the UBC (Ultimate B-Boy Championship) and Red Bull BC One competitions.[22] The ability to directly trace some of Seattle's earliest breakers to their world champion descendants was the ultimate in hip-hop lineage.

Repeating the pattern of success, such as being invited to join Rock Steady Crew or winning R16, and then returning to serve the community, had been the local blueprint. The methodology of that service was crucial. Intentional programming like "Way of the B-Girl" provided important spaces for a variety of participants to engage hip hop without the bravado and machismo that is often present. These approaches provided quality depth and diversity as new generations entered the scene.

The local dance community was shaken when on June 5, 2014, a lone gunman opened fire with a shotgun on the campus of Seattle Pacific University. One student was killed and two wounded in the attack by a local man who was not a student at the school and ultimately pled not guilty to the crime by reason of insanity. The single fatality was nineteen-year-old Paul Lee, from Portland, Oregon, who had been a member of SPU's student hip-hop dance club Ante Up. In response to the tragedy, the University of Washington Hip-Hop Student Association and Ante Up collaborated to produce a tribute video called *Dance for Paul Lee*. The four-minute video featured clips of dancers from Seattle and Portland but included others from locations around the world as far away as Turkey.[23]

Graffiti Locations Expand

As dynamic and well-known as the hip-hop dance scene was in Seattle, graffiti also maintained an active, albeit less-famous, presence. This was partially highlighted by the demolition of an unofficial local graffiti landmark. The building, located in the University District, had been an hourly Jacuzzi rental business known as Tubs from the early 1980s. When Tubs closed its doors in 2007, the property was purchased by an owner who essentially turned the entire building into a "free wall," which meant the Graffiti Nuisance Ordinance did not apply. Designs and color schemes took turns rotating on walls that had ample room for several grand design paintings. The building was finally torn down in 2014 to make room for a mixed-use residential and commercial building.[24]

The elements of unsanctioned graffiti continued to be countered somewhat as around the city walls in areas such as downtown and other parts of North Seattle served as spots for invited graffiti. Several of these locations were free walls, while others were sites where property owners hired graffitists to paint walls that had been continuously hit up illegally. Some of the featured artists included members of the pioneering DVS Crew, the female graffiti collective Few and Far, as well as Eras, Merlot, Video, Weirdo, and Huemr.[25]

Questions about Seattle Hip Hop's National Popularity

The steady, growing optimism of journalists who covered Seattle hip hop seemed to indicate a coming upswing. If a creative community's life lies in the depth of its variety, the local scene was strong and healthy. New waves of Seattle street rap mixed with more abstract material that embraced, among other things, queer identity. While shows and tours provided valuable cultural programming in smaller cities and college towns around the region, there were still questions about the negative influence of artists who felt entitled and whether it was actually necessary to leave town in order to make it. Questions about the dynamics around what was becoming known as "frat rap" raised issues of racial and cultural appropriation. Alternative funding methods appeared as business models in the industry shifted, as did recognition for music production, and the question who's next from Seattle was soon answered.

Over the decades the already immense regional power of Seattle culture was magnified even more by the emergence of local hip hop. By 2010 the numerous college towns, smaller cities, and rural communities scattered around the Pacific Northwest looked to Seattle as essentially the only lifeline by which to experience live hip hop. "In fact, the regional TPOB tour (Bellingham, Pullman, Ellensburg, Yakima) can be seen as a kind of service that Seattle (the big cultural center of the region) provides to small towns and remote college campuses," Charles Mudede pointed out. For those more rural parts of the region, hip hop, which has its foundation in the urban experience, represented another world that could be accessed through radio, the Internet, and television. "Pinder, GMK, Dyme Def, Royce the Choice, and Eighty4 Fly (men who've cut their teeth in the hoods and streets of a big city)," Mudede wrote, "present these outposts with an opportunity to see and be near the real deal."[26]

There was also a familiar sentiment in local media around the age-old question of Seattle hip hop's popularity outside the Northwest. With seemingly all the necessary ingredients present in the local scene to build a national following, the questions of why it had not happened yet became louder. "What will it take for this scene to

earn a country-wide audience on a par with those of, say, Atlanta or
St. Louis?" asked an article in the *Seattle Weekly*. "After all, we've got
the producers, the recording studios, the MCs, the venues, an endless
supply of traveling acts, and a solid local and regional fan base on
which to build," wrote journalist Kevin Capp. "And after massively
successful events like Go! Machine, it can be tempting to believe that
Seattle's hip-hop scene is playing at a higher level than it actually is."
Blue Scholars manager Dave Meinert added: "There's a lot of local
hype that never amounts to anything outside of Seattle." As a result,
the article concluded, "Seattle is great at breeding mediocrity.... The
city's hip-hop scene, long home to a multitude of sounds and styles,
saw the emergence in 2009 of something bordering on a cohesive
aesthetic: fun-loving, often spaced-out and danceable grooves that
would seem to provide those outside Seattle with something to latch
onto—a flare in the sky to guide them."[27]

When rising local artist J.Pinder—who had worked with Sportn'
Life Records and Jonathan Moore, Vitamin D, and Jake One—relocated to Atlanta in 2010, the question burned: Is leaving Seattle necessary to make it? "Pinder's move does hurt Seattle's scene because
it subtracts from its diversity," Mudede argued. "If Seattle is to be the
next home of hip-hop—and that is not an impossibility—then it needs
a wide spectrum of rappers, modes, and positions. We need gangsters,
lesbians, Afro-futurists, hardcore hipsters and rappers who possess
Pinder's sense of the theatrical."[28]

Alternative Funding Sources and Battling Originality

The apparent dilemma of whether to stay or go coincided with a
shift in the traditional recording industry business model. As overall album sales fell by half in the aftermath of Napster and digital
file sharing that began in the early 2000s, artists, especially independent ones, were finding new and different ways to get their music
out to listeners. With the release of the 2011 album *Cinemetropolis*,
Blue Scholars added yet another layer to their business methodology.
Cinemetropolis was funded through the website Kickstarter, where
projects and ideas are financed by other people. It only took a few
days for Blue Scholars to raise more than $10,000, and Macklemore,
who used Kickstarter to fund his "Wings" video, nearly doubled his
$10,000 goal in just two weeks.[29] The Physics—Gathigi "Thig Natural"
Gishuru, Njuguna "Monk Wordsmith" Gishuru, and Justin "Justo"

Hare—also turned to Kickstarter with a goal of $8,000 and raised more than $11,000 to produce their 2012 album *Tomorrow People*.[30]

There were aspects of ingenuity and creativity in these alternative methods of raising funds that pushed and challenged the scene. But these were sometimes countered by elements of entitlement and exaggerated self-importance. "There are a million terrible rappers who believe they're owed a living because they keep turning out mediocre shit," wrote Larry Mizell Jr. in 2011, "and then there are some who do it because they simply have to."[31] Issues around a willingness or ability to be artistically different and original seemed to be front and center. "In case you haven't noticed, artists parroting that mainstream party line in Seattle aren't finding a lot of success here. The folks who want to hear that kind of shit are already programmed to treat it like disposable background music. There's no real support for it here," Mizell cautioned. "I think, for reasons specific to our region, far more people want to hear something from the soul, something that speaks to them."[32] Later that year, he wrote: "Or you can just bitch about it not being about you, or your boy, or your crew; surely your bitter and self-centered approach is what the town needs more of."[33]

Sub Pop Expands Its Hip-Hop Roster

Indeed, as local hip-hop music expanded, variety of artistic content and approach seemed to be a driving force, including instances that directly challenged long-held conventions of mainstream hip-hop culture. Despite the anonymous nature of their initial release, the buzz and critical acclaim for Shabazz Palaces increased. In 2010 Ishmael Butler reached out to Jonathan Moore, who called on Megan Jasper, executive vice president at Sub Pop Records. Jasper, with more than twenty years at Sub Pop, was well aware of the label's past experiences with hip hop. However, Shabazz Palaces' experimental approach and artistic charisma convinced Jasper and Sub Pop to sign the group. Well before the signing, nearly everyone who worked at Sub Pop had been infatuated with the EPs *Shabazz Palaces* and *Of Light*.[34]

"Shabazz's almost subliminal messages are universal: 'Find out who you are and see it/Find out what you are and free it/Find out who you love and need it/Find out what you can and be it,'" wrote Charles Mudede. "It's a timely sentiment for Seattle hip-hop, which, after years of self-negating/hating or looking too much to the Bay Area and Brooklyn for direction, is enjoying a creative surge and homegrown industry that is—no bullshit—changing the landscape of Seattle music."[35] Larry Mizell Jr. agreed: "Seeing as how Sub Pop has an international rep for showcasing game-changing talent, and being that Shabazz are about the most revolutionary shit I've heard in years, I'm anticipating some cool developments."[36] Shabazz Palaces became the first rappers to appear on the cover of *The Stranger*. The duo was announced as recipients of the first Stranger Genius Award for Music. "Shabazz's songs aren't built with the usual sixteen-bars/chorus/repeat structure of most hip-hop—they take a more free-flowing form," *The Stranger* said. "When Butler locks into a groove, he often rides it until it's comfortably exhausted, or lets one otherwise unobtrusive line repeat until it becomes a mantra or a chant, not so much a traditional, song-anchoring chorus."[37]

Performances by Shabazz Palaces in New York City drew attention from major media outlets like the *New York Times*. Music writer Jon Caramanica wrote that the duo's show "made an awkward mess, fascinating in the details but harsh enough to thin an already thin crowd." He described the group's music as "unexpectedly beautiful juxtapositions of the digital and analog, hard drum-machine beats set against softer bongos or the resonant sweetness of an mbira" and "dense, curious, emotional and a little ferocious."[38] Following the release of their debut album *Black Up* in 2011, Shabazz Palaces was profiled in the *New Yorker*. "Shabazz Palaces uses sonic fog and unusual mixing to obscure its charms—a sly and unpredictable lead m.c. and a clutch of sonorous tones—not because the group is dissuading anyone from entering its world but because it is committed to high-resolution disorientation," wrote critic Sasha Frere-Jones. "All of this is keyed to pleasure. 'Black Up' would once have been called a 'headphones album': it is rich and striated, and was made for the closeup of the in-ear speaker."[39]

Back in Seattle, THEESatisfaction also signed with Sub Pop Records in 2011. The duo of Stasia "Stas" Irons and Catherine "Cat" Harris-White continued Seattle's practice of going against traditional hip-hop norms. "Almost exactly a year ago, local 'psychedelic space-rap/jazz' duo THEESatisfaction played Neumos for the first time," wrote journalist Andrew Matson. "It was one of Stasia Irons and Catherine Harris-White's earliest concerts as a group, and the girlfriends only had seven or eight songs in their repertoire. They were nervous as all get out." The group had since become veteran performers, regularly playing shows all over the city. "They work rooms with confidence that says, yes, Seattle *will* accept gay, Afrocentric musicians that vocalize jazz over low-key hip-hop instrumentals and dance like New Jack Swing hippies."[40] When THEESatisfaction released their debut album *awE naturalE* in 2012, national music media outlets such as *Pitchfork* picked up on the group, calling them "ultra-positive Queens of the Stoned Age who prioritize uninhibited genre exploration and good vibe-seeking above all" and "a pleasantly surprising resurrection Pacific Northwest-via-Brooklyn hippie-hop that we never might have anticipated a few years ago."[41]

Acceptance of Seattle Street Rap

While groups like Shabazz Palaces and THEESatisfaction represented new and alternative forms of hip hop, rap from a street perspective symbolized the mainstream status quo. Street rap from Seattle did not emerge as it had in other parts of the country during the late 1980s. Many artists from California became famous for misogynistic themes and resolving conflict with gunplay in their songs. This was not the case with Sir Mix-A-Lot, who rapped about intervening in a domestic dispute using mace. Could street rap from Seattle really ever catch on, and what had traditionally prevented this from happening? "There's the fact that it's Seattle, meaning not Chicago's South Side or something," explained Larry Mizell Jr. "Yeah, there are real hoods here (FYI, 'hood' means more than just an impoverished locality, it also refers to the folks representing it), but a person from another city (or a better-off section of this one) might never believe it." He continued: "Mainstream Seattle, aka middle-aged-to-old white men and women, as it stands, have nothing to gain from helping proliferate the messages of a marginalized people's pain and anger." The push for this would have to be grassroots, coming from the streets themselves. However, those same "streets" often failed to provide the necessary support—physical, financial, or both—found in other healthy local scenes such as Atlanta, Oakland, and Detroit. Still, there was another possibility. "The grand majority of Seattle street rap (there's a lot) has sucked, historically," Mizell contended. "Why should the hood support or keep supporting an artist (buy product, spread the word, go to shows) who doesn't think they deserve better than hella outdated, cheap-sounding beats, zero personality or detectable rap skills, and rehashed clichés they can hear executed far better via devilish commercial TV and radio?"[42]

Jesse "Nacho Picasso" Robinson, who announced his presence with his release *Blunt Raps* in 2010, emerged with a different style of local street hip hop. Nacho and the BAYB (Badd AzzYellowBoyz) brought "a wild new energy to Seattle street rap, a subgenre whose best participants have mastered a steely mastermind cool. Instead, BAYB's Jarv, Steezie, and Nacho rage shirtless, gold-toothed, and tatted to the wrists."[43] Larry Mizell Jr. summarized Picasso's position this way: "To the yang that characterizes some of Seattle's most well-known hip-hop—bright, ultra-posi[tive], upward-seeking—Nacho and BSBD [producers Blue Sky Black Death] are the yin: dark, colder, seeking the low places." This so-called "cult of the villain" style was described as "drug-induced thug noir" and "suicidal shoegaze thug-wave."[44] Nacho Picasso's 2011 album, *For the Glory*, received national recognition, including being named on *Spin* magazine's 50 Best Mixtapes of 2011 and the music websites *Stereogum* and *Pitchfork*. "Robinson is Nacho and Picasso, part fast food, part real deal. He is the hardcore hood nerd, the walking talking paradox writ large. Nacho openly claims he's an arrogant asshole, not to be trusted, a bridge burner, and a numbnuts. And *For the Glory* is basically a paean to girls, guns, tattoos, chronic, and comics," wrote Jeff Weiss on *Pitchfork*. "Picasso references his internal turmoil but never delves too deep. Nor does he need to. *For the Glory* is one of the best rap debuts of the year, one that simultaneously manages to say everything but reveal nothing."[45] Along with Nacho Picasso came his crew, the primarily Beacon Hill neighborhood–based Moor (Militia Organization Order Returns) Gang. Among the members of this collective were Gifted Gab, Thaddeus David, Jarv Dee, Steezi Nasa, Jerm D, Cam The Mac, and Kris Kasanova.

Seattle Hip Hop in the National Spotlight

Discussions about rap from Seattle often focused on vocals as opposed to production, although widespread critical acknowledgment of local musical talent was not only reserved for MCs. Over the course of two decades, Jake One had continued to build on a tradition of dynamic Seattle producers who were actively courted by some of the biggest names in music. A few of the artists Jake has produced include De La Soul, E-40, Tupac Shakur, 50 Cent, Rakim, Cypress Hill, T.I., Pitbull, Ghostface Killah, and Snoop Dogg. In December 2012, he received a Grammy nomination for production credit on the album *Some Nights* by the American indie pop band Fun. Jake One secured another nomination for his production on the song "3 Kings" by Rick Ross, featuring Dr. Dre and Jay-Z. Ross's album *God Forgives, I Don't* was nominated for the Best Rap Album award.[46] The stars kept calling as Jake One produced the 2013 song "Furthest Thing" for Canadian superstar Drake.

Jake One's Grammy-level recognition was part of a wave that put Seattle hip hop in the spotlight like never before. Another seemingly unlikely rise was framed within an unorthodox approach. In 2011 Macklemore's local profile was cemented by a string of successes. Perhaps sensing what was coming, Larry Mizell Jr. wrote in January of that year: "This dude Macklemore is going off right now. If you get the impression that a whole lot of folks are tripping over themselves to declare 2011 the Year of the Mack, it's only because that's exactly what it's looking like."[47] Indeed, a few months later, Macklemore appeared above the fold on the front page of the *Seattle Times*. He and Ryan Lewis sold out concerts on three consecutive nights at the Showbox in record time, where at the final show Sir Mix-A-Lot appeared as a guest onstage to perform "Posse on Broadway" and literally pass a torch to Macklemore. "I hand the baton to you," Mix-A-Lot said. "Run baby run!"[48] Macklemore also appeared on the cover of national rap magazine *XXL* as part of its "Freshman Class of 2012."

With the rising popularity of Macklemore and others, the inevitable discussion about the impact and contributions of white hip-hop artists returned. The fact that a subgenre of white hip hop now had an identifier—"frat rap"—indicated that changing racial dynamics were occurring within the culture. Pittsburgh artist Mac Miller, who died in 2018, exemplified the "frat rap" archetype, as he helped open the door to the phenomenon. After his appearance, "all the beer-pongin'-ass second-rate Millers are pouring in (there's some good beer-based jokes here, seeing as one of these fools actually calls himself Sam Adams)," observed Larry Mizell Jr. "But I also believe in *it ain't where you from, it's where you at*, as long as where you're at is a place called 'respecting what came before' and 'actually decent at rapping.'" Another example, Chris Webby, headlined a show at the Crocodile in Seattle. "This guy," Mizell cracked, "would've been lucky to get a buck on the nerdcore circuit four years ago, and now you probably can't kick the YouTube machine without some of his shittiness falling out. Such is life. Some of the old heads, upon seeing shit like this, scream, 'Battle stations!' but I'm more like, 'Abandon ship!'"[49]

Macklemore's more thoughtful content and reflective approach distinguished him from the frat rap blueprint and kept local opinion generally in his favor. This helped set the stage for a fateful fifteen-month run in the careers of Macklemore and Ryan Lewis. They released their album *The Heist* in October 2012 and soon the question of who would be the next rapper from Seattle to make a national impact was answered. While the album was released on Macklemore's label—Macklemore LLC—manager Zach Quillen worked with the Alternative Distribution Alliance (ADA), an independent arm of Warner Music Group, to help expand *The Heist*'s reach beyond the Seattle market and push pop radio promotion.[50]

The duo completely financed the production of their videos, and things moved quickly. "First, this," wrote Mizell in October. "As of this writing, Macklemore & Ryan Lewis have had the number one album—*The Heist*—in the US (and a few other spots) on iTunes for the past few days, above the album from Mack's fellow 2012 *XXL* freshman Machine Gun Kelly, Jay-Z's *Live in Brooklyn*, and the *Pitch Perfect* soundtrack." He explained the significance of the moment: "What we have here is a big deal—as well as a true DIY success story. As a witness to Mack's dues-paying, self-examination, and hard work over the last seven years, I am goddamn proud of him and RL."[51] Macklemore and Ryan Lewis made national television appearances on the *Ellen DeGeneres Show* in October and *Late Night with Jimmy Fallon* in December. In January 2013 the single "Thrift Shop" featuring Michael "Wanz" Wansley reached number one on the *Billboard* "Hot 100," where it spent six weeks. The song broke the record for longest-running number one rap song in the history of *Billboard*'s "Hot R&B/Hip-Hop" chart.[52] "Thrift Shop" sold several million copies, and the video accumulated more than 1.3 billion views on YouTube.[53] In May 2013 the duo's next single, "Can't Hold Us," featuring Ray Dalton, hit number one on the *Billboard* chart. Macklemore and Ryan Lewis became the first duo to have its first two singles reach number one in more than fifty years of the *Billboard* "Hot 100." The single "Can't Hold Us" sold more than four million copies and remained the number one song for five weeks.[54]

Released as a single in July 2012, "Same Love" featuring Mary Lambert was the rare rap song that openly supported gay rights and same-sex marriage. "I'm somebody that spends my life working on fighting fear. Realizing the fear that I have in myself, seeing fear in society and trying to address it and bring it to the surface,"

Macklemore explained. "When it comes to the arguments against same-sex marriage, if you strip away the biblical, the religious shit, it all comes down to fear. Fear of something that you don't know. And that has been the root of negativity in humanity since humans have been walking around this earth."[55] Referendum 74, approved in November 2012, legalized same-sex marriage in Washington State with "Same Love" serving as an anthem for the campaign. Macklemore, Lewis, and Lambert gave high-profile performances of the song on the *Ellen DeGeneres Show* and at the 2014 Grammy Awards, where they were joined on stage by Madonna and Queen Latifah, who presided over the weddings of more than thirty gay and straight couples. "Same Love" eventually reached number eleven on the *Billboard* chart while also stirring up controversy when teachers in Michigan and North Carolina were suspended after playing the song in class.[56]

Macklemore and Lewis concluded their world tour in support of *The Heist* in December 2013 by playing three consecutive nights of sold-out shows at the seventeen-thousand-plus-seat Key Arena with Sir Mix-A-Lot as the opening act. *The Heist* peaked at number two on the *Billboard* album chart and has sold more than one million copies to date. It won the title Favorite Rap/Hip-Hop Album and Macklemore and Ryan Lewis won Favorite Rap/Hip-Hop Artists at the 2013 American Music Awards. When nominations were announced for the 2014 Grammy Awards, *The Heist* was included for Best Rap Album as well as Album of the Year. In addition, Macklemore and Ryan Lewis were nominated for Best New Artist, "Thrift Shop" received nominations for Best Rap Performance and Best Rap Song, "Can't Hold Us" was nominated for Best Music Video, and "Same Love" was nominated for Song of the Year.[57]

After a staggering seven nominations, the duo took Best New Artist, *The Heist* won Best Rap Album, and "Thrift Shop" received Best Rap Performance and Best Rap Song at the fifty-sixth annual Grammy Awards in January 2014. Following the ceremony, Macklemore sent an apology via social media to Los Angeles artist and fellow Best Rap Album nominee Kendrick Lamar for *The Heist* winning over Lamar's *Good Kid, m.A.A.d. City*, which Macklemore felt was more deserving. With songs like "Thrift Shop" and "Same Love," Macklemore went directly against two of the most well-established norms in mainstream rap culture—namely bling (the wearing of expensive jewelry and brand-name clothing) and homophobia.

Undoubtedly the liberal nature and relative isolation of the greater Seattle area, combined with Macklemore's whiteness, contributed to his ability to successfully engage these topics through the lens of hip hop.

"Thrift Shop" sounded like nothing else out there at the time. "As Sir Mix-A-Lot raps only like Sir Mix-A-Lot, Macklemore raps only like Macklemore," Charles Mudede wrote in *The Stranger*. "Indeed, many of the comments on his YouTube videos compare him to Tupac, not because they sound similar, but because they share a style that feels honest and direct. Finally, 'Thrift Shop' also returned laughter to the dance floor and the pop charts." Because Seattle was so disconnected from the mainstream in the northwest corner of the United States, Mudede continued, it could never produce "the kind of predictable rappers who are obsessed with gold everything (Atlanta's Trinidad James) or have a serious boner for fucking problems (NYC's A$AP Rocky). Our rappers are instead asking girls to buy them drinks (Don't Talk to the Cops!), or having Christmas on the moon (THEESatisfaction), or celebrating the greatness of a Filipino deli on Beacon Hill (Blue Scholars), or feeling like $1,000 in 1988 (Fresh Espresso), or dealing with an old beat-up Volvo (Grynch)." Mudede concluded that "'Thrift Shop' will sound like something that came straight out of the blue if you don't come from 'The Town.'"[58]

Hip-Hop Occupies and Africatown

The activist and community-service component of hip-hop culture had long been present in Seattle, both in demonstrations and organizations. Past protests against radio station KUBE and Mayor Paul Schell were complemented by the work of organizations like Seattle Hip-Hop Summit Action Network (SHHSAN) and 206 Zulu. The growth of local infrastructure allowed for the emergence of new and different methods, such as protesting a protest, establishing an African American cultural preservation movement in the Central District, rhymes on the op-ed page of the newspaper, underlying hip-hop connections to two massive political outcomes, and the acknowledgment of ten years of service from two different sources.

Not limited to traditional paths of resistance, local hip hop found itself confronting issues of inequity within an emergent and popular social justice movement. In September 2011 the Occupy Wall Street movement received mainstream media attention when protesters used New York City's Zuccotti Park as a base for their activities throughout the Financial District in Manhattan. The Occupy movement stood against social and economic inequality and argued that the power enjoyed by large corporations and the global financial system disproportionately benefited a small minority of people. The term "the 99%" was popularized during this period, which referred to the concentration of wealth among the top 1 percent of earners versus the remaining 99 percent. The group stated: "We are the 99 percent. We are getting kicked out of our homes. We are forced to choose between groceries and rent. We are denied quality medical care. We are suffering from environmental pollution. We are working long hours for little pay and no rights, if we're working at all. We are getting nothing while the other 1 percent is getting everything. We are the 99 percent."[59]

In less than a month, Occupy protests sprung up in dozens of communities around the United States and in numerous countries around the world. In Seattle protesters gathered downtown outside the Federal Building and at Westlake Park. When Seattle police began removing protesters from Westlake, some of them relocated to City Hall at the invitation of the mayor. By the end of October, the Occupy encampment had settled on the campus of Seattle Central College. From the beginning, there were racial, cultural, and socioeconomic tensions within Seattle's Occupy movement, and soon a hip hop–based offshoot of Occupy Seattle, Hip-Hop Occupies, was formed. The group's first action, "Rise and Decolonize: Let's Get Free," was held November 18 in Westlake Park.

Among the leaders of Hip-Hop Occupies in Seattle was Julie C, a longtime local artist and activist. Larry Mizell Jr. asked in *The Stranger* whether "decolonize" was a rebuttal to the concept of "occupation." Julie C responded: "Decolonization of the world, our neighborhoods, and our hearts is the movement, and has been. Decolonization shows solidarity to our indigenous comrades, POC [people of color], and allies in the third world who experience the term 'occupation' very differently than the white liberal reformists who seem to be the popular faces and loudest voices emerging from Occupy." She further explained: "At the same time, we embrace the term 'occupation' as it has been reclaimed by militant workers of color globally to describe a strike back against oppressive forces." Other high-priority issues for Hip-Hop Occupies were youth justice, education disparities, corruption in the school district, diversion of money for youth crime prevention away from community organizations, and economic displacement, specifically the demolition of Yesler Terrace, the lone public-housing complex in the Central District. Asked about the movement's successes in Seattle, Julie C cited protest actions that had taken place at Chase Bank and the Sheraton Hotel downtown, which displayed the resolve and commitment among occupiers. "It was reported as a riot," she said, "but on the ground, it was beautiful. People were not allowing their allies to be arrested. They formed barricades to prevent arrests. They showed police they were in control. Cops didn't know what to do. That's a good sign."[60]

The activist nature of Hip-Hop Occupies was complemented by efforts aimed at historic community preservation, led by a longtime hip-hop advocate. In 2003 census data indicated that for the first time that more African Americans lived in suburban areas outside Seattle than inside the city limits.[61] Partially in response to this, an initiative called Africatown was launched in 2011 with Wyking Garrett as a member of the core advisory team. Using a model based on Seattle's Chinatown/International District, Africatown sought to create a core area of economic, educational, and cultural development in the CD. Garrett argued: "[Asian Americans] have a Chinatown–International District Preservation Authority—to preserve and develop. It's about the past and it's about the future. This is the only African-American community."

Africatown briefly occupied the vacant Horace Mann School building on Cherry Street and immediately used the space to offer classes for youth, Black history immersion, technology access, and a middle school for Muslim girls. "Part of the solution Africatown represents is that this is not lower Capitol Hill, this is not west Leschi, not upper Madison Park," Garrett said. "All these different ways they seek to ignore or marginalize, or devalue the people who have made their lives here and contributed to the richness that Seattle offers to the world." Africatown was envisioned as eventually being a destination for all people who valued the contributions and history of African Americans. After watching an Africatown presentation by Garrett, Mayor Ed Murray said he felt "the city should refer to the area as Africatown–Central District."[62] The proposal stood in the face of continued and accelerated gentrification in the CD, propelled primarily by new arrivals working well-paying jobs, skyrocketing real estate values, and the increased property taxes that accompanied them.

Performance Op-Ed in the *Seattle Times*

Instances of activism and service among the local hip-hop community took a variety of different forms. Protests, occupations, and civil disobedience had all served useful and important purposes. Eventually these methods also included the newspaper editorial page. In early 2012 a rash of shootings shook the Seattle area. These included the murder of four patrons at a coffee shop in the north side of the city and several suspected gang- or drug-related killings in the south end. Following this violent trend, George "Geologic/Prometheus Brown" Quibuyen of Blue Scholars wrote an op-ed in the *Seattle Times*. He had written an article for *Al Jazeera* in 2011, voicing support for the emerging Occupy Wall Street movement.[63] This time, he created an op-ed that was a song and video performance:

> Never heard of this, city getting murderous—
> occupation dangerous like Philippine journalists.
> Crazy and deranged they describe him in the same pages
> that would call him terrorist, if not for the melanin deficiency.
> Gang problem bigger than just juvenile delinquency.
> Gangs is survival if environments is grimy.
> To begin with—speaking of which, let's be consistent—
> Today is called a tragedy, yesterday a statistic.
> I'm listening, before I ever speak upon insisting.
> My name is young Prometheus and this is my opinion:
> Watch "The Interrupters," see ordinary civilians
> can police themselves before they have to call police for help.
> At least a little space to breathe, if you believe all violence
> is abhorrent to your being, then why you oversee it?
> If the killer wears a uniform but if the killer's me,
> it's normal if the victim also looks like me.
> Shots fired in the south end, nobody cares.
> Shots fired in the north end, everybody scared.
> Nothing they can do for us that we can't do ourselves.
> Point the finger at the mirror instead of somebody else.
> Can't lie, I know the music can be influential,
> but not as influential as desperation. They saying
> that you gotta act right if you wanna have rights,
> but what if you were born into a wrong situation?

Moral relativity—that passive aggressive city stuff—
becoming history quicker than you can blink at me.
Rule 1: Protect yourself at all times.
Rule 2: Always end but never start a fight.
Came up in the era of the hand-to-hand scrapping
'til the drugs happened, now it's bloodshed at transactions.
I'm calling time out like Samuel L. Jackson
playing DJ Love Daddy with the African medallion.
Tryin'a do the right thing. I don't have the answers,
but neither does a person who practices double standards.
If every death's a tragedy then join us when we're chanting,
and not just when we're singing and dancing.[64]

Sociopolitical statements in rhyme form by hip-hop artists were not a new thing, except on the op-ed page of Seattle's oldest newspaper. The willingness of a traditional institution like the *Times* to publish such a nontraditional editorial was a different look for hip hop in Seattle. Similar to the *Legacy of Seattle Hip-Hop* exhibit at MOHAI and hip hop being the cultural focus at the Folklife Festival in 2015, the op-ed piece signaled increasing acceptance of hip hop by the local mainstream. This level of recognition by the *Seattle Times* came around the same time as two enormous statewide political events with hip-hop connections.

Landmark Legislation and Anniversaries

The elections of November 2012 were historic, both nationally and locally. Barack Obama, the country's first African American president, earned a second term over Republican challenger Mitt Romney, winning Washington State by a wide margin. Locally, the passage of two measures in particular reflected evolving norms that placed Washington at the forefront of the cultural curve. Referendum 74 legalized same-sex marriage in the state and rode Macklemore's "Same Love" as a theme to victory. The other was Initiative 502, which would "license and regulate marijuana production, distribution, and possession for persons over 21. It would tax marijuana sales and earmark marijuana-related revenues. The new tightly regulated and licensed system would be similar to those used to control alcohol."[65]

Once ratified, Washington joined Colorado as the only two states in the country to sell recreational marijuana legally. Before this, the high-quality reputation of Northwest cannabis had already been embraced and celebrated by the local hip-hop community. Examples extend from a song like "Sunshine" by D.M.S. to Nacho Picasso's *Blunt Raps* album to the Stay-High Brothers, aka Vitamin D and Maineak B. This open-minded stance on same-sex marriage and legalization of marijuana, issues considered controversial in other parts of the country, further solidified Seattle's progressive reputation. In Washington the voting power of the greater Seattle-Tacoma metro region was enough to overcome the accumulation of more conservative smaller cities and rural communities, particularly in the eastern part of the state. A by-product of this mindset has been hip hop's consistent willingness to serve the scene on various levels.

While most hip hop–related community service was grassroots in nature, sometimes it came from the framework of media. By the time Larry Mizell Jr.'s "My Philosophy" in *The Stranger* celebrated its tenth anniversary in 2014, the column had become a local hip-hop fixture. In terms of its tenure, the column stood alone in the history of covering the Seattle hip-hop scene. Mizell remained remarkably consistent since he came in following the departure of Sam Chesneau and the Dan Savage fiasco. After taking over in July 2004, Mizell posted twenty-five columns for the remainder of the year, and wrote at least fifty columns every year between 2005 and 2014. Aside from Shockmaster Glen Boyd in the 1980s, no other writer has documented the Seattle hip-hop landscape more thoroughly over a longer period than Mizell. A performer and manager himself, Mizell dealt with the inevitable conflicts of interest that face someone who covers a scene in which they also participate.

"I have mixed feelings about mine still being the name at the top of this column, to be honest. Integrity is very important to me—and in my eyes, this particular soapbox carries some responsibility to a deep and once-underserved community of artists," Mizell reflected. He wondered if he was doing the scene a disservice by not moving on and letting someone else's point of view take over the column. "A decade down the line, I'm a walking conflict of interest," he wrote. "Stewarding not just this but other things, among them a radio show and the interests of the artists I help manage (who are some of the best in these Northwest states, and who I've always advocated for), but I try my best to be transparent about all of it."[66]

Hip hop's increasing maturity in the Northwest remained strengthened by dedicated and consistent media coverage, which over the decade had helped provide foundations for success. The development of this scene received the support of extended community activity. 206 Zulu celebrated its own decade of service on Valentine's Day weekend 2014. All programming took place at 206 Zulu's headquarters, in historic Washington Hall on 14th Avenue in the Central District, and featured three days of "true school hip-hop." Zulu Nation founder Afrika Bambaataa and Bay Area–based world champion DJ Qbert hosted the opening ceremonies. Other events included a three-on-three b-boy/b-girl battle with a $1,000 cash prize and performances by Los Angeles artist Rass Kass and numerous other MCs and DJs. The event culminated with a free "Meeting of the Minds" community forum and potluck.[67]

The anniversary produced a nineteen-track compilation album featuring such local artists as Specs Wizard, Gabriel Teodros, Derrick X aka Silver Shadow D, Orbitron, Sista Hailstorm, and Julie C. This practice of compilation albums persisted despite point number seven from Strath Shepard's 1997 piece in *The Rocket* titled "Moving Seattle Hip-Hop Forward: Ten Points of Light." Shepard wrote: "No more compilations. People don't buy compilations because they tend to be overwhelming for press and radio and often don't get the attention they deserve." After nearly two decades, however, the community-centric spirit around local hip hop remained.

Immigration and Seattle Hip Hop

The Macklemore era brought renewed attention to Seattle hip hop on multiple levels. Making the transition from local artist to being internationally recognized has potential ripple effects not only for a newly famous artist but for the scene they came from. Many events helped push the hip-hop community forward in Seattle: the immigrant experience, national outlets ranking local talent, continued female influence, an up-and-comer on Sub Pop Records, a historic and semicontroversial connection between Sir Mix-A-Lot's and the Seattle Symphony, and a critical read on gentrification in the Central District. As immigration from Asian and Pacific Island countries shaped the historical ethnic makeup of Seattle, so did the more recent arrival of those from Africa. During the 1960s and 1970s a handful of African-born immigrants settled in the Northwest. In 1858 it was Manuel Lopes, a native of the Cape Verde Islands off the West Coast of Africa who became Seattle's first Black resident. As time passed, new residents arrived from eastern and southern African countries such as Kenya, Tanzania, Uganda, and Zimbabwe. Dumisani "Dumi" Maraire arrived at the University of Washington as an artist-in-residence in 1968. The native of Zimbabwe taught ethnomusicology courses on campus and marimba and mbira classes in the community. Dumi Sr.'s sons Tendai (of Shabazz Palaces) and Dumi Jr. (aka "Draze's" group CAVE), along with brothers Gathigi and Njuguna Gishuru of The Physics, helped bring some African flavor to Seattle hip hop.[68]

Local immigration patterns increased during the 1980s and 1990s in large part because of political crises, civil wars, and widespread drought and resulting famine around the Horn of Africa. This brought greater numbers of African immigrants to the Pacific Northwest, seeking the opportunity for a better life. By 2008 an estimated twenty-three thousand Eritreans, Ethiopians, Kenyans, Somalis, Sudanese, and Ugandans called King County home. Almost as many African immigrants resided in King County in 2008 as the total Black population of the county in 1960. Indications of this presence were found in the form of mosques, markets, and restaurants primarily in the Central District and the Rainier Valley. Suburban towns such as Tukwila and Sea-Tac also had high concentrations of Somalis, but almost every community in King County had some East Africans or their descendants among their residents. East African children comprised a high percentage of Black students in the county's public schools. Community-based support agencies such as the Refugee Federation Service Center and the Refugee Women's Alliance continue to provide valuable services for people upon arriving in the United States for the first time.[69]

Members of these local communities began to use the lens of hip hop to express themselves. One example was the local hip-hop hotspot Hidmo restaurant, opened by sisters Asmeret and Rahwa Habte in 2006. Another was the Somali-American group Malitia Malimob (Chino'o and Krown) and their 2012 debut album *Riots of the Pirates*. Larry Mizell Jr. encouraged listeners to "peep the uncut perspective of these young, street-active Somali cats over beats that are at once riotously trill, deep, and ancient-sounding." The album's name played on something that Somalia had become known for in the 2000s—the seizure of foreign containerships by Somali pirates for ransom in the Indian Ocean off of Africa's East Coast. This phenomenon was dramatized in the 2013 film *Captain Phillips*, starring Tom

Hanks. "Also on this show is Malitia Malimob, Seattle's own amped-up
Somali American headbussas," Mizell reported. "On their new *Riots
of the Pirates*, they have a unique and coherent take on aggressive
trap braggadocio, evoking the brutal imagery of the Somali pirate
much like U.S.-born street rappers have invoked mob figures."[70] The
group's outlook and message evolved over time, moving away from
the stereotypical hardcore visual approach of champagne and cars.
According to Chino'o, "This whole thing is really about us doing our
part for our country, for our community. Really we plan on being
activists, not just rappers. We're African. We're proud."[71] Artists like
Malitia Malimob highlighted the diverse perspectives that emerged
from Seattle hip hop. Coverage of these perspectives was carried
on various homegrown media platforms, from *The Stranger* column
"My Philosophy" to *Hip-Hop 101 TV* to the website MissCaseyCarter
.com, which remained active and community-focused. However, after
the global success of Macklemore, national media weighed in on the
local scene. In June 2013, New York–based *XXL* magazine released
what it called a "New New" list of "15 Seattle Rappers You Should
Know." The magazine prefaced the list by saying, "With the New New,
XXL tries to spotlight burgeoning acts who we feel haven't gotten
the shine they deserve, but what makes this edition special is that we
feel the entire city of Seattle hasn't gotten the attention it deserves."
The featured artists were Avatar Darko, Black Stax, Brothers from
Another, Champagne Champagne, Eighty4Fly, Fatal Lucciauno, Fresh
Espresso, J.Pinder, Jarv Dee, Kung Foo Grip, Mack E, Nacho Picasso,
Sam Lachow, Shelton Harris, Sol, and Thaddeus David.[72]

Although the list shined a light on Seattle hip hop, it also produced
some hard feelings and revived criticisms within the local scene. Silas
Blak of Black Stax went so far as to say, "You know, I almost kind of
wish I wasn't on the list—you won't believe the kind of hate that's out
there. It's more trouble than it's worth." Reacting to Blak's reaction,
Charles Mudede wrote: "Blak is profoundly intelligent, intensely sensitive, very perceptive, and generally positive. So to see him all down
like this about a great piece of publicity for his crew meant that things
were really, really rotten in Denmark." He added: "I later even heard
someone, who will remain unnamed, state that Black Stax made the
list because their trumpeter, Owuor Arunga, tours with Macklemore."
Local producer Rob Castro commented: "Macklemore and that *XXL*
article is making people crazy. It doesn't say anything about Seattle

but what the industry thinks about Seattle. There is this rapper I know and really respect, but I had to yell at him to stop talking about that list. IT'S JUST A FUCKING LIST!" Mudede was struck by one post in particular as he viewed the comments section of the article online, which read: "If you ever wondered why Seattle rarely gets national attention for hip hop—scroll down and watch the crabs in the bucket."[73]

The national spotlight shone again in December 2013, when *XXL* published another list, "15 Female Rappers You Should Know," which included Seattle's Gifted Gab of Moor Gang. The magazine said that Gifted Gab had an "aged, classic-hip hop flow," similar to the New York sound of classic female lyricists like Queen Latifah. "Repping Moor Gang, Gifted Gab seems serious about putting the Northwest on the hip-hop map, crafting an impressionable image with her nonchalant flow yet hard-hitting lyrics," *XXL* wrote. "With her self-touted title 'Queen LaChiefa,' which is also the title of her latest EP, Gifted Gab carries a sound that has the potential to contribute to, or even spurn, a new age of quality female lyricism in the industry."[74]

More national attention for Gab followed when *Time* magazine included her in a 2014 article titled "The 7 Female Rappers You Should Be Listening to Right Now." After concluding that Macklemore and Ryan Lewis had "finally made people pay attention to the Northwest's hip-hop scene," groups like Common Market, Nacho Picasso, Blue Scholars, and Moor Gang "have all been working in the city's rap trenches for years. In their ranks is Gifted Gab, a Seattle rapper, with a throwback flow and a way with words. She has made no secret of the fact that Queen Latifah is her biggest inspiration—in fact, she named her debut album *Queen La'Chiefah*."[75]

Local praise for Gab was present as well. "Her excellently titled [EP] *Queen La'Chiefah* . . . harks back to the '90s heyday of cold females on the mic via the name and the cover (a take on Queen La's [1991 album] *Nature of a Sista'*). Gifted Gab has widely been regarded as one of the best female rappers from this corner of the country. The fact is Gab isn't just one of the best female rappers in the NW, she's one of its best rappers, period," wrote Larry Mizell Jr. "Gab's a classic: a boys-club-proven, boom-bap-devouring devotee of real rap's hoodies-and-Timbs heyday—and a real woman reflecting on weak dudes in the rearview. Not exactly as concerned with sexism as Dana [Queen Latifah] Owens, Gab has her own pimpish West Coast twist to the blueprint."[76]

Porter Ray on Sub Pop and Classical Sir Mix-A-Lot

The flurry of sudden and intense national attention on the local scene brought with it both positive and negative dynamics. Similar to the aftermath following Nirvana's rise in the 1990s, the search for up-and-coming talent in the post-Macklemore era was ongoing. In this climate another talented local MC, one mentored by a hip-hop elder, earned recognition. Although Porter Ray Sullivan flirted with poetry and MCing during his high school years, it was not until 2009 when his younger brother was murdered that he looked to music as a serious expressive outlet. By the time his debut mixtape *BLK GLD* was released in 2013, Porter Ray had created substantial underground buzz. As Larry Mizell wrote in *The Stranger*: "Porter had low-key become the prince of the city in reputation but hadn't released a damn thing—and, by my count, had played all of one show."

After one listen, Mizell labeled *BLK GLD* a classic local debut that "more than lives up to the considerable hype placed on his name's shoulders. Porter is a classically gifted master of poetic, slick shit—no hyperbole meant, but my first instinct was to compare his ice-water style to that of Nas and *Reasonable Doubt*–era Jay[-Z]." Hyperbole, whether intended or not, seemed inevitable when drawing parallels between a new local artist and an international superstar like Jay-Z. Still, the comparison included thoughtful analysis. "Unlike most young heads looking to evoke their titanic cool, however, he never gets lost in a wordy haze. Even more important to his appeal, he at times kicks perfectly gameful bars for ladies without having to resort to basic-ass Drake-isms," Mizell observed. "What we appear to have in Mr. Ray is an MC of rare sensitivity, deftness, and subtlety—and I for one am damned excited to see what it is he does next."[77]

Porter Ray released two more mixtapes in 2013—*WHT GLD* and *RSE GLD*. He received greater exposure, such as an in-studio interview and performance on KEXP's show *Street Sounds* as well as a *City Arts* magazine article naming *WHT GLD/RSE GLD* as its album of the month for August. "He writes with rare selflessness, equally comfortable as narrator, protagonist and side character. Ray stacks active-verb snapshots to form a wide-angle view of the early-onset adulthood facing him and his peers," wrote music critic Clayton Holman. "His firmly structured flow is more vehicle than destination, its strong, consistent template allowing space for narrative detail.

Here and elsewhere, Ray's concern for his people is fluid, expressed through dialogue and observation. He doesn't moralize; he relates."[78]

Porter Ray's rising star and association with Seattle super producer Jake One led to an offer from industry giant Interscope Records in late 2013, which Porter declined. Digable Planets and Shabazz Palaces cofounder Ishmael Butler had become an A&R (artist and repertoire) at Sub Pop Records in 2013. Butler made Porter Ray his first signee to Sub Pop in May 2014. While working on his debut album *Watercolor* for Sub Pop, Porter Ray released a digital album called *Fundamentals* in 2014.

With artists like Porter Ray representing new generations of local hip hop, one artist who represented the first generation continued to earn attention. Sir Mix-A-Lot assumed a hip-hop emeritus status of sorts, not necessarily recording new music but still making occasional appearances within popular culture, both locally and nationally. In June 2014 the Seattle Symphony's *Sonic Evolution* program featured original works by young composers based on local blues, rock, or hip hop. Past installments of Sonic Evolution had been inspired by Jimi Hendrix, Kurt Cobain, and Quincy Jones.[79] For this edition three original compositions were premiered: "FrisLand" by Luis Tinoco based on jazz guitarist Bill Frisell, "Hundred Heads" by Du Yun based on singer/songwriter Ray Charles, and "Dial 1-900 Mix-A-Lot" by Gabriel Prokofiev.

Following Prokofiev's piece, Sir Mix-A-Lot himself made his way to the stage of regal Benaroya Hall, home of the Seattle Symphony. He performed "Posse on Broadway" with symphony accompaniment, followed by a rendition of his Grammy Award–winning classic "Baby Got Back." Charles Cross in the *Seattle Times* described the event this way: "Before Friday night's 'Sonic Evolution' program, I'd never seen 40 women jump onstage in front of the symphony—at Sir Mix-A-Lot's invitation—and shake their butts for 10 minutes to the sounds of hip-hop. It was an explosion of raucous energy unlike any symphony program at Benaroya before." He continued: "Mix asked if 'a couple' of ladies could help him out. Soon the stage was quickly mobbed and the symphony hidden, and a party started. Yet for everyone at Friday's concert—new to Benaroya, patrons, or old vets—it was a night to celebrate. 'Tell 'em to shake it,' Mix-A-Lot urged."[80]

A video of the performance posted on YouTube went viral, amassing more than eight million views. Despite the national buzz, some in the world of classical music were unimpressed. In his review of the show for the *New York Times*, James R. Oestreich wrote: "I won't presume to review things so far outside my ken as Sir Mix-A-Lot. But I am left to wonder what a symphony orchestra can meaningfully add to this kind of repertory, notwithstanding Gabriel Prokofiev's rudimentary orchestrations here."[81]

Among other things, Sir Mix-A-Lot represented the long tradition of hip-hop artists making songs about their hometown, which dates back to the beginning of the hip-hop culture. Locally this practice took a decidedly sociological turn with a musical examination of a specific neighborhood: the Central District. Major changes to the CD as the seat of Seattle's Black community ironically enough could be traced to the "open housing" movement pushed by local civil rights groups. The Seattle City Council passed the ordinance on April 19, 1968, just fifteen days after Dr. Martin Luther King's assassination in Memphis. While open housing made it possible for African Americans to move wherever they wanted, it also contributed to the eventual fragmentation of the Black community, primarily toward South Seattle and outlying cities farther south such as Renton, Kent, Auburn, and Federal Way. Meanwhile, the 1980s and 1990s saw a steep increase in CD property values, which meant a corresponding rise in property taxes.[82]

Dumi "Draze" Maraire Jr. released the single and video "The Hood Ain't the Same" in 2014, which addressed gentrification in the CD. Shot around the Central District and the south end, the lyrics and images focused on historic people and places that traditionally marked Seattle's Black community. For instance, the building that for decades was the home of *The Facts*, Seattle's oldest Black newspaper founded in 1961 by Fitzgerald Beaver, located on the corner of Martin Luther King Way and Cherry Street, had turned into a dog daycare and groomer. Also highlighted was the phenomenon of longtime residents who wished to remain in the community, but the sudden steep increase in property values made paying the taxes on their homes nearly impossible on a fixed income.[83]

Food and Local Hip Hop

Hip hop's interdisciplinary style had always allowed, and even encouraged, the building of bridges within its surroundings. Relationships developed naturally as the culture and its participants found ways to make meaning of their environment. Some unique local trends that emerged from these dynamics were around Seattle hip hop's connection with food, its link to sports, and the inevitable impact of the next generation. The term "flavor" has long been slang within hip hop equating to "style" or "swag," and that was the name of the Seattle-based hip hop magazine published between 1992 and 1996. Over the years, local artists such as Vitamin D symbolically played on this connection by releasing mixtapes with names like *Table Manners*, *Table Manners 2*, and *Hip-Hop Kitchen*, which included the original song "Local Produce."[84] DJ100proof produced the mixtape series *Backyard BBQ*, and the Blue Scholars ("Fou Lee") and Amos Miller ("Roger's Thriftway") have released songs about specific local grocery stores.[85]

Some artists moved beyond symbolism and into actual culinary creation. Hillside Quickie's Vegan Sandwich Shop in the University District, managed by local artist Ayinde Howell and his sister Afi, was known as Seattle's only health-conscious hip hop–oriented deli. With items like the Crazy Jamaican Burger, the New York Deli Tofu Sub, and Tempehestrami TLT, Hillside Quickie's fell within the realm of "progressive" hip hop. Some of the more well-known customers included Philadelphia hip-hop band The Roots, slam poet Saul Williams, R&B superstar Erykah Badu, and Source of Labor. As Charles Mudede wrote in *The Stranger*, "This is not the sort of place that 50 Cent or Memphis Bleek would much care for; the break from the conventional American foods is too extreme—and as a consequence not macho enough—for their gangsta temperaments."[86] This animal-free approach was complemented by the Seattle chapter of Hip-Hop Is Green, an organization founded by Keith Tucker that hosted community vegan dinners and promoted health and wellness resources.

Seattle artist DT, or Deep Thoughts, was known as the Thuggin Chef. He produced cooking videos on YouTube, featuring dishes such as herb-crusted halibut, paprika fried chicken, and shitake mushroom and green pea risotto pancakes. Along with other recipe suggestions, the Thuggin Chef provided restaurant reviews for different types of food establishments all over the city.[87] Jimaine "Maineak B" Miller went by the title Def Chef. He served chicken and waffles, tacos, pies, and meat turnovers direct to customers through orders placed by email and through social media. Evidence of Def Chef was on display in the video for the song "Home" by Jake One as Miller delivered his verse from behind a smoking barbeque grill.

Other examples included musician and producer Bubba Jones, owner of the highly popular Jones Barbeque in South Seattle, and longtime rapper Jeremy "Jerm" DuBois, whose Mattie Bell Catering Company features family recipes developed over generations. Silas Blak of Silent Lambs Project and Black Stax served as a chef at the Kingfish Café, the landmark soul food restaurant in the Central District that opened in 1997. Picking up on the rapidly growing trend of mobile eats, poet and painter Jesse "Akil" Lee came up with the My Sweet Lil Cakes truck, which served hotcakes on a stick, filled with fruits, vegetables, meats, or cheeses, along with custom dipping sauces.[88]

George "Geologic" Quibuyen, also known as Prometheus Brown, remained musically active in 2014, joining Los Angeles–based fellow Filipino-American rapper Bambu to form The Bar and release their album *Barkada*. Quibuyen and his wife, Chera Amlag, started a monthly restaurant pop-up featuring Filipino cuisine called Food and Sh*t. Food and Sh*t was hosted at Inay's, a Filipino restaurant in the Beacon Hill neighborhood.[89] Quibuyen and Amlag combined traditional with nontraditional to come up with dishes like pork sisig tacos, pan de sal bistek sliders, inasal chicken wings, and buko pan-dan cheesecake. Food and Sh*t was at the center of what *Seattle* magazine called a rising "Filipino food movement" in the area.[90]

Seahawks, the Super Bowl, and the Younger Generations Making Moves

Although the combination of hip hop and food seemed to be a relatively recent trend, the intersection of hip hop and sports was not. Sir Mix-A-Lot's "Not in Our House," Kid Sensation and Ken Griffey Jr.'s "The Way I Swing," and Gary Payton's "Livin Legal & Large" were all local examples of this relationship from the 1990s. When the Seattle Seahawks rose to prominence as a National Football League power in the 2010s, the names of such players as quarterback Russell Wilson, the "Legion of Boom" with defensive backs Richard Sherman, Earl Thomas, and Kam Chancellor, and wide receiver Doug Baldwin all became trending topics in various aspects of popular culture. The most polarizing figure of the Seahawk's back-to-back Super Bowl appearances of 2014 and 2015 was running back Marshawn Lynch. Famous for his fearless, bruising running style, Lynch was a favorite of the notably loud Seattle fan base known as the "12s," a representation of fans as a "12th" player on the field during a game. One of the biggest storylines in the days leading up to both Super Bowls was the conflict between Marshawn Lynch and the massive amounts of media from around the world on hand to cover the event.

As part of the collective bargaining agreement between the NFL players' union and team owners, all players were required to be available to the media after games. Lynch's sometimes adversarial relationship with reporters often led him to respond to every question with the same answer. In the lead-up to the Seahawks Super Bowl XLVIII 43–8 victory on February 2, 2014, over the Denver Broncos in East Rutherford, New Jersey, much was made of the friction between Lynch and the media. Pro Football Hall of Famer and NFL Network personality Deion Sanders spoke with Lynch during Super Bowl media day, asking Lynch about speaking to the media. Lynch's response—"I'm just 'bout that action, boss"—spread across social media, and within days several versions of songs and remixes sampling the line had sprung up on YouTube.[91] The scenario repeated itself in the lead-up to Super Bowl XLIX on February 1, 2015, against the New England Patriots. Lynch, who had been fined $100,000 earlier in the season for not speaking with reporters after a game, showed up to required Super Bowl media events and answered every question by simply saying, "I'm just here so I don't get fined" and "You know why I'm here." Again, Seattle's hip-hop community posted tracks and remixes based on Lynch's responses, this time with the title "Thanks for Asking (So I Won't Get Fined)."[92]

Following Seattle's first Super Bowl championship, the city threw a downtown parade for the Seahawks on February 4, 2014. Of the more than 750,000 people who turned out to celebrate, a good number of them gathered at Westlake Park, where DV One, the team's official DJ, rocked the crowd from atop the Westlake Mall. Supreme also collaborated in playing alongside DV One at the parade, which will arguably go down as the biggest party in Washington State history. Although the prestigious, shiny world of professional sports has had a long relationship with local hip hop, youth have always been the lifeblood of the culture. The spread and accessibility of hip hop has meant more opportunities for newer generations of young people to engage on various levels. One example was local b-boy Jalen "Jstyles" Testerman. Born in 2001, Jstyles became interested in dancing while watching the 2004 dance film *You Got Served*. His skill led to performances at Seattle SuperSonics games; guest spots on the Maury Povich, Oprah Winfrey, and Ellen DeGeneres shows; television appearances on Nickelodeon and reality shows *Live to Dance* and *Dance Moms* (Season 3); as well as movie roles in the films *Step Up 3D* (2010) and *Jack and Jill* (2011).[93] It is telling that local young people like Jstyles were able to find personal entry points into hip-hop culture through elements besides MCing. Another instance of this was Lenox "Yung Lenox" Buringrud. Born in 2007, Lenox became a nationally recognized artist from Seattle who drew old school rap album covers after being introduced to them by his father Skip "Skip Class" Buringrud.[94] Lenox's father posted Yung Lenox's drawings on Instagram, which eventually landed Lenox a spot in the 2013 Frieze Week art fair in New York City.[95]

Yung Lenox frequently drew his own versions of classics like the cover for Wu-Tang Clan member Raekwon's debut album *Only Built For Cuban Lynx* (1995). Jenson Karp, owner of Gallery 1988 West in Los Angeles, held a 2014 showing of Yung Lenox's work titled *L.A.'s Most Wanted*. "Raekwon vividly talks about drug sales and violence on his classic first solo album," Karp said, "and to see the cover redrawn in a childlike, coloring-book style—no matter the age—it's an ironic take on something so iconic in the minds of my generation."[96] Yung Lenox's work included albums by Tupac, NWA and Ice Cube, and he has drawn the attention of rap artists such as Ultramagnetic MCs member Kool Keith, Raekwon, and Cam'ron. A Kickstarter campaign raised more than $17,000 to fund a documentary film about Yung Lenox, *Live Fast Draw Yung*.[97]

— —

Macklemore and Ryan Lewis's four-trophy triumph at the 2014 Grammy Awards was arguably one of the most significant moments in Seattle's cultural history. General community expectations that accompanied this level of success within hip hop have traditionally included the idea that the bright lights focused on Macklemore and Ryan Lewis would bring shine to others within the scene. Expectations were that the duo would use their status to help facilitate the development of local artists and their projects. Past examples of this ethos have been the Sir Mix-A-Lot–produced compilation album *Seattle . . . The Darkside* in 1993 and more recently Ishmael Butler's mentorship of Porter Ray.

At the grassroots end of the spectrum, social action and commentary remained key elements around the scene. Wyking Garrett's involvement in Africatown strove to preserve historical aspects as well as build up Seattle's African American community in the Central District, while Draze followed up "The Hood Ain't the Same" with "Irony on 23rd," which commented on the presence of a white-owned marijuana dispensary located at the corner of Twenty-third Avenue and Union Street in the Central District. The irony lay in the fact that for decades, numerous people of color—and African Americans specifically—were arrested all around this same corner and taken to jail for selling, among other things, marijuana. However, as it had in the past, the story of local hip hop always circled back to the youth. The breaking of JStyles, which symbolized multiple generations of hip-hop dance in Seattle, has been seen in several movies and television shows. The visual arts of Yung Lenox represented his crayon-rendered version of numerous classic hip-hop album covers that were released well before he was born. While rap music traditionally remained the most popular route to hip-hop engagement, decades of growth and development within the scene created sustained spaces for alternative paths. It is examples like these, and countless others over some forty years, that demonstrate how each new generation consumes and reinterprets not just local hip-hop culture but overall Seattle culture as well.

CONCLUSION

"Back when Empire Way became MLK"

O N January 20, 1966, Reverend John H. Adams of First AME Church told the Advisory Committee to the US Civil Rights Commission Hearing, "Seattle is one of the few cities left in America which can solve its racial problem before it becomes unsolvable." In this statement, Adams spoke for numerous Black, Latino, Native, Asian, and white residents who "still summoned the courage to believe in a peaceful racial future for the city and the nation," wrote Dr. Quintard Taylor in *The Forging of a Black Community*. But that optimism has yet to be fully justified. Over ensuing decades, racial tensions have been further enflamed by such issues as police misconduct, educational inequities, and increasing gentrification. Taylor concluded: "Indeed, Seattle's apparent success, and its underlying failure, in its race relations paradigm has been its meticulously crafted image which promoted the illusion of inclusion."[1]

When it came to actual inclusion, hip hop led the way. Legendary New York MC KRS-One once stated that hip hop was less about race and ethnicity, and more about skill, ideology, and authenticity. Past examples of racial diversity in hip hop included Puerto Rican contributions to the development of break dancing and the acceptance of white rap groups in the late 1980s and early 1990s such as the Beastie Boys and 3rd Bass in New York City as well as Latino artists like Kid Frost and Cypress Hill in Los Angeles. The local scene in Seattle demonstrated this multiracial dynamic early on with the seminal meeting of Filipino DJ "Nasty" Nes Rodriguez and young Sir Mix-A-Lot at the Rotary Boys & Girls Club in the Central District. It could be argued that Seattle is one of the more inclusive environments in all of hip hop, as over time African Americans, Africans, Asian/Pacific Islanders, Native Americans, whites, Latinos, women, the disabled, homeless, and others have all been represented within various elements of local hip hop. Potentially complex interactions between diverse groups of people could be simplified with hip hop functioning as a common point of cultural interest.

As it relates to inclusion, it is worth specifically noting the shift in hip-hop discourse around LGTBQ issues, albeit provided by straight-identifying Macklemore and Ryan Lewis's "Same Love," which up to that point had been overwhelmingly demeaning and homophobic. In the song's aftermath, New York artist Young MA, whose 2016 debut single "Ooouuu" went multiplatinum, credited coming out as the turning point in her career. Jay-Z released the track "Smile" on his 2017 album *444*, in which his mother revealed she was a lesbian. Lil Nas X announced he was gay in 2019 while his smash single "Old Town Road" was in the process of breaking the record for longest running number-one hit of all time atop the *Billboard* "Hot 100." The fact that space had been created for one of the great established figures in hip-hop history, along with record-breaking, history-making newcomers, to challenge hip hop's LGTBQ status quo speaks to a legacy of local music, which literally extended concepts of liberation and equity worldwide.

Although inclusion existed, there is no question that misogynistic attitudes and inappropriate behavior—a characteristic of hip hop and society in general—were also present in Seattle. As such, local hip hop was not immune to the backlash, both directly and indirectly, associated with survivors of abuse coming forward and seeking justice. In 2016 Afrika Bambaataa, founder of the Universal Zulu Nation, parent organization of 206 Zulu, faced accusations of sexually abusing boys and young men dating back to the early 1980s. Russell Simmons, cofounder of the Hip-Hip Summit Action Network (HHSAN), which also had a local chapter, and local promoter and businessman Dave Meinert, former manager of the group Blue Scholars, were both accused of past sexual assaults in 2017 and 2018 respectively, as the #metoo movement emerged and demanded accountability.

As the second decade of the twenty-first century drew to a close, several trends asserted themselves within Seattle hip hop. One of these represented the continuation of the relationship between hip hop and local politics, as activism entered the electoral process. Beginning in the late 1990s, Seattle went from one mayor publicly blaming hip hop for a nightclub shooting (Paul Schell) to the next mayor instituting the annual Mayor's Award for Excellence in Hip-Hop (Greg Nickels). The vacancy left by disgraced Mayor Ed Murray's resignation amid charges of sexual misconduct meant Seattle would have a new mayor in 2017. Enter attorney, activist, and spoken word artist Nikkita Oliver, who represented the Seattle Peoples Party. The connection between hip hop in Seattle and spoken word had been reinforced in 2005 when Melissa Noelle Green was awarded the Mayor's Award for Excellence in Hip-Hop in the Spoken Word category and by the work of people like Laura "Piece" Kelley. Oliver's candidacy connected with disenfranchised voters and highlighted such issues as police reform, homelessness, and affordable housing—all of which resonated within the local hip-hop community. She ultimately received the third most votes in the mayoral primary, narrowly missing a chance to advance to the general election.

One of the hallmarks of Seattle hip hop has been the use of innovative approaches and styles to generate both artistic and economic success. Local super producer Jake One demonstrated impressive musical range by joining with Los Angeles–based, Grammy-nominated singer Mayer Hawthorne in 2015 to form the funk/soul duo Tuxedo, which released and toured behind three acclaimed albums. This trend remained a defining characteristic of the region as Seattle's book-end Grammy Award–winning artists announced new nonmusic business ventures in 2019 when Macklemore became part owner of Major League Soccer's Seattle Sounders FC franchise, which subsequently won the 2019 MLS cup. Sir Mix-A-Lot introduced his line of custom slot machines for casinos called "I Like Big Buck$." His venture raises an interesting point. The immovable staying power of the message and continued relevance of this song some thirty years after its release—from comprising an answer on the game show *Jeopardy*, a recipe for "Baby Got Back Ribs" in Snoop Dogg's 2018 cookbook *From Crook to Cook*, to countless other references and parodies—suggest "Baby Got Back" may not only have had the greatest impact on modern popular culture of any rap song but perhaps any other song in any other genre period.

Some newer names who began to increase their profile musically benefited from a helping hand. Similar to Sir Mix-A-Lot, Macklemore's meteoric rise allowed him a platform to promote other local artists. On the 2017 single "Corner Store" Macklemore featured two up-and-coming artists, Dave B and Travis Thompson. Following a performance of the song on the *Tonight Show Starring Jimmy Fallon*, Dave B opened for Macklemore in front of a sold-out house at Seattle's Key Arena and headlined a show himself at the Neptune Theater in the University District in advance of his 2018 album *Pearl*. Coming off his collaboration with Macklemore, Thompson, from the southern suburb of Burien, signed a deal with Epic Records and released his album *Reckless Endangerment* in 2019.

From hip hop's beginnings in the Central District and the South End, its cultural ripple effects, in addition to relentless gentrification, have expanded the traditional borders of Seattle hip hop. The manner in which up-and-coming local artists earned their notoriety reflected both old school and new school methods. If one of the older methods of gaining artistic traction was getting "put on," or receiving support from a more established name, and scaffolding within the local scene, then the newer style was more Internet-based. Lil Mosey, from the northern suburb of Mountlake Terrace, posted his music on Soundcloud in 2016 and rose to fame by amassing nearly thirty million views on YouTube for his video "Pull Up." In 2018 he released his debut album *Northsbest* and was named to the 2019 *XXL* magazine freshman class.

"Nasty" Nes Rodriguez, without a doubt one of the most pivotal figures in Seattle hip-hop history, influenced the local scene with producing the group The High Children, billed as the "only true electronic hip-hop band in the music business." They appeared on the legendary national radio show *Sway in the Morning* in 2017. Meanwhile, Gifted Gab of Moor Gang highlighted the quickly shifting landscape of the Central District, joining with Bay Area artist Blimes Brixton to form the duo Blimes and Gab (aka BAG). The pair filmed the video for their 2018 single "Come Correct" in front of the soon-to-be demolished Red Apple Market on the Paul Allen–purchased corner of Twenty-third Avenue and Jackson Street. Dave B and BAG toured nationally together in 2019.

However, in the seemingly never-ending fight against gentrification, Africatown continued landing solid blows. The Africatown Land Trust was formed in 2016 following a historic development agreement for the Liberty Bank Building at Twenty-third and Union. Soon after opening in 2019 with 115 units, the building received the Affordable Housing Finance Award in the Urban Development category. The project across the street, Africatown Plaza, has nearly 150 affordable units planned.

These trends indicated the high level of activity and change within the scene as arguably the most successful decade in Seattle hip-hop history came to a close. This success was reflected in the embrace of hip hop by venerable local cultural institutions such as MOHAI and the annual Folklife Festival. An extension of this movement was the 2018 establishment of the 206 Hip-Hop Archive at the University of Washington by Dr. Third Andresen. This collection, a tribute to the creativity and durability of the local scene, elevated the UW among high-profile institutions that have initiated hip-hop archives and collectives. They include Stanford, the University of Michigan, Columbia, and Harvard. The 206 Hip-Hop Archive recognized that which remained local, such as 206 Zulu and its fifteenth anniversary celebration in 2018. Others aspects, like the Seattle hip-hop media landscape, shifted in 2016 as Larry Mizell Jr. who—after twelve years, had become the longest tenured journalist to continually cover hip hop in Seattle—left *The Stranger* as well as radio hosting duties on his KEXP show *Street Sounds*. Stas Thee Boss (Stasia "Stas" Irons), formerly of THEESatisfaction, was named as Mizell's replacement. This movement in local radio continued in 2019 as Casey Carter was named host of *The Come Up* Sunday nights on KUBE.

For most of the 1980s, much of the world outside the Pacific Northwest regarded Seattle hip hop dismissively, if at all. The double whammy of geographic isolation combined with an initial hesitation by the national mainstream to embrace hip hop created a lag that the region has subsequently made up for. Today there is no question that the accumulated expressions, successes, and innovations over forty years have cemented the city's legacy as a creative force within hip hop. However, for all of the achievements produced over the decades, the nature of the culture is less about looking back and more about forward movement. Awards, championships, and incorporated entities can inform local legacy, but with its focus on youth, creativity, experimentation, and new forms of expression, hip hop remains oriented toward the future. This future only takes shape as fresh generations of DJs, graffiti writers, artists, b-girls and b-boys, MCs, beatboxers, teachers, journalists, fashion designers, researchers, promoters, broadcasters, filmmakers, activists, and others interpret what hip hop means to them in the context of their own lives and experiences.

TIMELINE OF SEATTLE HIP HOP

1979

The Rocket
The Rocket, a local alternative arts and music newspaper, is launched.

Sugarhill Gang
The Sugarhill Gang release their landmark single "Rapper's Delight" on New Jersey–based Sugar Hill Records on September 16.

Robert L. Scott
KYAC 1250 AM program director Robert L. Scott plays "Rapper's Delight" on Seattle radio for the first time in October.

1980

KFOX
Radio station KYAC 1250 AM changes its call letters to KKFX (KFOX).

Emerald Street Boys
Eddie "Sugar Bear" Wells and James "Captain Crunch" Croone form The Terrible 2. They lose a rap contest to Gary Jam and Big Boss Cross (aka Jam Delight), at Lateef's, Seattle's first hip-hop club.

FreshTracks
1250 KKFX's (KFOX) *FreshTracks* hosted by "Nasty" Nes Rodriguez becomes the first all-rap radio show on the West Coast.

Glen Boyd
Glen Boyd begins working at Penny Lane Records in Tacoma, Washington.

1981

KNHC
Radio station KNHC 89.5 FM begins playing hip hop.

Silver Chain Gang
Duke of Earl, Sir Wesley, Jazzy D, and Foxy combine to form the Silver Chain Gang.

West Side Threat
The West Side Threat is formed.

Emerald Street Boys
Eddie "Sugar Bear" Wells, James "Captain Crunch" Croone, and Robert "Sweet J" Jamerson form the Emerald Street Boys. "Nasty" Nes Rodriguez is the DJ.

Street Life
Steve Sneed and Reco Bembry produce the play *Street Life*, which includes a dance scene featuring the Emerald Street Boys.

1982

Emerald Street Girls
Cousins Mia "Angel Face" Black and Doretha "Playmate" Johnson form the Emerald Street Girls.

Emerald Street Boys
The Emerald Street Boys perform in February 1982 in a benefit at the National Guard Armory on Elliot Avenue. The show is reviewed in *The Rocket*.

Emerald Street Girls
The Emerald Street Girls perform at On The Boards Fifth Anniversary Party on November 13, 1982.

1983

Emerald Street Boys versus Silver Chain Gang
The Emerald Street Boys and the Silver Chain Gang perform in the Black Community Festival at Judkins Park.

Whiz Kid
Tacoma resident Whiz Kid (Harold McGuire) releases "Play That Beat Mr. DJ" on Tommy Boy Records.

Sir Mix-A-Lot
Sir Mix-A-Lot begins playing parties at the Rainier Vista Boys & Girls Club.

Emerald Street Boys
Seattle's first rap record, *Christmas Rap* (B side "The Move"), by the Emerald Street Boys, is produced by Tony B and released on his label Telemusic Productions.

Emerald Street Girls
Bobbie "Luscious Lynn" Solomon and Jenell "Black Velvet" Cole join the Emerald Street Girls.

1984

Grandmaster Flash
Grandmaster Flash and The Crash Crew perform at the Music Hall.

Afrika Bambaataa
Afrika Bambaataa plays the Gorilla Gardens.

Emerald Street Boys
Emerald Street Boys open for The Treacherous Three at the Seattle Center Exhibition Hall.

Summer Break '84
Summer Break '84 break-dance competition is televised on KOMO Channel 4.

Sir Mix-A-Lot
Sir Mix-A-Lot begins playing parties at the Central District Boys & Girls Club. "Nasty" Nes Rodriguez meets Mix-A-Lot there and invites him to air his material on KFOX. Sir Mix-A-Lot becomes KFOX's most requested artist.

Graffiti
DC3 and Kuo "Mr. Clean" Yang paint the first block-long burner on the side of the Nordstrom department store in downtown Seattle.

Breaking
The *Seattle Times* runs a feature story on breaking in the Arts and Entertainment section in February 1984.

Beat Street
Producer Harry Belafonte and pioneering New York break-dancers Rock Steady Crew arrive in Seattle to promote the film *Beat Street* in June 1984.

1985

NastyMix Records
Ed Locke, "Nasty" Nes Rodriguez, Sir Mix-A-Lot, and Greg Jones form NastyMix Records.

High Performance versus New York City Breakers
High Performance defeats the New York City Breakers at the Tacoma Dome.

Teen Dance Ordinance
City Council president Norm Rice proposes a Teen Dance Ordinance, which is later passed by the Seattle City Council.

Frostmaster Chill
John "DJ Frostmaster Chill" Funches and the Freeze MCs, Daddy D, Col. G, and Mellow Mike open for L.A. Dream Team at the Seattle Trade Center.

Sir Mix-A-Lot
Baron Von Scratch and Sir Mix-A-Lot battle Rainier Valley crew Kings Of Cutting (KOC).

Graffiti
David "Image 8000" Toledo and Sean "Nemo" Casey paint a piece titled *ImageNemo* at Gas Works Park.

Colman School occupation
In November 1985 a group calling itself the Citizens Support Committee for the African American Heritage Museum/Cultural Center occupies the vacant Colman School building and demands the space be used to house a Black history museum and community center.

1986

Sir Mix-A-Lot
Sir Mix-A-Lot plays Fresh Fest in London.

Boss Cross
Big Boss Cross releases his single "Party Invader" on Macola Records.

Run DMC
Run DMC plays the New Year's Eve show at the Tacoma Dome with El DeBarge and Bobby Brown.

Billboard
Billboard mockingly refers to Seattle as a "hip-hop hotbed."

Frostmaster Chill

Frostmaster Chill, DJ JOC (Jammin On Cuts), and Robert "MC Le Rap" Spikes record the single "Breakdown."

Boys Will B-Boys

Steve Sneed and Reco Bembry produce the play *Boys Will B-Boys* at On the Boards; the Emerald Street Boys, originally set to star in the production, are eventually replaced by the Silver Chain Gang.

Egyptian Lover

Los Angeles artist Egyptian Lover plays shows on consecutive nights in the Colman School gymnasium in support of the occupation by the Citizens Support Committee for the African American Heritage Museum/Cultural Center.

Crack

The *Seattle Times* runs its first story on the spread of crack cocaine in the Seattle area on May 28, 1986.

1987

Vitamix

Portland, Oregon, artist Vitamix releases his single "That's the Way Girls Are" on Profile Records.

Incredi-Crew

Incredi-Crew releases the single "High Powered Hip-Hop" on their label Gemini Records.

KCMU

Radio station KCMU 90.3 FM debuts the program *Shock Frequency* with "Shockmaster" Glen Boyd.

Sir Mix-A-Lot

Sir Mix-A-Lot releases the single "Posse on Broadway."

DI-RA Boys

The DI-RA Boys record the singles "The Times" and "Crack Get Back."

Beverly's Records & Tapes

Beverly's Records & Tapes opens at the corner of Twenty-third Avenue and Jackson Street.

RICO-1

Reggie Brown and Robert Lomax establish RICO-1, a mobile DJ unit that plays parties at various local venues.

DURACELL Crew

DURACELL (Def Undisputed Rhymes Are Cuts Especially Long Lasting) Crew, Derrick "Silver Shadow D" Seals, Clifton "Chilly C/SOZ" Seals, Bruce "Incredible B/Horton B" Griffith, Lawayne "Crazy Waves" Rainwater, and Jason "JG" Gavin win the first All-City Talent Show held at Franklin High School and become the first hip-hop artists to perform at the annual Folklife Festival at the Seattle Center.

Chelly Chell

Chenelle "Chelly Chell" Marshall records the single "He's Incredible."

Crips and Bloods

The *Seattle Times* runs a story on June 28, 1987, about the arrival of Crips and Bloods in Seattle with the headline "Gangs Increasing in Seattle–L.A. Toughs Leave Slums for New Turf."

1988

Sir Mix-A-Lot

Sir Mix-A-Lot's debut album *Swass* is released on NastyMix Records.

Rap Attack

The radio program *Rap Attack*, hosted by "Shockmaster" Glen Boyd and "Nasty" Nes Rodriguez, debuts on KCMU.

Chilly Uptown

Chilly Uptown releases "I Got Rules" on Ever Rap Records.

Peer Pressure

Steve Sneed and Reco Bembry produce the play *Peer Pressure*, featuring Derrick "Vitamin D" Brown.

DJ Jazzy Jeff and the Fresh Prince

Four people receive minor injuries in October 1988 in a drive-by shooting outside a Sea-Tac hotel where DJ Jazzy Jeff and the Fresh Prince are staying after a concert at the Paramount. The *Seattle Times* follows with a story probing "the connection" between rap music and violence.

Ingraham Rams

The Ingraham Rams become the first Metro League team to win the Washington State high school football championship, using Public Enemy's "Don't Believe the Hype" as their motto and theme song, on December 3, 1988.

1989

DJ DD
DJ DD of DI-RA Boys is shot to death.

Kid Sensation
Kid Sensation releases the single "Back 2 Boom" on NastyMix Records.

Swass
Sir Mix-A-Lot's album *Swass* is certified gold (500,000 copies sold).

PD2
PD2 releases the single "You Ain't Got No Bass."

Ice Cold Mode
Ice Cold Mode releases the single "Union St. Hustlers."

Seminar
Sir Mix-A-Lot releases his second album, *Seminar*.

Battle for Seattle Supremacy
Greg B and Eaze win the DJ and MC competitions in the Battle for Seattle Supremacy at the Moore Theatre.

Source of Labor
Jonathan "Wordsayer" Moore and Negus 1 combine to form the group Source of Labor.

Sir Mix-A-Lot
Yo! MTV Raps films an episode in Seattle featuring Sir Mix-A-Lot.

Vitamin D
The recording studio in the basement of Vitamin D's house in the Central District is created and dubbed "The Pharmacy."

1990

Kid Sensation
Kid Sensation releases the album *Rollin' with #1* on NastyMix Records.

Sir Mix-A-Lot
Sir Mix-A-Lot leaves NastyMix Records.

Criminal Nation
Criminal Nation from Tacoma releases its debut album, *Release the Pressure*, on NastyMix Records.

Brothers of the Same Mind
Brothers of the Same Mind is featured in the "Unsigned Hype" section of *The Source* magazine.

High Performance
High Performance releases the EP *Here's a Party* on NastyMix Records.

Tony B
Tony B begins hosting *Street Beat*, an hour-long urban community forum show on radio station KUBE 93 FM, which discusses relevant social issues and features local music.

Frankie Wells and PDQ Crew
Frankie Wells and PDQ Crew release the single "I Need Bud."

Sir Mix-A-Lot
The Black Entertainment Television (BET) series *Rap City* visits Seattle to profile Sir Mix-A-Lot and NastyMix Records in January 1990.

Music Inner City
Gordon Curvey debuts *Music Inner City* on Seattle's Public Access Network (SCAN) in December 1990.

1991

Brothers of the Same Mind
Brothers of the Same Mind releases self-titled EP on Conspiracy Records.

Love Sick Rhymers
Love Sick Rhymers release "Hold Tight to the Rhythm" on Blackstyle Records.

King of Kuts
KOK opens for King Tee and MC Lyte at the NCO club at Fort Lewis.

Sir Mix-A-Lot/Rhyme Cartel Records
As part of a deal signed with Rick Rubin's Def American Records, Sir Mix-A-Lot creates and becomes CEO of his own label, Rhyme Cartel Records. Ricardo Frazer serves as president.

Vanilla Ice
Vanilla Ice is accused of plagiarizing lyrics from Sir Mix-A-Lot's 1986 song "I'm a Trip."

Coolout Network
Georgio Brown broadcasts the first episode of *Coolout Network* on Seattle's Public Access Network (SCAN) on April 4, 1991.

1992

B-Mello
B-Mello DJs HBO's *Def Comedy Jam* at the Paramount Theatre.

PD2
PD2 releases the single "Flavin in Bumpcity."

Sir Mix-A-Lot
Sir Mix-A-Lot releases the album *Mack Daddy* on Def American Records.

NastyMix Records
NastyMix Records is dissolved.

Ice Cube concert
Four people are shot and wounded outside an Ice Cube concert at the Paramount Theatre.

Langston Hughes Performing Arts Institute
Jonathan "Wordsayer" Moore begins holding regular hip-hop shows and activities at the Langston Hughes Performing Arts Institute, beginning with the show *African Echoes—A Hip-Hop Continuum.*

Kun Luv
Chukundi "DJ Kun Luv" Salisbury throws a birthday barbeque at a house in the Central District, an event that becomes the annual Virgo Party.

Source of Labor
Kamikaze becomes the DJ for Source of Labor.

DVS Crew
Fever One, Soul-One, Sneke, and Rey form DVS (Droppin Vicious Styles) Crew.

KCMU
"Shockmaster" Glen Boyd leaves NastyMix Records and KCMU's *Rap Attack* program for a position with Def American Recordings in Los Angeles.

Summer Jam
Radio station KUBE 93 holds the first annual Summer Jam at Cheney Stadium in Tacoma and includes performances by Kid Sensation, Nice and Smooth, Das EFX, and Pete Rock.

Ken Griffey Jr. and Kid Sensation
Ken Griffey Jr. and Kid Sensation record the single "The Way I Swing."

Censorship
House Bill 2554, which banned the sale of "erotic sounding" recordings
to anyone under eighteen, is passed by the Washington State Legislature and signed into law only to be repealed four months later by a
Superior Court judge in Seattle.

The Flavor
The March 1992 debut issue of *The Flavor*, an international hip-hop
magazine based in Seattle, features Cypress Hill on the cover.

Rodney King
Civil unrest occurs in downtown Seattle in the aftermath of the Rodney
King verdict on May 1, 1992.

Weed and Seed
The Seattle City Council adopts "Weed and Seed," a federal anticrime
program, in December 1992.

1993

Digable Planets
Digable Planets, a group led by Seattle artist Ishmael Butler, aka
Butterfly, releases its debut album, *Reachin' (A New Refutation of Time
and Space)*.

Seattle ... The Darkside
The compilation album *Seattle ... The Darkside* is released by Rhyme
Cartel through Def American Records.

Sir Mix-A-Lot
Sir Mix-A-Lot wins American Music and Grammy Awards for the single
"Baby Got Back."

Supreme
Supreme and Sure Shot form Conception Records.

The Foundation at the Art Bar
DVS Crew, Supreme, Kutfather, B-Mello, and Source of Labor crew with
DJ Kamikazee combine to launch The Foundation, a weekly hip-hop
night at the Art Bar.

Colman School occupation
The occupation of the Colman School by the Citizens Support
Committee ends. The action is cited as the longest running act of
civil disobedience in US history.

Greg B
Greg B releases the cassette *Listen to the Greg B* on Wicked Dungeon Records.

Music Inner City
The program *Music Inner City* receives a Billboard Award nomination for Top Rap/R&B Video Show.

E-Dawg
E-Dawg and Filthy Rich release the single "Drop Top" (B side "Little Locs").

Black Anger
The group Black Anger (Kendo, E-Real, Sayeed, and Wicked D) forms in Tacoma, Washington.

Summer Jam 2
KUBE 93 Summer Jam 2 is held in Monroe, Washington, and includes Tupac Shakur, Run DMC, Pharcyde, Onyx, Immature, Funk Doobiest, Tag Team, and Guru from the group Gangstarr.

Sir Mix-A-Lot
Sir Mix-A-Lot releases the single "Not in Our House," an anthem for the Seattle SuperSonics during the 1993 NBA playoffs.

Shabazz Coalition
Fleeta Partee, Sean Malik, John Doe (John Elder), and C Black (Chris Bailey) perform together under the name Shabazz Coalition.

Silver Shadow D
An article on Silver Shadow D is featured in *Vibe* magazine in September 1993.

Source of Labor
Source of Labor plays the Crocodile Café in Belltown, bringing Seattle's second generation of hip hop downtown for the first time in October 1993.

Autumn Jam
Autumn Jam, a concert showcasing local teen hip hop, rock, R&B, and gospel artists from the Multimedia and Performance Program of CAYA (Central Area Youth Association), is held at Broadway Performance Hall in November 1993.

RKCNDY
Ghetto Youth present "Sound Check" at RKCNDY with performances by Ghetto Children, Jace and the Fourth Party, Source of Labor, and Six in the Clip on December 23, 1993.

1994

The Flavor

The Flavor's second anniversary party at Club Moe features Nas, Coolio, Casual, Supernatural, The Fugees, Kurious, The Whooliganz, Ed O.G. and Da Bulldogs, and Jamal-Ski.

Digable Planets

Digable Planets win a Grammy for their song "Rebirth of Slick (Cool Like Dat)."

RKCNDY

Jonathan "Wordsayer" Moore establishes a weekly event at the RKCNDY featuring local MCs and DJs as well as open mic nights.

Digable Planets

Digable Planets release their second album, *Blowout Comb*.

Darkset

Darkset—Frostmaster Chill, MC (Sugar) Bear, DJ Pace, I Double L, and Shan Dog—release "Krakerbashin" on CD Raised Records.

DMS

Local group DMS signs with Bay Area label D-Shot Records and releases the EP *Takin Ends*.

Sir Mix-A-Lot

Sir Mix-A-Lot's song "Just da Pimpin' in Me" receives a Grammy nomination for Best Solo Rap Performance.

Sinsemilla

Sinsemilla—DJ Topspin, H-Bomb, and Francis—release the single "If They Only Know."

Funk Daddy

Funk Daddy, formerly Greg B, releases the album *Funk You Right On Up* on D Shot Records.

Sin Q

Sin Q releases his album *Deathflow* on Seattle-based Mutiny Records.

DJ Kamikaze

DJ Kamikaze releases the mixtape *One Love*.

Prose and Concepts

Prose and Concepts, formerly Six in the Clip, releases *Procreations*. The album is on Loosegroove Records, founded by Pearl Jam guitarist Stone Gossard and distributed nationally by Epic/Sony.

Jasiri Media Group
Jonathan Moore and Upendo Tookas of Source of Labor and Erika "Kylea" White of Beyond Reality form Jasiri Media Group.

Graffiti Nuisance Ordinance
The City of Seattle enacts the Graffiti Nuisance Ordinance, which requires property owners to remove graffiti within ten days or face fines of one hundred dollars per day. The Seattle Public Utilities Graffiti Prevention Program enforces the ordinance.

Sir Mix-A-Lot
Sir Mix-A-Lot releases the album *Chief Boot Knocka*.

TRED
Prolific local graffiti writer Travis "TRED" Edwards serves three weeks in jail, receives one thousand hours of community service, and is put on probation for two years.

Graffiti Rangers
Seattle Public Utilities forms the Graffiti Rangers, a six-member crew to clean up public property.

Silver Shadow D
Silver Shadow D self-releases his album *Sleepless—Tha BricKKKs* on Lost and Found Recordings.

Folklife Festival
"The Flavor Magazine Showcase" premiers at the Folklife Festival.

Graffiti comic book
David Toledo and Michael Owsley publish *Urban*, a comic book based on the duo's real-life adventures as graffiti artists.

Mecca International
Mansa and Nebra Square Musa start The Mecca at Twenty-third and Union featuring live music, drum and Swahili classes, open mic nights, chess club, and hip-hop night.

Moving Target
Andre Bostic forms Sexy Sounds Management and releases the compilation album *Moving Target* with production by DJ Supreme and Tyrone Dumas.

RKCNDY
Source of Labor, Ghetto Children, Six in the Clip, and Blind Council play "to a packed house" at the RKCNDY on January 21, 1994.

Seattle Hip-Hop Forum

The second annual Hip-Hop Forum is held on February 12, 1994, at the Seattle Center. Panelists include Mike Clark, J-Styles, Jonathan "Wordsayer" Moore, B-Self, Mr. Supreme, Blaac, B-Mello, Soul One, and organizer Jace.

Kun Luv

Chukundi "DJ Kun Luv" Salisbury receives the Seattle King County Generations United Hand in Hand Award for promoting positive inter-generational relationships on May 5, 1994.

CITR DJ and MC Soundwar

Seattle performers win three of four competitions at the CITR DJ and MC Soundwar in Vancouver, British Columbia, when B-Mello wins the DJ competition, Blind Council wins the group award, and DVS Crew wins the dance contest in November 1994.

1995

Glen Boyd

Glen Boyd returns to Seattle and becomes the owner of iconic hip-hop record store Music Menu.

Tribal Productions

Tribal Productions releases the compilation album *Untranslated Prescriptions*.

Kun Luv

Chukundi "DJ Kun Luv" Salisbury releases the mixtape *Big Fella Blends Part II*.

Gary Payton

Seattle SuperSonics all-star point guard Gary Payton records the single "Livin' Legal & Large" as part of the compilation album *B-Ball's Best Kept Secret*.

Funk Daddy

Funk Daddy releases his debut album, *Funk Daddy Is the Source*.

MAD Krew

MAD Krew is formed.

Kev The Rap'N Rev

Kev The Rap'N Rev and Sister Harmony release the album *Bible Stories* on Seattle-based New City Records.

DJ Topspin
DJ Topspin releases *101.1 KTOP FM [Fat Mixtapes]—Broadcast #1.*

CAVE
Tendai Maraire, Dumi "Draze" Maraire Jr., and Merm and Mall combine to form CAVE (Christ Anoint Verbal Evangelist).

Sir Mix-A-Lot
Sir Mix-A-Lot stars in the TV drama series *The Watcher* on the fledgling UPN network in January 1995.

Kevin Gardner
Seattle's Kevin Gardner produces the song "Smoke 'n' Drank" on E-40's album *In a Major Way* in March 1995.

B-Mello
B-Mello is named DJ of the month in the national magazine *RapSheet* in March 1995.

The Ghetto Children
The Ghetto Children win the Black Student Union Talent Show at the University of Washington in March 1995.

Funk Daddy
Seattle's Funk Daddy produces three songs—"Sideways," "It's All Bad," and "Fed"—on E-40's album *In a Major Way* in March 1995.

Boss Crew
The Late Night Teen Program at Rainier Beach Community Center sponsors a break-dance battle on March 24, 1995. Boss Crew wins.

The Flavor
The Flavor magazine sponsors "Homegrown Hip-Hop II" at the Folklife Festival in May 1995.

Evergreen State College
Evergreen State College in Olympia hosts the all-day hip-hop event "Phunky Phat '95" on June 3, 1995.

Northwest Hip-Hop Forum
The Northwest Hip-Hop Forum, organized by Robert Brewer, is held at the Showbox Theater on November 19, 1995.

Funk Daddy
Funk Daddy is on the cover of *The Flavor* magazine, one of only two such covers featuring Seattle artists, in December 1995.

1996

Tribal Productions
Tribal Productions releases the compilation album *Do the Math.*

The Flavor
The Flavor publishes its final issue.

Silent Lambs Project
Jace and Silas Blak form the Silent Lambs Project.

Sir Mix-A-Lot
Sir Mix-A-Lot releases the album *Return of the Bumpasaurus.*

Street Level Records
Street Level Records is founded by David "D-Sane" Severance III.

ENYCE
Seattle native Tony Shellman along with Evan Davis and Lando Felix cofound the hip-hop fashion company ENYCE in March 1996.

Prose and Concepts
Mic Dub of Prose and Concepts dies by suicide on December 31, 1996.

1997

Rap Attack
"Nasty" Nes Rodriguez leaves KCMU's *Rap Attack* and moves to Los Angeles.

Rap Attack
Vancouver, BC, DJ Maximus Clean takes over as host of *Rap Attack* on Seattle radio station KCMU.

KUBE 93 FM protest
Silver Shadow D, James Croone, Curtis Elerson, and Gordon Curvey lead a protest against KUBE 93 FM, charging the radio station with failure to play local and independent hip-hop artists.

The Virgo Party
The Virgo Party, held at the Showbox on First Avenue, is linked in the newspaper to a downtown "riot and looting spree" allegedly committed by teens who had been turned away at the door.

Word * Sound * Power
Jasiri Media Group releases the compilation album *Word * Sound * Power,* featuring Beyond Reality, Felicia Loud, Theaster Gates, Source of Labor, and Cecil Young.

Prose and Concepts
The final album of Prose and Concepts, *Everything Is Nice*, is released.

Sharpshooters
Sharpshooters, Mr. Supreme and Sure Shot, release their album *Choked Up*.

Beyond Reality
Beyond Reality releases the twelve-inch single "I Reality" on the Jasiri Media Group record label.

Circle of Fire
Seattle b-boy crew Circle of Fire is formed.

artsEdge Festival
The inaugural artsEdge Festival featuring experimental music, theater, dance, performance art, spoken word, video, film, and visual art from emerging Northwest artists is held at the Seattle Center.

Dark Diamond Records
Dark Diamond Records is formed by Cedric Prim and Steven Johnson. Step One Mobb, 2-Tyght, and Hustlers For Life combine to form the collective Mobb Tyght Hustlers and release a self-titled compilation album on Dark Diamond.

Deuce 8 Records
Benjamin "Mr. Benjamin" Smith forms Deuce 8 Records.

Break Battle at The Rec
Sigrid Batara organizes the Inaugural Break Battle at The Rec in Shoreline, Washington.

14 Fathoms Deep
The compilation album *14 Fathoms Deep* is released on Loosegroove Records on January 28, 1997.

Sub Pop Records
Seattle-based Sub Pop Records, best known for first signing grunge rock band Nirvana, agrees to a distribution deal with Conception Records in May 1997.

Rating the local scene
Asked by *The Rocket* in July 1997 to rate the local hip-hop scene on a scale of one (worst) to ten (best), a panel of eight leading Seattle hip-hop figures give an average answer of five.

1998

Kun Luv
Chukundi "DJ Kun Luv" Salisbury launches Seaspot.com.

Wyking Garrett
Twenty-one-year-old Kwame Wyking Garrett runs for state representative Position 1 from Seattle's Thirty-seventh District.

Fever One
Seattle native Fever One becomes a member of the Rock Steady Crew in New York City.

Street Sounds
Mr. Supreme and Kutfather take over as hosts of *Street Sounds* (formerly *Rap Attack*) on radio station KCMU.

Walkman Rotation
Conception Records releases the compilation album *Walkman Rotation*.

Jake One
Jake One produces several tracks on the Conception Records compilation album *Walkman Rotation*.

Evil Tambourines
Seattle-based Evil Tambourines becomes the first hip-hop act to sign with Sub Pop Records.

Beyond Reality
Beyond Reality opens for Salt-N-Pepa at the Showbox.

Classic Elements Compilation
Classic Elements Compilation is released on Olympia, Washington–based K Records.

Enter the Madness
MAD Krew releases the local hip-hop documentary *Enter the Madness*.

1999

Sit & Spin
Jonathan "Wordsayer" Moore establishes the all-ages friendly Sure Shot Sundays at the Sit & Spin in downtown Seattle.

Massive Monkees
Two Beacon Hill–based break-dance crews, Massive and Untouchable Style Monkees, combine to form Massive Monkees.

Student Hip-Hop Organization of Washington (SHOW)

SHOW is established at the University of Washington.

Skratchcast.com

Joshua Kusske and Jason Schluter launch Skratchcast.com.

Source of Labor

Jasiri Media Group releases Source of Labor debut album *Stolen Lives* in partnership with New York's Subverse Records.

Vitamin D

Vitamin D releases the mixtape *Table Manners 2*.

Hip-Hop 101

King Khazm, DJ Scene, Dirty Dev, and the MAD Krew create *Hip-Hop 101* on Seattle public-access television.

Subset

Sir Mix-A-Lot and Seattle-based alternative rock band The Presidents of the United States of America combine to form the group Subset.

Evil Tambourines

The Evil Tambourines release their debut album, *Library Nation,* in July 1999.

2000

Macklemore

Ben "Macklemore" Haggerty performs live for the first time at the Sit & Spin as part of the group Elevated Elements at Sure Shot Sundays.

The Rocket

The Rocket publishes its final issue.

Music Menu

Music Menu closes permanently.

Massive Monkees

Juse Boogie and Twixx from Massive Monkees win the B-Boy Summit in Los Angeles.

Kylea

Kylea performs as a part of Jumbalaya starting at the 700 Club and ending at the Baltic Room.

Vivid Vixens

Jenna Hikida, Fides "Anna Banana Freeze" Mabanta, and Kasi Farrar form the b-girl crew Vivid Vixens.

Silent Lambs Project

The Silent Lambs Project release their album *Soul Liquor*.

Graffiti

Consolidated Works gallery presents *Evidence*, an exhibit of contemporary graffiti writing.

Circle of Fire

Circle of Fire participates in the Battle of the Year breaking competition held in Germany.

Student Hip-Hop Organization of Washington

SHOW brings Mos Def to perform at the Husky Union Building (HUB) in January 2000.

Mayor blames hip hop

Seattle mayor Paul Schell publicly blames hip hop for a shooting outside the Bohemian Backstage, a club in Pioneer Square, in September 2000.

Hip Hop rally

Close to 150 people gather in Westlake Park to protest Mayor Paul Schell blaming hip hop for a shooting outside the Bohemian Backstage in September 2000.

The Tablet

The Tablet, a new alternative newspaper, publishes its first issue in October 2000. Sam Chesneau becomes the paper's hip-hop writer, and his column is basically a calendar that highlights local artists and events.

Mayor's Award for Excellence in Hip-Hop

Benjamin "Mr. Benjamin" Smith is the first winner of the Mayor's Award for Excellence in Hip-Hop.

2001

DV One

Seattle DJ Toby "DJ DV One" Campbell is invited to join Rock Steady Crew as a DJ and dancer.

Brainstorm Battle

Student Hip-Hop Organization of Washington and MAD Krew present the first Brainstorm Battle, a freestyle rap competition with forty MCs from around the United States. Preliminary rounds are held at the Sit & Spin, finals at the Paradox Theater. Local MC Khingz wins the $500 first prize.

KEXP
KCMU 90.3 FM changes its call letters to KEXP.

Oldominion
Oldominion releases their debut album *One.*

Vera Project
The Vera Project is founded as a response to a lack of all-age music venues resulting from Seattle's Teen Dance Ordinance.

Merciful
Merciful releases his CD *Fugazi/East Union Street Hustlers.*

Lords of the Floor
Red Bull presents Lords of the Floor, a break-dance battle held at the Sand Point Naval Station, in May 2001.

Byrdie
Byrdie releases his debut album, *Poetic Epidemic,* in September 2001.

2002

Sportn' Life Records
Sportn' Life Records is established.

Blue Scholars
Alexei Saba "DJ Sabzi" Mohajerjasbi and George "Geologic" Quibuyen form Blue Scholars.

Brainstorm Battle
The second annual Brainstorm Battle presented by SHOW ends in controversy when a white MC from Chicago named Presence wins the $2,500 first prize using numerous racist lines against his Asian competitors.

Nocturnal Rage
The Seattle group Nocturnal Rage records a remix for their single "Miss Mary Jane" featuring Rick James.

Seattle Hip-Hop Summit Action Network
The Seattle Hip-Hop Summit Action Network is established as an affiliate of the Hip-Hop Summit Action Network, founded in New York by Russell Simmons and Dr. Benjamin Chavis in 2001.

Circle of Fire
Circle of Fire produces Red Bull Lords of the Floor breaking competition.

Ishmael Butler
Ishmael Butler stars in the short film *I Am Ali.*

911 Amerika
911 Amerika, a local hip-hop compilation reflecting on the aftermath of the 9/11 attacks, is released on MADK/Pangea.

Teen Dance Ordinance
Seattle's Teen Dance Ordinance, instituted in 1985, is repealed.

Art of Movement (AOM)
B-boy crew AOM (Art of Movement) is formed.

Summer Jam
One man is shot to death following the tenth KUBE 93 Summer Jam featuring LL Cool J, Nelly, Jermaine Dupree, and Da Brat held at the Gorge Amphitheater in George, Washington.

X104
Mercer Island High School radio station KMIH aka X104 switches to a hip-hop/R&B format.

2003

Sam Chesneau
Sam Chesneau begins writing "The Truth," a weekly hip-hop column in the alternative weekly *The Stranger.*

Brainstorm Battle
At the third Brainstorm Battle, Geologic, who is Filipino, eliminates defending champion Presence in the round of sixteen while making references to Presence's numerous racist lines used against Asian competitors the year before.

"Yo, Son!"
The weekly Sunday night hip-hop event "Yo, Son!" begins at Capitol Hill venue Chop Suey.

Sir Mix-A-Lot
Sir Mix-A-Lot releases the album *Daddy's Home.*

Mayor's Award for Excellence in Hip-Hop
Jonathan Moore is presented with the Mayor's Award for Excellence in Hip-Hop.

Coolout Network
Coolout Network adjusts its format, incorporating more electronic music and renaming the show *Coolout 2GX.*

Tupac Shakur course
Graduate student Georgia Roberts develops and begins teaching the course "The Textual Appeal of Tupac Shakur" at the University of Washington.

Hip-Hop Theory and Culture
A new course titled "Hip-Hop Theory and Culture" is developed and offered at Seattle Central Community College.

Gentrification
For the first time, data indicates that more African Americans live in suburban areas outside Seattle than live inside the city limits.

Art Primo
Art Primo, a Seattle–based art supply company specializing in graffiti and aerosol materials, opens.

Saba Seven
Logic "Saba Seven" Amen releases his album *Free Saba: The Lost Scriptures of Frank Talk.*

Geologic
George "Geologic" Quibuyen curates the exhibit *It's Like That: APA's (Asian Pacific Americans) and the Seattle Hip-Hop Scene* at Wing Luke Asian Museum in July 2003.

Brainstorm Battle
The third annual Brainstorm Battle in November 2003 attracts more than fifty contestants from around the country. Preliminary rounds are held at Chop Suey with the finals at the Husky Union Building (HUB), where California MC Bo-Rat wins the $2,500 first prize.

2004

Massive Monkees
Massive Monkees win the World B-Boy Championships held in London.

Laura "Piece" Kelley
Laura "Piece" Kelley performs her spoken-word piece "Central District" on the HBO program *Russell Simmons Presents Def Poetry.*

Ishmael Butler
Ishmael "Butterfly" Butler stars in the film *Men Without Jobs.*

Wyking Garrett
Wyking Garrett runs again for state representative Position 1 from the Thirty-seventh District as a Lincoln Republican.

Blue Scholars
Blue Scholars independently release their self-titled debut album, which is named album of the year by *Seattle Weekly.*

Mayor's Award for Excellence in Hip-Hop
Seattle Mayor Greg Nickels presents Georgio Brown's *Coolout Network* with the Mayor's Award For Excellence in Hip-Hop.

Brainstorm Battle
The fourth annual Brainstorm Battle has regional prelims in Ann Arbor, Michigan; Chicago; Los Angeles; New York; Portland, OR; and Seattle. Finals are held at Bumbershoot, where New York MC Iron Solomon takes the $2,500 first prize.

Rhymesayers Entertainment
Minneapolis-based Rhymesayers Entertainment signs local artists Vitamin D, Grayskul, and Boom Bap Project.

Obese Productions
Melissa "Meli" Darby launches Obese Productions.

Massive Monkees
Massive Monkees begin performing at Seattle SuperSonics home games as the Sonics' "Boom Squad."

Grynch
Grynch releases his debut EP *The Seven Deadly Sins* as a senior at Ballard High School.

Mr. Supreme
Mr. Supreme produces music for the hit HBO crime drama series *The Sopranos.*

Soul Gorilla
The promotion company Soul Gorilla is founded.

DV One
Toby "DJ DV One" Campbell becomes the DJ for the Seattle Seahawks.

206 Zulu
King Khazm establishes 206 Zulu, the Seattle chapter of the Universal Zulu Nation, in February 2004.

ENYCE
Liz Claiborne Inc. purchases ENYCE for $114 million in February 2004.

Massive Monkees
Mayor Greg Nickels declares "Massive Monkees Day" in Seattle on April 26, 2004.

The Stranger
After releasing Sam Chesneau as writer of the weekly hip-hop column "The Truth" in May 2004, substitute columnist and *Stranger* editor Dan Savage, who is white, repeatedly calls *Stranger* colleague Charles Mudede, who is Black, "scholar nigger."

Larry Mizell Jr.
Larry Mizell Jr. replaces Sam Chesneau writing the weekly hip-hop column for *The Stranger*, renaming it "My Philosophy" in July 2004.

Back to Its Roots
The second annual Back to Its Roots spoken word and hip-hop festival at the Langston Hughes Performing Arts Institute is held in October 2004. It includes Jessica Care Moore, Beyond Reality, Blue Scholars, Toby "DJ DV One" Campbell, Circle of Fire, and Massive Monkees.

Hip-Hop Hope Seattle
In December 2004 local nonprofit Power of Hope releases *Hip-Hop Hope Seattle*, an album of original songs and spoken word produced by teens in the Hip-Hop Hope after-school program.

5th Element Beatbox Battle
SCIONtific Records holds the inaugural 5th Element Beatbox Battle at the Vera Project in December 2004. Prizes include $500 and a SHURE SM58 microphone.

2005

Sunday Night Sound Session
Jonathan "Wordsayer" Moore and DJ Hyphen begin hosting *Sunday Night Sound Session* on KUBE 93 FM.

Zulu Radio
Zulu Radio, hosted by King Khazm, Gabriel Teodros, and WD4D, premieres on KBCS 91.3 FM.

Music Inner City
The program *Music Inner City*, hosted by Gordon Curvey and originally broadcast on public access television, is made available On Demand on Comcast.

Grayskul
Grayskul releases their debut album, *Deadlivers*, on Rhymesayers Entertainment.

Framework

Framework releases his debut album, *Hello World*.

Boom Bap Project

Boom Bap Project release their debut *Reprogram* on Rhymesayers Entertainment.

Abyssinian Creole

Abyssinian Creole (Gabriel Teodros and Khingz) releases the album *Sexy Beast* on MADK Productions.

Grynch

Grynch releases his debut album, *This Is What I Do*.

Mayor's Award for Excellence in Hip-Hop

Melissa Noelle Greene, Patrick Lagreid, and Sir Mix-A-Lot win the Mayor's Award for Excellence in Hip-Hop.

Graffiti

Police data indicates that half the people arrested for graffiti offenses in Seattle actually live in outlying areas such as Mercer Island, Kirkland, Bellevue, and Tacoma, Washington.

Tsunami relief

Mix for Relief, a benefit for victims of the Indian Ocean tsunami, is held in January 2005 at the Showbox, featuring Sir Mix-A-Lot, Byrdie, DJ B-Mello, and a contingent of KUBE 93 DJs.

Source of Labor

Source of Labor plays its final show at the Crocodile Café in May 2005. Eddie "Sugar Bear" Wells of the Emerald Street Boys DJs the event, and Sir Mix-A-Lot is the host.

Hip-Hop Appreciation Week

SCIONtific Records and the Temple of Hip-Hop present Hip-Hop Appreciation Week in Seattle in May 2005 with a kick-off event at the Vera Project hosted by Laura "Piece" Kelley with performances by local DJs, MCs, and b-girls and b-boys.

Hip-Hop Festival for Kids

Hip-Hop Festival for Kids is held in May 2005 at Rainier Beach Community Center, a four-hour program that includes a variety of seminars and workshops on topics such as writing and marketing.

Big Tunes

Vitamin D hosts the inaugural Big Tunes challenge, a local production/beat-making competition, at the War Room in July 2005.

Vitamin D
The "Power Bill," a regular series presented by Vitamin D and The Pharmacy at the War Room, features Kylea, Felicia Loud, Piece, and Choklate in August 2005.

Common Market
Common Market, Ryan "RA Scion" Abeo and Saba "Sabzi" Mohajerjasbi, release their self-titled debut album in October 2005.

2006

Wyking Garrett
Wyking Garrett runs for state representative Position 2 from the Thirty-seventh District.

Raindrop Hustla
Raindrop Hustla becomes the first blog focused on Seattle hip hop.

Dope Emporium
Jace ECAJ organizes the first Dope Emporium, a free, all-ages family-friendly event promoting local hip-hop artists and culture.

Hidmo
Sisters Asmeret and Rahwa Habte buy Hidmo restaurant, which becomes a hip-hop hot spot in the Central District.

Shocked on the Buzz
In January 2006, Shocked on the Buzz, a local talent showcase sponsored by SCIONtific Records, Obese Productions, KEXP, and *The Stranger*, features Common Market, Specs One, Cancer Rising, and Macklemore.

Emerald Street Girls
Mia "Angel Face" Black of the Emerald Street Girls passes away on February 9, 2006.

Hip-Hop Appreciation Week
SCIONtific Records and the Temple of Hip-Hop present Hip-Hop Appreciation Week in Seattle in May 2006.

Blue Scholars
Blue Scholars launch their own record label, Mass Line Records, in July 2006.

D. Black
D. Black releases his debut LP, *The Cause & Effect*, on Sportn' Life Records in July 2006.

Local showcases
"The Derby Liberation Front Summer Hip-Hop Extravaganza" and "NW Stand Up" showcase up-and-coming local hip-hop talent in July 2006.

DV One
Toby "DJ DV One" Campbell is arrested in September 2006 and charged with third-degree assault after attempting to intervene in an altercation between his teenage daughter and a Seattle police officer.

Mayor's Award for Hip-Hop Excellence
The Mayor's Award for Hip-Hop Excellence recipients are awarded in October 2006 to Mr. Supreme (Pioneer Award), Gordon Curvey (Media Award), and King Khazm (Unsung Hero Award).

B-Mello
B-Mello is named West Coast DJ of the Year at the DJ Power Summit held in the Dominican Republic in October 2006.

2007

Laura "Piece" Kelley
Kelley releases her album *Street Smartz*.

Massive Monkees
The Seattle Arts Commission presents Massive Monkees with the Mayor's Arts Award in honor of the group's continued contributions to the local arts.

Jake One
Seattle native Jake One produces the 50 Cent song "All of Me" featuring Mary J. Blige.

Beyond Reality
Beyond Reality release their album *A Soul's Journey*.

Fatal Lucciauno
Fatal Lucciauno releases "The Only Forgotten Son" on Sportn' Life Records.

Fatal Lucciauno is arrested on firearms charges after a shooting outside the Tabella nightclub. He is eventually convicted and serves an eighteen-month prison term.

Sir Mix-A-Lot
Sir Mix-A-Lot appears with Ice-T, MC Breeze, King Tee, Candyman, and Conscious Daughters on the West Coast remix of Nas's tribute song "Where Are They Now."

Mass Line Media and Blue Scholars
Mass Line Media agrees to a partnership with New York–based Rawkus Records to distribute Blue Scholars' second album, *Bayani*, in June 2007.

Big Tunes
Red Bull becomes title sponsor for Vitamin D and Jonathan Moore's Big Tunes producer battle, adding dates in cities around the country.

Gabriel Teodros
Gabriel Teodros releases his album *Lovework*.

Dyme Def
Dyme Def (Fearce Villain, S.E.V., and Brainstorm) release their album *Space Music*.

Battle of Burien
The inaugural Battle of Burien break-dance competition is held at Burien Community Center.

UW Hip-Hop Student Association
The UWHHSA is formed.

Asian Hip-Hop Summit
The Asian Hip-Hop Summit Tour makes a stop in Seattle at the University of Washington's Ethnic Cultural Center.

Silas Blak
Silas Blak releases the album *Silas Sentinel*.

The Physics
The Physics release their album *Future Talk*.

Seattle Young People's Project
The MLK Day Hip-Hop Show of the Seattle Young People's Project features headliners D. Black and Macklemore in January 2007.

Massive Monkees
Massive Monkees and Big World Breaks host "4 the Love—A Tribute to James Brown" in February 2007.

Laura "Piece" Kelley
Laura "Piece" Kelley produces and stars in the one-woman show *Street Smarts: The Story of a True School B-Girl* at the Rainier Valley Cultural Center in South Seattle in April 2007.

DV One

Despite significant amounts of support from the local hip-hop community, Toby "DJ DV One" Campbell is found guilty of assaulting a police officer in October 2007.

Blue Scholars

Blue Scholars organize The Program, a five-day event celebrating the region's hip-hop culture, in December 2007.

2008

Jake One

Jake One releases his debut album *White Van Music.*

Dyme Def

Seattle's Dyme Def are featured in the "Unsigned Hype" section of *The Source* magazine.

Blue Scholars

Blue Scholars are named one of *Playboy* magazine's "Ten to Watch in 2008."

Mad Rad

Mad Rad (Terry Radjaw, Buffalo Madonna, and P Smoov) release their debut album, *White Gold.*

Saturday Knights

The Saturday Knights (Barfly, Tilson, and Suspence) release their debut album.

Hip-Hop Photo Book

Emerald City Hip-Hop—a book of pictures, lyrics, and memorabilia from the Seattle hip-hop scene compiled by Alexis Wolfe—is released, with the foreword written by Bay Area artist Shock G.

Mr. Supreme

Mr. Supreme contributes a song to the soundtrack of the hit HBO crime drama series *The Wire.*

Way of the B-Boy

Fever One and Jeromeskee are featured in the documentary film *Way of the B-Boy.*

ReignCity

Obese Productions, one of Seattle's premier hip-hop concert booking agencies, becomes ReignCity.

Valentine's Day Riot
The Valentine's Day Riot takes place on February 14, 2008, at Evergreen State College in Olympia during a performance by the group dead prez.

Vicious Puppies Crew
Seattle b-boy collective Vicious Puppies Crew is formed in May 2008.

Asian Hip-Hop Summit Tour
The Asian Hip-Hop Summit Tour makes a stop in Seattle in August 2008 and features local talent Sonny Bonoho, Orbitron, DJ Soul One, and DJ B-Girl.

Massive Monkees
Massive Monkees host Crash Test, a breaking competition at the Paramount Theatre with crews from around the United States as well as Korea, Brazil, and Europe, in November 2008.

2009

Hip-Hop Is Green
Hip-Hop Is Green hosts a vegan dinner at the Mount Baker Community Center.

Wyking Garrett
Wyking Garrett becomes a candidate for mayor of Seattle.

Jake One
Jake One releases the single "Home" featuring Vitamin D, Maineak B, C-Note, and Ish.

Macklemore
Macklemore releases his single "The Town."

Jake One
Jake One produces the single "Won't Be Long" by Rakim.

Shabazz Palaces
Tendai Maraire and Ishmael Butler form Shabazz Palaces and release the EPs *Shabazz Palaces* and *Of Light*.

D. Black
D. Black releases *Ali'Yah* on Sportn' Life Records.

Massive Monkees
Massive Monkees place third on Season 4 of the MTV program *America's Best Dance Crew.*

Street Sounds
Larry Mizell Jr. begins hosting *Street Sounds* on KEXP 90.3 FM.

Fresh Espresso
Fresh Espresso (Rik Rude and P Smoov) release their album *Glamour*.

Kung Foo Grip
Suburban Eastside group Kung Foo Grip releases "Sonny Cheeba," a song about riding the bus into Seattle.

Fatal Lucciauno
Fatal Lucciauno's single "Gangsta" is included on the local digital music and video compilation *GIVE*, which benefits Arts Corps and Seattle-area food banks.

Helladope
Helladope (Tay Sean and Jerm) release their EP *Return to Planet Rock*.

They Live!
They Live! release the album *They LA Soul*.

Grynch
Grynch releases his album *Chemistry 1.5* and is featured in an interview in *Billboard* magazine.

Champagne Champagne
Champagne Champagne releases their self-titled debut album.

Northwest Hip-Hop Leadership Conference
The first annual Northwest Hip-Hop Leadership Conference is held at Seattle Central Community College in March 2009.

Big Tunes
Red Bull Big Tunes, created by Vitamin D and Jonathan Moore, premieres on Black Entertainment Television (BET) in April 2009.

206UP.com
Hip-hop blog 206UP.com is launched by Chul Gugich in July 2009.

MTV
A Seattle episode of the MTV local music series *$5 Cover* features THEESatisfaction and Champagne Champagne in August 2009.

Blue Scholars
Blue Scholars release "Bayani Redux" in September 2009.

Go! Machine
Go! Machine, a two-day showcase featuring twelve local hip-hop acts, is held at the Crocodile in December 2009.

2010

Macklemore

"Can't Hold Us" by Macklemore and Ryan Lewis is named local song of the year on KUBE's *Sunday Night Sound Session.*

Shabazz Palaces

Shabazz Palaces signs with Sub Pop Records. Shabazz Palaces becomes the first rappers on the cover of *The Stranger* and also wins the first ever Stranger Genius Award for Music.

Nacho Picasso

Nacho Picasso releases the album *Blunt Raps.*

Black Stax

Black Stax (Felicia Loud, Silas Blak, and Jace ECAJ) release their debut album, *Talking Buildings.*

Grynch

Grynch releases the video for his single "My Volvo."

OCnotes

OCnotes releases the mixtape *From Me to You.*

Helladope

Helladope release their self-titled debut album.

Yuk

Bean One and Fearce Villain launch their clothing/music project titled Yuk.

Fice

Tacoma, Washington, native Fice releases the single "Two Five Three."

Kevin Collabo

Seattle group Truckasaurus hosts Kevin Collabo, a live show collaboration with more than thirty local MCs.

SPECSONE

The exhibit *The Visual Art of SPECSONE* premieres at the Throwbacks NW gallery.

Mr. D.O.G.

Tacoma resident Mr. D.O.G. releases the single and video for "Hilltop."

OCnotes

OCnotes releases his album *Doo Doo.*

Jstyles

Nine-year-old Seattle-born b-boy Jalen "Jstyles" Testerman appears in the movie *Step Up 3D.*

Suntonio Bandanaz

Suntonio "Asun" Bandanaz releases his debut album, *Who Is Suntonio Bandanaz?!*

Haiti Relief Show

In response to the earthquake in Haiti, Sol presents and performs in the Haiti Relief Show at Neumos in February 2010, featuring Common Market, The Physics, Dyno Jamz, The Flying Sneakers Crew, and Khingz benefiting Doctors Without Borders.

Blue Scholars

Blue Scholars headline three consecutive nights of sold-out shows at the Showbox in March 2010. Also on the bill are DJ Soul One and Macklemore.

South by Southwest

Seattle artists Blue Scholars, D. Black, Dyme Def, THEESatisfaction, Shabazz Palaces, and Grynch perform at the South by Southwest Music Festival in Austin in March 2010.

Emerald Street Boys

The Emerald Street Boys reunite for a show at the Crocodile in April 2010.

Spoken Word

Local MCs participate in an all-ages event of spoken word poetry in the Penthouse of the Sorrento Hotel in April 2010.

Jake One

Jake One releases his compilation/mixtape *Town Biz* in April 2010.

Seattle Hip-Hop Career and Business Expo

The Seattle Hip-Hop Career and Business Expo: Business at the Speed of Hip-Hop, a day-long event of workshops, panels, and networking, is held at the Vera Project in October 2010.

Blue Scholars

Blue Scholars become the first local rap act to headline a bill at the Paramount Theatre in October 2010.

Hip-Hop History Month

On November 1, 2011, Mayor Mike McGinn proclaims November as Hip-Hop History Month in Seattle.

2011

Shabazz Palaces
Shabazz Palaces releases their debut album, *Black Up*.

Nacho Picasso
Nacho Picasso releases "Ziplock Hip-Hop" with BAYB (Jarv Dee and Steezie NASA) and *For the Glory*.

Metal Chocolates
Metal Chocolates (OCnotes and Rik Rude) release their self-titled debut album.

Chevy Shann
Chevy Shann releases his album *Been Ridin*.

Africatown
Africatown, an initiative focused on African American–centered economic, educational, and cultural development in the Central District, is launched.

Neema
Neema releases his EP *Black Roses*.

Sam Lachow
Sam Lachow releases his debut album, *Brand New Bike*.

10.4 Rog
Renton producer 10.4 Rog releases the EP *Late* in February 2011.

Macklemore
Macklemore is featured above the fold on the front page of the *Seattle Times* in February 2011.

Macklemore and Ryan Lewis
Macklemore and Ryan Lewis sell out shows on three consecutive nights at the Showbox in March 2011.

Seattle City Breakers
The Seattle City Breakers celebrate their thirty-year reunion in May 2011.

Blue Scholars
Blue Scholars release the album *Cinemetropolis* in June 2011.

THEESatisfaction
Stas and Cat, aka THEESatisfaction, signs with Sub Pop Records in July 2011.

Red Bull Emsee Freestyle Battle
The Red Bull Emsee Freestyle Battle, hosted by Bun B and featuring judges Casual, Crooked I, and Too $hort, is held at the Crocodile in July 2011.

MissCaseyCarter.com
Casey Carter launches the independent artist, event, and lifestyle website MissCaseyCarter.com in July 2011.

Grand Groove
Members of Shabazz Palaces, THEESatisfaction, Metal Chocolates, and others begin holding a monthly event in August 2011 called Grand Groove, which is a "celebration of art, community, culture and life."

Shabazz Palaces
Shabazz Palaces is profiled in the *New Yorker* magazine in August 2011.

Hip-Hop Occupies
Hip-Hop Occupies, an off-shoot of the Occupy movement, is established in Seattle in October 2011.

Prometheus Brown
Blue Scholars MC Prometheus Brown (aka Geologic) writes an op-ed on the Occupy Wall Street movement for *Al Jazeera* in November 2011.

2012

Massive Monkees
Massive Monkees become the first American crew to win the prestigious R16 World B-Boy Masters Championship held in Seoul, South Korea.

Macklemore
Macklemore and Ryan Lewis release their album *The Heist*.

Nacho Picasso
Nacho Picasso releases the "Lord of the Fly," "Exalted," and "Black Narcissus."

Fleeta Partee
Fleeta Partee releases his debut solo album, *LifeMuzik*.

Raz Simone and Sam Lachow
Raz Simone and Sam Lachow release the EP *5 Good Reasons*.

Reign Supreme
UWHHSA founder Mike Huang organizes the first annual Reign Supreme break-dance competition.

Malitia Malimob

Somali-American group Malitia Malimob releases their album *Riots of the Pirates*.

50 Next

50 Next: Seattle Hip-Hop Worldwide, a short film by Avi Loud, is released.

Sol

Sol releases his album *Yours Truly* then leaves to travel the world for nine months after receiving a fellowship.

The Physics

The Physics release their album *Tomorrow People*, crowd-funded entirely on Kickstarter.com.

Stop Biting

Stop Biting, a regular hip-hop night at Lo-Fi, is turned into a compilation album and mini-documentary.

Champagne Champagne

Champagne Champagne releases their album *Swine? My Brother . . .*

Fatal Lucciauno

Fatal Lucciauno releases the album *Respect* on Sportn' Life Records in February 2012.

THEESatisfaction

THEESatisfaction releases their debut album, *awE naturalE*, in March 2012.

Gifted Gab

Gifted Gab releases her debut EP *Queen La'Chiefah* in March 2012.

Macklemore

Macklemore appears on the cover of *XXL* magazine as part of the "Freshman Class of 2012" in April.

Emerald Street Boys

The Emerald Street Boys release the single "When Folks Was Real (Back in the Dayz)" in July 2012.

Jake One

Jake One receives Grammy nominations for production credits on the album *Some Nights* by the group Fun and the single "3 Kings" from the Rick Ross album *God Forgives, I Don't*, nominated for Best Rap Album, in December 2012.

2013

Jake One
Jake One produces the single "Furthest Thing" by Drake.

Porter Ray
Porter Ray releases the mixtapes *BLK GLD* and *WHT GLD/RSE GLD*.

Shabazz Palaces
Ishmael Butler of Shabazz Palaces becomes a member of Sub Pop Records Artist and Repertoire (A&R) team.

Nacho Picasso
Nacho Picasso releases "Vampsterdam" and "High and Mighty."

Raz Simone
Raz Simone releases his debut solo EP *Solomon Samuel Simone*.

Massive Monkees
Massive Monkees open The Beacon, a dance studio located downtown.

Way of the B-Girl
Anna Banana Freeze of Massive Monkees teaches the class "Way of the B-Girl" at The Beacon, Massive's home studio.

Macklemore
Macklemore and Ryan Lewis's single "Thrift Shop" hits number one on the Billboard "Hot 100" chart in February 2013.

XXL Magazine
XXL magazine prints a story called "The New New: 15 Seattle Rappers You Should Know" in May 2013.

Jake One
The Best Men, a DJ duo from Switzerland, release "The Jake One-ders," a collection of Jake One–produced songs in July 2013.

Seattle Hip-Hop History
The panel "From Emerald St. to Pike St.: A History of Seattle Hip-Hop 1980–2013" is held in November 2013 with Fever One, Julie C, Larry Mizell Jr., and Sir Mix-A-Lot in the Broadway Performance Hall at Seattle Central Community College.

Macklemore and Ryan Lewis
Macklemore and Ryan Lewis play three consecutive nights of sold-out shows at Key Arena with Sir Mix-A-Lot as opening act in December 2013.

Byrdie
Byrdie passes away at age thirty-five in December 2013.

2014

Nacho Picasso
Nacho Picasso releases *Trances with Wolves: The Prixtape*.

Gifted Gab
Gifted Gab releases her debut album, *Girl Rap*.

206 Zulu
206 Zulu celebrates its tenth anniversary.

Shabazz Palaces
Shabazz Palaces releases the album *Lese Majesty*.

Grynch
Grynch releases his album *Street Lights*.

Raz Simone
Raz Simone releases *Cognitive Dissonance: Part One*.

Hip-Hop History Month
Mayors Marilyn Strickland of Tacoma, Stephen Buxbaum of Olympia, Andy Ryder of Lacey, and Patty Lent of Bremerton all proclaim November as Hip-Hop History Month in their respective cities.

Hip-Hop History Month
Governor Jay Inslee proclaims November as Hip-Hop History Month in the state of Washington.

Yung Lenox
Seven-year-old Seattle hip-hop artist Lenox "Yung Lenox" Buringrud has his first solo gallery show in Los Angeles and is profiled in *LA Weekly*.

Tubs
The University District building that once housed the hourly hot tub rental business Tubs, which had subsequently become a destination "free wall" for graffiti, is torn down.

Dance for Paul Lee
A video tribute titled *Dance for Paul Lee* is produced by UWHHSA and Seattle Pacific University hip-hop dance club Ante Up in honor of Paul Lee, an SPU student and Ante Up member who was shot and killed on campus.

Draze
Draze releases the video for his song "The Hood Ain't the Same," which discusses gentrification in the Central District.

Macklemore
Macklemore and Ryan Lewis win four Grammy Awards in January 2014.

MOHAI
The Museum of History and Industry (MOHAI) hosts an event called "The Legacy of Seattle Hip-Hop" in February 2014.

Porter Ray
Porter Ray signs with Sub Pop Records on May 21, 2014.

Sir Mix-A-Lot
Sir Mix-A-Lot performs "Posse on Broadway" and "Baby Got Back" with the Seattle Symphony at Benaroya Hall in June 2014.

Porter Ray
Porter Ray releases the digital album *Fundamentals* in August 2014.

Gifted Gab
Gifted Gab releases her EP *G-Shit* in November 2014.

2015

Raz Simone
Raz Simone releases "Cognitive Dissonance: Part Two."

Folklife Festival
For the first time, hip hop is the cultural focus of the annual Folklife Festival held at Seattle Center.

Gyasi Ross
"Big Indian" Gyasi Ross releases the single "Marlon Brando" featuring Sacred Water.

OCnotes
OCnotes is nominated for *The Stranger* Genius Award in Music.

THEESatisfaction
THEESatisfaction release their album *EarthEE* in February 2015.

Legacy of Seattle Hip-Hop
MOHAI presents the exhibit *The Legacy of Seattle Hip-Hop* in September 2015.

NOTES

Introduction

The lyric in the chapter title is from Sir Mix-A-Lot's "Posse on Broadway" (Seattle: NastyMix Records, 1987).

1. Quintard Taylor, *The Forging of a Black Community: Seattle's Central District from 1870 through the Civil Rights Era* (Seattle: University of Washington Press, 1994), 5.

Chapter 1. Seattle, the Central District, and the Arrival of Hip Hop

The lyric in the chapter title is from Boom Bap Project, "Welcome to Seattle" (Minneapolis: Rhymesayers Entertainment, 2005).

1. City of Seattle, "Seattle Municipal Archives: Brief History of Seattle." www.seattle.gov/cityarchives/seattle-facts/brief-history-of-seattle (accessed April 2, 2014).
2. Daudi Abe and Quintard Taylor, "From Memphis & Mogadishu: The History of African Americans in Martin Luther King County, Washington, 1858–2014," October 3, 2014, BlackPast.org, www.blackpast.org/memphis-and -mogadishu-history-african-americans-martin-luther-king-county -washington-1858-2014.
3. George Tamblyn, "Grose, William (1835–1898)," BlackPast.org, January 26, 2007, www.blackpast.org/aaw/grose-william-1835-1898.
4. Abe and Taylor 2014.
5. Greg Lange, "Billboard Reading 'Will the Last Person Leaving SEATTLE—Turn Out the Lights' appears near Sea-Tac International Airport on April 16, 1971," Essay 1287, June 8, 1999, HistoryLink.org.
6. Abe and Taylor 2014.
7. Dale Soden, "Congress of Racial Equality (CORE) Seattle Chapter (1961–1970)," January 27, 2010, www.blackpast.org/aaw/seattle-chapter-core -congress-racial-equality-1961-1970.

8. Quintard Taylor, *The Forging of a Black Community: Seattle's Central District from 1870 through the Civil Rights Era* (Seattle: University of Washington Press, 1994).

9. David Wilma, "Seattle City Council Approves Open Housing Ordinance on April 19, 1968," Essay 1384, April 2, 2001, HistoryLink.org.

10. Anne LaGrelius Siqueland, *Without a Court Order: The Desegregation of Seattle Schools* (Seattle: Madrona Press, 1981).

11. Nikolaus Wirth, "Student Nonviolent Coordinating Committee (1960–1973)," December 16, 2007, www.blackpast.org/aah/student-nonviolent-coordinating -committee-1960-1973.

12. Priscilla Long, "Stokely Carmichael Speaks to 4,000 at Seattle's Garfield High School on April 19, 1967," Essay 3715, March 2, 2002, HistoryLink.org.

13. David Wilma, "Riots Erupt in Seattle's Central Area after Franklin High Protestors Are Sentenced on July 1, 1968," Essay 1515, June 4, 2000, HistoryLink.org.

14. Alan J. Stein, "Bobby Seale Names Aaron Dixon Head of Seattle Black Panthers on April 13, 1968," Essay 1382, June 4, 1999, HistoryLink.org.

15. Alan J. Stein, "Seattle Police Raid Black Panther Office in Central Area, Setting Off Riots, on July 29, 1968," Essay 1530, January 1, 2000, HistoryLink.org.

16. Seattle Civil Rights and Labor History Project, "Seattle Black Panther Party History and Memory Project," University of Washington, http://depts .washington.edu/civilr/BPP.htm (accessed January 9, 2014).

17. Taylor 1994.

18. Henry McGee Jr., "Gentrification: Integration or Displacement? The Seattle Story," August 19, 2007, www.blackpast.org/perspectives/gentrification -integration-or-displacement-seattle-story.

19. Taylor 1994.

20. Paul de Barros, *Jackson Street after Hours: The Roots of Jazz in Seattle* (Seattle: Sasquatch Books, 1993).

21. Ray Charles and David Ritz, *Brother Ray: Ray Charles' Own Story* (New York: Dial Press, 1978).

22. Quincy Jones, *The Autobiography of Quincy Jones* (New York: Doubleday, 2001).

23. Mary Willix, "Hendrix, Jimi (1942–1970)," January 17, 2007, www.blackpast .org/aah/hendrix-jimi-1942-1970.

24. Murray Forman in "Represent: Race, Space, and Place in Rap Music," in *That's the Joint! The Hip-Hop Studies Reader*, edited by Murray Forman and Mark Anthony Neal (New York: Routledge, 2004), 217.

25. Pavitt as quoted in Forman 2004: 218.

26. Jonathan Raban, *Bad Land: An American Romance* (New York: Vintage Books, 1996).

27. Charles Mudede, "Beyond the Sea," *The Stranger*, September 19, 2002.

28. Steven Hager, "Afrika Bambaataa's Hip-Hop," in *And It Don't Stop: The Best American Hip-Hop Journalism of the Last 25 years*, edited by Raquel Cepeda, 12–26 (New York: Faber and Faber, 2004).

29. Craig Castleman, "The Politics of Graffiti," in Forman and Neal 2004: 21–29.

30. Sacha Jenkins, "The Writing on the Wall: Graffiti Culture Crumbles into the Violence It Once Escaped," in Cepeda 2004: 288–99.
31. Juan Flores, "Puerto Rican and Proud, Boyee!: Rap, Roots and Amnesia," in *The Hip-Hop Reader*, edited by Tim Strode and Tim Woods, 30–40 (New York: Pearson, 2008).
32. Sally Banes, "Breaking," in Forman and Neal 2004: 13–20.
33. Nelson George, "Hip-Hop's Founding Father's Speak the Truth," in Forman and Neal 2004: 45–55.
34. Russell Simmons, *Life and Def: Sex, Drugs, Money, and God* (New York: Three Rivers Press, 2001), 37.
35. David Toop, *Rap Attack 3* (London: Serpent's Tail, 2001).
36. Simmons 2001: 52.
37. Sugarhill Gang, "Rapper's Delight," Sugar Hill Records, 1979.
38. Sugarhill Gang, "Rapper's Delight," Sugar Hill Records, 1979.
39. Ice-T as quoted in Daudi Abe, *6 'n the Morning: West Coast Hip-Hop Music 1987–1992 and the Transformation of Mainstream Culture* (Los Angeles: Over the Edge Books, 2013), 31.
40. Eddie Wells, personal communication with the author, June 2008.
41. Vince Canby, "'Wild Style,' Rapping and Painting Graffiti," *New York Times*, March 18, 1983.
42. Charlie Ahearn, dir. *Wild Style* (Los Angeles: Rhino Home Video, 1982).
43. Robert Newman, personal communication with the author, March 2015.
44. *Seattle Times*, October 30, 1983.

Chapter 2. Seattle Hip Hop in the 1980s

The lyric in the chapter title comes from Sir Mix-A-Lot, "Posse on Broadway" (Seattle: NastyMix Records, 1987).
1. Eddie Wells, personal communication with the author, June 2008.
2. James Croone, personal communication with the author, March 2008.
3. David Wilma, "Seattle Becomes the Emerald City in 1982," Essay 3622, October 24, 2001, HistoryLink.org.
4. Peter Blecha, "Seattle's 'Underground' Hip-Hop Scene Breaks Out with Big Exhibition Hall Gig on August 17, 1984," Essay 9778, May 1, 2011, HistoryLink.org.
5. Robert Newman, "Armory Rap-Up," *The Rocket*, February 15, 1982.
6. Karl Kotas, "Notable Examples of Local Mixes," *The Rocket* June 1982, p. 37.
7. Johnny Renton, "Lip Service," *The Rocket*, December 1982, p. 9.
8. Nes Rodriguez, personal communication with the author, June 2007.
9. Robert Newman, personal communication with the author, August 2014.
10. Tony B, personal communication with the author, May 2015.
11. Robert Newman, "They're Fresh!!!" *The Rocket,* September 1984, p. 34.
12. Eddie Wells, personal communication with the author, June 2008.
13. Newman 1984.
14. Steve Sneed, personal communication with the author, March 2015.

15. Sheila Anne Feeney, "Break Dancing: Waves and Tics and Baby Rolls Keep Body and Soul Together," *Seattle Times*, February 19, 1984, p. F1.

16. Belafonte as quoted in John Hartl, "Belafonte Backs Film on 'Hip-Hop' Culture," *Seattle Times*, June 8, 1985, p. D3.

17. John Vorhees, "NBC Is Hoping for a News Start on Sunday Nights," *Seattle Times*, June 30, 1984, p. D8.

18. Maysha Watson, "The History of the Seattle Center," *Seattle Magazine*, February 2012.

19. Blecha 2011.

20. ZiggyFan2012, "4 Generations of B-Boys Come Out To Celebrate 30 Years of Hip-Hop Culture at the 'Seattle City Breaker's Reunion,'" *King County News*, August 5, 2012, http://kingcountynews.org/2012/08/05/4-generations-of -b-boys-come-out-to-celebrate-30-years-of-hip-hop-culture-at-the-seattle -city-breakers-reunion.

21. Mandalit Del Barco, "Style Wars: Documenting Graffiti Artists," *NPR Morning Edition,* April 25, 2003, www.npr.org/templates/story/story.php?storyId =1242898.

22. JP Scratches, "Deepest Roots: 30 Years of Hip Hop in Seattle," *King County News,* November 11, 2014, http://kingcountynews.org/2014/11/11/deepest -roots-30-years-of-hip-hop-in-seattle.

23. David Toledo, personal communication with the author, June 2015.

24. Nes Rodriguez, personal communication with the author, March 2007.

25. Glen Boyd, "The Northwest's Hottest Funk DJs Square Off," *The Rocket,* May 1985, p. 9.

26. "Boss Cross," *The Rocket,* November 1986, p. 9.

27. Glen Boyd, "The Big Chill: Seattle Funk DJs and MCs Square Off," *The Rocket,* March 1985, p. 9.

28. Boyd 1986.

29. Glen Boyd, personal communication with the author, November 2014.

30. Mary Henry, "African American History Museum," Essay 8602, April 21, 2008, HistoryLink.org.

31. Daudi Abe, *6 'n the Morning: West Coast Hip-Hop Music 1987–1992 and the Transformation of Mainstream Culture* (Los Angeles: Over the Edge Books, 2013).

32. Earl Debnam, personal communication with the author, March 2015.

33. Roberta Penn, "The Monastery," *The Rocket,* June 1985, p. 14.

34. Penn 1985: 14.

35. "Parents In Arms," *The Rocket,* June 1985, p. 35.

36. Ben Jacklet, "The Return of the Demon," *The Stranger*, September 2, 1999.

37. "Teen Dance Club Regulations Proposed," *The Rocket,* June 1985, p. 35.

38. Amy Jenniges, "Black Listed," *The Stranger,* September 21, 2000.

39. Seattle Teen Dance Ordinance Project, https://seattletdoproject.wordpress .com (accessed June 8, 2014).

40. Dennis P. Eichhorn, "Third Avenue Freeze Out," *The Rocket,* February 1986, p. 17.

41. Krist Novoselic, "City, Artists Crafted Ordinance to Assure Safe, All-Ages Events," *Seattle Post-Intelligencer*, September 6, 2002.
42. Carlton Smith, "Crack—Cheap Form of Cocaine Spreading across Nation, into Seattle Area," *Seattle Times*, May 28, 1986, p. A1.
43. Smith 1986: A1.
44. Dan Satterberg, personal communication with the author, November 2014.
45. Daudi Abe 2013.
46. "Washington State Cocaine/Crack Crimes," Violation of the Uniform Controlled Substances Act, www.vucsa.com/cocaine-crack (accessed January 4, 2014).
47. Carrie Johnson, "Justice Dept. Backs Changes Affecting Cocaine Sentencing," *Seattle Times*, April 30, 2009, p. A9.
48. Gabe Morales, "Overview of Gang History in the Pacific Northwest," Gang Prevention Services, www.gangpreventionservices.org/ganghistory.asp (accessed January 26, 2014).
49. Don Duncan, "Gangs Increasing in Seattle—L.A. Toughs Leave Slums for New Turf," *Seattle Times*, June 28, 1987, p. A1.
50. "Seattle Gang Territory," www.google.com/maps/d/viewer?mid =zAH7tI3pUGmw.ka-c-NuLJ88I (accessed February 26, 2014). This disclaimer runs alongside the map: "The Seattle gang territory map gives a rough estimate of where certain gangs hang out and operate. By no means are the gangs listed here bounded by the colored area. Seattle gangs are very transient and often are allies with other gangs, therefore it is common to find gangs outside of their so-called area. Gang territories in Seattle are nothing like what you might come across in Los Angeles or Chicago."
51. Seattle Police Department, "The Number of Homicides in Seattle between 1985–1995," Public Disclosure Request # P2014-3688.
52. Glen Boyd, personal communication with the author, November 2014.
53. Glen Boyd, "Tacoma DJ Battle Mixmasters," *The Rocket*, November 1983, p. 12.
54. Tacoma DJ Bobby "Galaxy" Lewis and Phillip "G-Man" Gonzales as quoted in Glen Boyd, "Tacoma DJ Battle Mixmasters," *The Rocket*, November 1983, p. 12.
55. Glen Boyd, "Par-Tay in T-Town," *The Rocket*, August 1984, p. 13.
56. Glen Boyd, "The Royal Court of N.W. Rap," *The Rocket*, November 1987, p. 23.
57. "Miztah Zelle: Band History," Sound Click, www.soundclick.com/bands /default.cfm?bandID=171867 (accessed November 19, 2014).
58. Josh Rizeberg, "Tacoma's Own Miztah Zelle's Hip-Hop Journey Is Legendary," NorthwestMilitary.com, June 2012, www.northwestmilitary.com/music-and -culture/features-and-columns/2012/06/Tacomas-own-Miztah-Zelles -hip-hop-journey-is-legendary/.
59. Glen Boyd, "Born to Run," *The Rocket*, January 1986, p. 17.
60. Boyd 1987.
61. Mr. Supreme, personal communication with the author, July 2014.
62. Silver Shadow D, personal communication with the author, February 2015.
63. Davey D., "Jam on the Groove," *Hip-Hop Daily News*, May 20, 1997, www.daveyd.com/jamgroovenews.html.

64. Fever One, personal communication with the author, June 2014.

65. Glen Boyd, "Rap on the Map," *The Rocket*, June 1987, p.10.

66. Mike Clark, "DI-RA," *The Flavor*, May 1994, no. 14, p. 18.

67. Mix-A-Lot quotations in the following paragraphs are all from Glen Boyd, "To Sir with Funk," *The Rocket*, September 1986, p. 20.

68. Mix-A-Lot as quoted in Glen Boyd, "To Sir with Funk," *The Rocket*, September 1986, p. 20.

69. Mickey Hess, *Hip-Hop in America: A Regional Guide* (Santa Barbara: Greenwood Press, 2010).

70. Sir Mix-A-Lot, personal communication with the author, November 2014.

71. Hess 2010.

72. "He's Dreaming of a Gold Christmas," *The Rocket*, January 1989, p. 7.

73. Peyton Whitely, Dave Dirkland, and Patrick MacDonald, "Clues Hazy in Drive-By Shootings—Was Rap Music a Factor?" *Seattle Times*, October 8, 1988, p. A1.

74. John Peoples, "Mighty Metro! Rams Stun Juanita in OT," *Seattle Times*, November 12, 1988, p. D1.

75. Glen Boyd, "Wanted Badly: Public Enemy #1," *The Rocket*, July 1988, p. 29.

76. M. K. Asante, "Don't Believe the Hype," *New York Times*, February 17, 2012.

77. Steve Christilaw, "'Don't Believe the Hype'—Ingraham in Kingbowl—Lightly Regarded Rams Top Ferris in Semifinals," *Seattle Times*, November 27, 1988, p. C2.

78. John Peoples, "Ingraham Wins It All—Rams Blank Kentwood for AAA Title," *Seattle Times*, December 4, 1988, p. C1.

79. Andrew Matson, "Friday Favorites: Ice Cold Mode, DMS, Chelly Chell," *Seattle Times*, April 30, 2010.

80. Johanna Somers, "A Fast-Food Joint That's Heaven-sent," *Seattle Times*, August 5, 2012.

81. Matson 2010.

82. Glen Boyd, "Rap's Class of 1990: Straight Outta Seattle," *The Rocket*, June 1990, p. 12.

83. Roberta Penn, "Post Graduate Studies: Seminar Puts Sir Mix-A-Lot at the Head of the Class," *The Rocket*, December 1989, p. 29.

84. "Slice 'n Dice with Mix 'n Rice," *The Rocket*, February 1990, p. 6.

85. Roberta Penn, "Beyond Beepers and Boom," *The Rocket*, September 1990, p. 23.

86. Peter Blecha, "NastyMix Records Hosts Fifth Anniversary Party on November 29, 1990," Essay 9794, 2011, HistoryLink.org.

87. Patrick Macdonald, "A Mix Bag—Seattle's NastyMix Records Is Becoming a Key Player in the Highly Competitive, Rap-and-Rock Sound Business," *Seattle Times*, June 3, 1990.

88. Grant Alden, "Criminal Nation," *The Rocket*, April 1990, p. 20.

89. Greg Barbrick, "High Performance," *The Rocket*, September, 1989 p. 16.

Chapter 3. Seattle Hip Hop in the 1990s

The lyric in the chapter title comes from The Ghetto Children, "N's Don't L" (Seattle: Tribal Music Inc., 1996).

1. David Wilma, "Rioting Erupts in Seattle Following Verdicts in Rodney King Beating on May 1, 1992," Essay 3054, March 6, 2001, HistoryLink.org.

2. Seattle Police Department, "Weed and Seed Seattle: A Community Report," 2006, www.seattle.gov/police/publications/Community/2006_WeedSeed _AR.pdf (accessed October 25, 2014).

3. Terence Dunworth and Gregory Mills, "National Evaluation of Weed and Seed," National Institute of Justice: Research in Brief, US Department of Justice, Office of Justice Programs, 1999, www.ncjrs.gov/pdffiles1/175685.pdf (accessed February 8, 2014).

4. Brian King, "Weed & Seed Three Years On," *Washington Free Press* (October/ November 1994), http://wafreepress.org/12/Weed.html.

5. Dick Lily, "Seattle Wins Grant for 'Weed and Seed' Program," *Seattle Times*, April 6, 1992.

6. Elizabeth Grant, "Gangsta Rap, the War on Drugs, and the Location of African American Identity in Los Angeles, 1988–92," in *The Hip-Hop Reader*, edited by T. Strode and T. Wood, 159–72 (New York: Longman Publishing Group, 2008).

7. Alan Light, "About a Salary or Reality?" in *That's the Joint: The Hip-Hop Studies Reader*, edited by M. Forman and M. A. Neal, 137–45 (New York: Routledge, 2004), 138.

8. Barbara Serrano, "Bill Would Ban Sales of 'Dirty Music' to Minors— Some Stores Label Effort Censorship," *Seattle Times,* February 18, 1992.

9. Ricardo Frazer, personal communication with the author, July 2014.

10. Roberta Penn, "Money, Guns, & Lawyers," *The Rocket,* February 1992, p. 17.

11. Patrick Macdonald, "NastyMix Records to Close," *Seattle Times*, October 6, 1992.

12. Tad, "Missed Information," *Spin,* July 1991, p. 32.

13. Ed Christman, "Exclusive: Rick Rubin Brings American Recordings to Universal Republic," *Billboard*, August 22, 2012.

14. Roberta Penn, "Money, Guns, & Lawyers," *The Rocket*, February 1992, p. 17.

15. David Toop, *Rap Attack 3* (London: Serpent's Tail, 2001).

16. Daniel McDermon, "'Baby Got Back' Story: Sir Mix-A-Lot Was an Early Interactive Success," *New York Times*, June 10, 2014.

17. Casey McNerthney, "Sir Mix-A-Lot's 'Baby Got Back': Seattle's Last No. 1 Hit," *Seattle Post-Intelligencer*, February 25, 2010.

18. As quoted in Charles Mudede, "Seattle Saves Hip-Hop Again," *The Stranger*, January 30, 2012.

19. Jane Birnbaum, "Sir Mix-A-Lot Defends 'Baby Got Back,'" *Entertainment Weekly*, June 12, 1992.

20. Patrick Macdonald, "An Odd Night at the Grammys," *Seattle Times*, February 25, 1993.

21. Matthew Jacobs, "'Baby Got Back' Turns 21," *Huffington Post*, May 7, 2013.

22. Jessica T., "Sir Mix-A-Lot Explains How Publishing Beats Out Royalties," *VladTV*, June 6, 2015, www.vladtv.com/article/212464/sir-mix-a-lot-explains -how-publishing-beats-out-royalties.

23. Vladimir Bogdanov, ed., *All Music Guide to Hip-Hop: The Definitive Guide to Rap & Hip-Hop* (San Francisco: Backbeat Books, 2003), 546.

24. Scott Griggs, "Hangin and Talkin Shit with Mix," *The Rocket*, July 6–20, 1994, p. 18.

25. Greg Barbrick, "NXNW: E-Dawg," *The Rocket*, September 1993.

26. "Beavis and Butthead: About the Show," www.beavisandbutthead.net/about .html (accessed October 25, 2014).

27. Chris Willman, "TV Reviews: 'Marker,' 'Watcher' Latest UPN Premieres," *Los Angeles Times*, January 17, 1995, http://articles.latimes.com/1995-01-17 /entertainment/ca-20809_1_kcop-tv-channel.

28. Joanne Weintraub, "UPN Lives, Dies by 'Marker' and 'Watcher,'" *Chicago Tribune*, March 18, 1995, http://articles.chicagotribune.com/1995-03-18 /entertainment/9503180068_1_off-road-vehicles-hawaiian-andy-bumatai.

29. Scott Griggs, "Hangin and Talkin Shit with Mix," *The Rocket*, July 6–20, 1994, p. 17.

30. Associated Press, "Melee Erupts after Rap Concert," *Spokane Spokesman-Review*, December 28, 1992, p. A10.

31. "Summer Jam Rosters (1992–2010)," KUBE 93 FM, www.kube93.com/photos /summerjam/summer-jam-rosters-19922010-236750/14000992/#/0/14000992 (accessed July 30, 2014).

32. "History," Central Area Youth Association, http://seattle-caya.org/about-us (accessed August 18, 2014).

33. Mary Elizabeth Cronin, "Program Teaches Teens to Work for Their Dreams—CAYA Helps Youth Put Lives into Focus," *Seattle Times*, November 1, 1993.

34. DJ B-Mello, "Seattle Regional," *The Flavor*, November 1995, p. 25.

35. Payton Carter, "Seattle Hip-Hop Forum Trips the Beat Tip," *The Rocket*, December 6–20, 1995, p. 9.

36. University of British Columbia, "The History of Radio at UBC," 2002, http:// bcradiohistory.radiowest.ca/Biographies/TheUBCRadioStory.htm (accessed April 1, 2014).

37. Mike Clark, "Cross the Globe: Seattle," *The Flavor*, December 1994, p. 28.

38. Quoted in Brian Coleman, *Check the Technique* (New York: Villard, 2007), 161.

39. Coleman 2007.

40. Greg Braxton, "Hip-Hop TV's Leading Edge: Along with Its Emmy Awards and Enviable Ratings, 'In Living Color' Has Attracted Criticism That the Show Deals in Negative Stereotypes," *Los Angeles Times*, November 4, 1990.

41. Coleman 2007.

42. Coleman 2007: 171.

43. Simon Vozick-Levinson, "Digable Planets Reissue 'Blowout Comb': Butterfly Looks Back," *Rolling Stone*, June 19, 2013.

44. Topher Sander, "Ishmael Butler: Cherrywine," *AllHipHop*, October 1, 2003, http://allhiphop.com/2003/10/01/ishmael-butler-cherrywine.

45. Bill Reader, "Did You Know Griffey Raps Too?" *Seattle Times*, April 5, 2009.

46. Brian Floyd, "Sir Mix-A-Lot's 'Not in Our House' Music Video Resurrected from the Dead." *SBNation*, May 25, 2011, http://seattle.sbnation.com/seattle -nba/2011/5/25/2190001/sir-mix-a-lot-not-in-our-house-music-video.

47. Eric Diep, "15 of the Best NBA Rappers," *XXL*, October 28, 2013, www.xxlmag .com/news/2013/10/15-best-nba-rappers/2.

48. Cynthia Rose, "Sharpshooters—Duo Adds a Hot New Chapter to Seattle's Jazz History," *Seattle Times*, August 17, 1995.

49. Payton Carter, "Northwest Interview: Sharpshooters," *The Rocket*, September 27–October 11, 1995, p. 12.

50. Mr. Supreme, personal communication with the author, July 2014.

51. Rich Marin, "Grunge: A Success Story," *New York Times*, November 15, 1992.

52. Jonathan Cohen, "Pearl Jam: Biography," *Rolling Stone*, 2001, www .rollingstone.com/music/artists/pearl-jam/biography (accessed June 17, 2014).

53. "Alice In Chains: Biography," *Rolling Stone*, www.rollingstone.com/music /artists/alice-in-chains/biography (accessed September 5, 2014).

54. Karen Ganz, "Soundgarden: Biography," *Rolling Stone*, www.rollingstone .com/music/artists/soundgarden/biography (accessed June 10, 2014).

55. "Nirvana Timeline," www.nirvana.com/bio (accessed November 1, 2014).

56. Charles Cross, *Here We Are Now: The Lasting Impact of Kurt Cobain* (New York: Harper Collins, 2014).

57. El Mafioso as quoted in Specs, "El Mafioso," *The Flavor*, April–May 1993, no. 6, p. 22.

58. Zola Mumford, "Langston Hughes Performing Arts Institute (Seattle)," Essay 10909, August 6, 2014, HistoryLink.org.

59. Jonathan Moore, personal communication with the author, August 2014.

60. Mickey Hess, *Hip-Hop in America: A Regional Guide* (Santa Barbara: Greenwood Press, 2010), 294.

61. Larry Mizell Jr., "My Philosophy: Hip-Hop Ya Don't Stop," *The Stranger*, August 18, 2005.

62. Novocaine, "Conscious Party," *The Rocket*, August 13–27, 1997, p. 17.

63. Steve Stav, "Pain in the Grass 2000 Previews: Beyond Reality," *The Rocket*, August 2000.

64. Hess 2010.

65. Frannie Kelley, "Singled Out: E-40's 'Function'," *NPR: The Record*, March 30, 2012, www.npr.org/sections/therecord/2012/03/30/149570066 /singled-out-e-40s-function.

66. Hess 2010.

67. Jason Birchmeier, "E-40: Biography," 2014, www.billboard.com/artist/276018 /e-40/biography (accessed January 21, 2014).

68. B-Mello, "Local Flavor: Silver Shadow D," *The Flavor*, April 1994, no. 13, p. 22.

69. Dove, "Tales of Anger: Black Anger," *Davey D's Hip-Hop Corner*, www.daveyd .com/blackangerinterview.html.

70. Dan Johnson, "Black Anger," *The Rocket*, October 9–23, 1996, p. 12.

71. Lynne K. Varner, "Race Has a Role in the 37th—Black, White, Asian and Native Candidates Vie," *Seattle Times*, September 3, 1998, p. B4.

72. Sara Jean Green, "4 Seek 2 Seats in Diverse District 37—Santos Again Faces Garrett," *Seattle Times*, October 23, 2004, p. B4.

73. David Bowermaster, "Democrats Dominate 37th, 43rd Legislative Districts," *Seattle Times*, October 7, 2006.

74. Vitamin D, personal communication with the author, December 2014.

75. Hess 2010: 301.

76. Vanessa Ho, "Ghetto Children: Relax, Kick Back, Gyrate If You Want To," *Seattle Times*, January 7, 1994.

77. Novocaine, "Seattle Hip-Hop Underground's Ready for Prime Time Players," *The Rocket*, November 20–December 4, 1996, p. 20.

78. Novocaine 1996.

79. Jason Sutherland, "Prose & Concepts: Clip the Six," *The Rocket*, December 21–January 18, 1995, p. 19.

80. Strath Shepard, "Planet Rock: Prose Close Up," *The Rocket*, May 14–28, 1997, p. 28.

81. Tom Scanlon, "For Evil Tambourines, Things Are Starting to Shake Out," *Seattle Times*, May 27, 1999.

82. "Sir Mix-A-Lot: Bio," http://sirmixalot.com/bio-3 (accessed March 19, 2014).

83. S. Duda, "The Beat Writers: A Seattle Hip-Hop Roundtable," *The Rocket*, July 9–23, 1997, p. 9.

84. Strath Shepard, "Planet Rock: This Is Progress? Is Seattle Hip-Hop Really Moving Forward?" *The Rocket*, August 27–September 10, 1997, p. 28.

85. Strath Shepard, "Post-Nes Mess," *The Rocket*, October 22–November 5, 1997, p. 38.

86. Charles Mudede, "Can You Hear Street Sounds?" *The Stranger*, October 21, 1999.

87. Tina Potterf, "Jam on The KUBE," *The Rocket*, May 28–June 11, 1997, p. 9.

88. Potterf 1997: 9.

89. Tony B, personal communication with the author, May 2015.

90. Chad Kangas, "Ralph McDaniels Celebrates 30 Years of Video Music Box," *Village Voice*, March 15, 2013.

91. Gordon Curvey, "Music Inner City: About," 2008, http://music.sportsinnercity .com/?page_id=2 (accessed September 5, 2014).

92. City of Seattle Office of Arts & Culture, "Mayor Nickels Announces Fifth Annual Awards for Excellence in Hip-Hop," 2006, www.seattle.gov/arts /news/press_releases.asp?prID=6592&deptID=1 (accessed April 2, 2014).

93. Georgio Brown, personal communication with the author, August 2014.

94. City of Seattle Office of Arts & Culture, "Mayor Greg Nickels Announces Third Annual Award for Excellence in Hip-Hop to Georgio Brown and The Coolout Network," 2004, www.seattle.gov/arts/news/press_releases .asp?prID=4476&deptID=1 (accessed January 9, 2014).

95. Alison Pember and Rachel Crick, personal communication with the author, August 2014.

96. Mission Statement, *The Flavor*, March 1992, no. 1, p. 3.

97. Pember and Crick, personal communication with the author, August 2014.

98. Cynthia Rose, "Hip-Hop's Changing Flavor—Seattle's 3-Year-Old Rap Mag Has an Audience That's Both Global and National," *Seattle Times*, July 14, 1995.

99. Pember and Crick, personal communication with the author, August 2014.

100. Rose 1995.

101. Pember and Crick, personal communication with the author, August 2014.

102. Payton Carter, "Where's the Flavor?" *The Rocket*, December 4–18, 1996, p. 42.

103. DJ Kun Luv, personal communication with the author, July 2014.

104. Jake Batsell and Vikki Ortix, "Videotape May Yield Riot Clues—Camera Recorded Looters at Downtown Shoe Store," *Seattle Times*, September 22, 1997.

105. Charles Mudede, "Beyond the Sea," *The Stranger*, September 19, 2002.

106. Erin Franzman, "Skratching to the Top: Skratchcast.com Brings Hip-Hop to the Cybermasses," *The Stranger*, September 2, 1999.

107. Jonathan Zwickel, "High Rolling," *The Stranger*, June 7, 2007.

108. Jake Ellison, "The '90s: When Seattle Hip-Hop Broke Out on Public Access TV," *Seattle P-I*, November 26, 2013.

109. Cynthia Rose, "The Mecca Guys Are Back to Launch a New, Urbane Line," *Seattle Times*, February 28, 1997.

110. Tony Shellman and Abby Ellin, "Executive Life: The Boss; Forget the Uniform," *New York Times*, October 13, 2002.

111. Rose 1997.

112. Liz Black, "Enyce Sold to Sean John," *Huffington Post*, November 22, 2008.

113. Nikki Duckworth, "Tony Shellman: Hip-Hop Trendsetter, Fashion Innovator and Parish Nation," *Clutch Magazine*, December 2007, www.clutchmagonline.com/2007/12/tony-shellman-hip-hop-trendsetter-fashion-innovator-parish-nation.

114. Jonathan Moore, personal communication with the author, August 2014.

115. Larry Mizell Jr., "Hip-Hop People," *The Stranger*, March 23, 2006.

116. S. K. Honda and Strath, "DVS Floor rockers," *The Flavor*, October 1995, no. 29, p. 14.

117. Payton Carter, "Planet Rock: Droppin' Vicious Styles," *The Rocket*, March 26–April 9, 1997, p. 30.

118. Fever One, personal communication with the author, June 2014.

119. Jeromeskee, personal communication with the author, July 2014.

Chapter 4. 206/2K

The lyric in the chapter title is from Jake One, "Home" (Minneapolis: Rhymesayers Entertainment, 2009).

1. Associated Press, "Hip-hop Blamed for Club Shooting," *Eugene Register-Guard*, September 24, 2000, p. 5C.

2. Melanie McFarland, "Hip-Hop Enthusiasts Stage Peaceful Protest," *Seattle Times*, October 1, 2000.

3. Seattle City Council, "Mayor to Present Hip Hop Awards at MUSICA Festival, Oct. 7," 2006, www.seattle.gov/council/newsdetail.asp?ID=6545&Dept=28 (accessed April 13, 2014).

4. Tina Potterf, "Mr. Benjamin Goes with 'Flow' While Directing Energy to Youth," *Seattle Times*, October 26, 2003.

5. Brian Goedde, "9/11 as Muse: Local Rappers Respond with Posturing, Poetry," April 18, 2002.

6. Dorit Kalev, "Rick James Joins Nocturnal Rage on Remix," *All Hip-Hop .com*, October 14, 2002, http://allhiphop.com/2002/10/14/rick-james-joins -nocturnal-rage-on-remix.

7. Larry Mizell Jr., "My Philosophy: SportN' Life Records: Ten Years of Seattle Hip-Hop Greatness," *The Stranger*, November 21, 2012.

8. Geologic, personal communication with the author, August 2014.

9. "The Blue Scholars," *Billboard,* July 10, 2006.

10. Charles Mudede, "We Got Next: Mass Line's Multiculti Boom Bap," *The Stranger*, June 22, 2006.

11. Larry Mizell Jr., "My Philosophy," *The Stranger*, December 1, 2005.

12. "Rhymesayers Entertainment: A Written History," www.rhymesayers.com /about (accessed November 19, 2013).

13. Joe Lynch, "50 Cent Admits Retirement Threat Was Just to Sell Records," *Fuse*, September 12, 2012, www.fuse.tv/2012/09/50-cent-admits-retirement -threat-was-just-to-sell-records.

14. Larry Mizell Jr., "My Philosophy," *The Stranger*, September 15, 2005.

15. Larry Mizell Jr., "My Philosophy," *The Stranger*, September 15, 2005.

16. Charles Aaron, "What the White Boy Means When He Says Yo," in *And It Don't Stop: The Best American Hip-Hop Journalism of the Last 25 Years*, edited by Raquel Cepeda (New York: Faber and Faber, 2004), 218.

17. Rowald Pruyn, "Beyond Reality: A Souls Journey," *Rap Reviews.com*, October 2, 2007, www.rapreviews.com/archive/2007_10_asoulsjourney.html.

18. Larry Mizell Jr., "My Philosophy," *The Stranger*, August 18, 2005.

19. Robert Jamieson Jr., "Mr. Mayor, Do You Hear Our Cries for Change?" *Seattle P-I*, August 20, 2008.

20. Marian Liu, "Seattle Spoken-Word Artist Has Music in Her Blood, Poetry on Her Soul," *Seattle Times*, March 19, 2009.

21. *Street Smarts: The Story of a True School B-Girl: A One Woman Show by Laura "Piece" Kelley Jahn*," Brown Paper Tickets, 2007, www.brownpapertickets .com/event/14188 (accessed January 26, 2014).

22. "#TBT Breaking Battles: Red Bull Lords of the Floor (2001–2002)," www .redbullbcone.com/en/blog/tbt-breaking-battles-red-bull-lords-floor-2001 -2002 (accessed March 15, 2014).

23. Tina Potterf, "Seattle Breakdance Crew Earns World Title—Massive Monkees Call London Competition 'Fun,'" *Seattle Times*, February 13, 2004, p. E3.

24. Gabrielle Nomura, "Massive Monkees Share Success with Community— 2013 Visionary Award Recipient," *Northwest Asian Weekly*, October 17, 2013, www.nwasianweekly.com/2013/10/massive-monkees-share-success -community-2013-visionary-award-recipient.

25. Jeromeskee, personal communication with the author, July 2014.

26. Larry Mizell Jr., "My Philosophy," *The Stranger*, December 1, 2005.

27. Larry Mizell Jr., "My Philosophy," *The Stranger*, February 1, 2007.

28. Larry Mizell Jr., "My Philosophy: Hip-Hop Ya Don't Stop," *The Stranger*, October 30, 2008.

29. "Battle of Burien Breakdancing Drew Huge Crowd Friday Night," *Highline Times*, February 12, 2012, www.highlinetimes.com/2012/02/12/news/update-battle-burien-breakdancing-drew-huge-crowd.

30. Quibuyen as quoted in Dove, "Hip-Hop Commentary: Are Backpackers Really Conscious?" *The FNV Newsletter*, 2002, www.daveyd.com/backpacker.html (accessed March 19, 2014).

31. Samuel Chesneau, personal communication with the author, December 2014.

32. Nolan Strong, "Man Shot and Killed at Seattle's KUBE Summer Jam," *All Hip-Hop.com*, July 22, 2002, http://allhiphop.com/2002/07/22/man-shot-and-killed-at-seattles-kube-summer-jam/.

33. Kim Nowacki, "Ludacris, Chingy Heat Up the Summer Jam Crowd," *Seattle Times,* July 22, 2003.

34. Charles Mudede, "Secret of Its Success," *The Stranger,* March 6, 2003.

35. Charles Mudede, "Panic on the Streets of Belltown," *The Stranger*, April 23, 2009.

36. Larry Mizell Jr., "My Philosophy," *The Stranger*, February 3, 2005.

37. Quibuyen as quoted in Tina Potterf, "The Spin on Asian-American Hip-Hop," *Seattle Times,* July 20, 2003.

38. Interview of Paul Javier by George Quibuyen, May 12, 2003.

39. Marian Liu, "Asian Hip-Hop Summit Headed to Seattle," *Seattle Times,* August 20, 2008.

40. Larry Mizell Jr., "My Philosophy," *The Stranger*, May 18, 2006.

41. CD News Staff, "Dope Emporium Brings Best in Seattle Hip-Hop to Washington Hall," *Central District News*, November 10, 2010, www.centraldistrictnews.com/2010/11/dope-emporium-brings-best-in-seattle-hip-hop-to-washington-hall/.

42. Larry Mizell Jr., "Pharmacy Direct," *The Stranger*, October 20, 2005.

43. Charles Mudede, "Make Music for My People," *The Stranger*, November 1, 2007.

44. Charles Mudede, "Vanguard or Vandalism?" *The Stranger,* March 30, 2000.

45. Leah Baltus, "Getting Up," *City Arts*, April 27, 2015, www.cityartsonline.com/articles/getting.

46. Jonah Spangenthal-Lee, "Tag Team: Seattle Graffiti Gang 3A: Artists or Assholes?" *The Stranger,* September 6, 2007.

47. Clout, "Tred BTM 3A Interview," *Clout Magazine*, March 17, 2012, www.cloutonline.com/2012/03/tred-btm-3a-interview/.

48. Jonah Spangenthal-Lee, "Lone Ranger," *The Stranger*, August 23, 2007.

49. Ericka Berg, "Wiping Out Graffiti: South End Citizens Focus on Persistent Street Vandals," *Beacon Hill News & South District Journal,* January 26, 2005, p. 1.

50. Andrew Matson, "The Visual Art of Seattle Abstract-Rap Pioneer SPECSONE 08/12/10 at Throwbacks NW," *Seattle Times*, July 16, 2010.

51. Brian Goedde, "End of Flight, Please Disembark: R.I.P. The Rocket," *The Stranger,* November 2, 2000.

52. Davey D, "Seattle's *The Stranger* Publishes a Racist Hip-Hop Article," *Davey D's Hip-Hop Corner*, May 17, 2004, http://hiphopandpolitics.com /2004/05/17/seattles-the-stranger-publishes-a-racist-hip-hop-article.

53. Larry Mizell Jr., personal communication with the author, October 2014.

54. Charles Mudede, "Gimme a Beat! I Want Hip-Hop Radio," *The Stranger*, December 14, 2000.

55. Charles Mudede, "Gimme a Beat! I Want Hip-Hop Radio," *The Stranger*, December 14, 2000.

56. "City of Mercer Island: Mercer Island Demographic Information," www .mercergov.org/Page.asp?NavID=592 (accessed February 5, 2014).

57. City of Seattle, Office of Arts & Culture, "Mayor Greg Nickels Announces Fourth Annual Awards for Excellence in Hip Hop," 2005, www.seattle .gov/arts/news/press_releases.asp?prID=5369&deptID=1 (accessed July 5, 2014).

58. Seattle Times Staff, "A&E Briefs: Source of Labor Singer Wins Mayor's Hip-Hop Award," *Seattle Times*, July 24, 2003.

59. Larry Mizell Jr., "My Philosophy," *The Stranger*, July 7, 2005.

60. Quoted in Larry Mizell Jr., "Pharmacy Direct," *The Stranger,* October 20, 2005.

61. Charles Mudede, "A New Morning of America," *The Stranger*, December 18, 2008.

62. Larry Mizell Jr., "My Philosophy," *The Stranger*, November 2, 2006.

63. Jonathan Zwickel, "Love Raindrop Hustla," *The Stranger*, June 5, 2007.

64. Tumblin' Erb, "What Are the Best Blogs for Regional Rap?" 2013, http:// tumblinerb.com/post/44201264285/what-are-the-best-blogs-preferably -curated-for (accessed June 8, 2014).

65. Chul Gugich, personal communication with the author, January 2015.

66. Casey Carter, personal communication with the author, February 2015.

67. Charles Mudede, "Up & Coming: Saigon, Dyme Def," *The Stranger*, May 14, 2009.

68. Andrew Matson, "Right Now, Seattle Is Making Hip-Hop History," *Seattle Times,* August 6, 2009.

69. Larry Mizell Jr., "My Philosophy: Seattle: All the Hip-Hop You Need," *The Stranger*, May 21, 2009.

70. Charles Mudede, "Separating the Music from the Murder: Why Chop Suey Should Keep Hosting Hip-Hop Shows," *The Stanger*, January 8, 2009.

71. Charles Mudede, "Separating the Music from the Murder: Why Chop Suey Should Keep Hosting Hip-Hop Shows," *The Stanger*, January 8, 2009.

72. Daudi Abe, "A Seattle Black Life That Almost Mattered in 1938," *The Stranger*, June 21, 2016.

73. Mike Romano, "Death by Pepper Spray?" *Seattle Weekly,* October 9, 2006.

74. Parrish Geov and Rick Anderson, "Death on Union," *Seattle Weekly*, October 9, 2006.

75. Jonah Spangenthal-Lee, "DV One Sentenced," *The Stranger*, December 14, 2007.

76. Nick Perry, "Evergreen State College Divided after Riot," *Seattle Times*, March 6, 2008.

77. "HSAN," Rush Communications, www.rushcommunications.com/community
-affairs/hip-hop-summit-action-network (accessed May 5, 2015).

78. "About," Seattle Hip-Hop Summit Youth Council, https://seattlehiphopsummit
.wordpress.com/about-2 (accessed June 24, 2014).

79. Brian Goedde, "Afterschool Special," *The Stranger*, February 28, 2002.

80. "What Is the Universal Zulu Nation?" Universal Zulu Nation, www.zulunation
.com/about-zulunation (accessed May 25, 2014).

81. 206 Zulu, "About 206 Zulu," www.206zulu.com/about.html (accessed
June 15, 2014).

82. 206 Zulu, "About 206 Zulu," www.206zulu.com/about.html (accessed
July 3, 2014).

83. Larry Mizell Jr., "My Philosophy," *The Stranger*, September 29, 2005.

84. Larry Mizell Jr., "Here Comes the Neighborhood: Despite What You've
Heard, Hip-Hop Is Saving America," *The Stranger*, December 13, 2007.

85. Julie Chang Schulman, "Seattle Hip-Hop Community Tackles Tough
Issues at NW Hip-Hop Leadership Conference," *Reclaim the Media*,
March 7, 2009, www.reclaimthemedia.org/arts/activism/seattle_hip
_hop_community_tack0710.

86. Mizell 2007.

87. Andrew Matson, "Seattle Hip-Hop Career & Business Expo 10/09/10 at
VERA," *Seattle Times,* October 7, 2010.

88. "About/History," The Vera Project, http://theveraproject.org/about/history
(accessed August 15, 2014).

89. Marian Liu, "Fresh and Local: It's the Live @ Hidmo Series at Central Area
Restaurant," *Seattle Times*, August 13, 2009.

90. Daudi Abe, "Hip-Hip and the Academic Canon," *Education, Citizenship and
Social Justice*, 4, no. 3 (2009): 7.

91. UWHHSA, personal communication with the author, March 2015.

92. "Multi-Ethnic Programs: Student Groups," Seattle Pacific University, http://
spu.edu/depts/mep/student-groups.asp (accessed July 30, 2014).

93. Jollee Pullig, "Promoting Hip-Hop at SPU," *The Falcon*, November 13, 2013,
www.thefalcononline.com/2013/11/promoting-hip-hop-at-spu.

94. "Young Northwest: Trailblazers," *DList Magazine*, September 2011, http://
issuu.com/dlistmagazine/docs/sept_2011/44 (accessed November 19, 2014).

95. Larry Mizell Jr., "Hip-Hop People: Meli Darby's Obese Productions Promotes
Artists on the Verge," *The Stranger*, March 23, 2006.

96. Charles Mudede, "Street's Disciples: Sportn' Life Records, Voice of the
Central District," *The Stranger*, August 16, 2007.

97. Manier as quoted in Charles Mudede, "Street's Disciples: Sportn' Life
Records, Voice of the Central District," *The Stranger*, August 16, 2007.

98. Charles Mudede, "Panic on the Streets of Belltown," *The Stranger*,
April 23, 2009.

99. Charles Mudede, "Blue Scholars Presents: The Program," *The Stranger,*
2007, www.thestranger.com/seattle/special/theprogram (accessed
April 20, 2014).

100. Larry Mizell Jr., "My Philosophy," *The Stranger*, February 21, 2008.

101. Andrew Matson, "Seattle's Hip-Hop Scene Comes into Its Own," *Seattle Times,* November 7, 2007.

102. Lalario as quoted in Andrew Matson, "Seattle's Hip-Hop Scene Comes into Its Own," *Seattle Times,* November 7, 2007.

103. Geologic as quoted in Larry Mizell Jr., "My Philosophy: Blue Scholars Stop Chasing That Big Record-Deal Unicorn," *The Stranger,* August 6, 2009.

104. Larry Mizell Jr., "My Philosophy: Blue Scholars Stop Chasing That Big Record-Deal Unicorn," *The Stranger,* August 6, 2009.

105. Humberto Martinez, "Photos and Review: Blue Scholars, Macklemore and Others Pack the Showbox," *Seattle P-I,* March 29, 2010.

106. Andrew Matson, "Native Hip-Hop at Folklife: Komplex Kai Raps a Rez Reality," *Seattle Times,* May 26, 2008.

107. Tom Breihan, "Nas's 'Where Are They Now' Remixes: Publicity-Stunt Greatness," *Village Voice,* February 2, 2007.

108. Andrew Matson, "Best Seattle Hip-Hop Video Ever: Jake One—'Home,'" *Seattle Times,* May 28, 2009.

109. Larry Mizell Jr., "My Philosophy," *The Stranger* June 4, 2009.

110. Larry Mizell Jr., "My Philosophy," *The Stranger,* November 6, 2008.

111. As quoted in Charles Mudede, "Where I'm From," *The Stranger,* June 7, 2001.

112. Matson 2009.

113. Larry Mizell Jr., "My Philosophy," *The Stranger,* October 1, 2009.

114. Tricia Romano, "Sci-Fi Beats with a Pacific Flavor," *New York Times,* August 1, 2014.

115. Larry Mizell Jr., "My Philosophy," *The Stranger,* July 2, 2009.

116. Andrew Matson, "Shabazz Palaces Conjures Nighttime in Seattle's Central District, Invents Boho-Gangster Rap," *Seattle Times,* November 1, 2009.

117. Cortney Harding, "Grynch Sounds Off on Seattle Hip-Hop," *Billboard,* September 3, 2009.

Chapter 5. Traditions Change and Continue

The lyric in the chapter title is from Draze's self-released single "The Hood Ain't the Same," Seattle, 2014.

1. "SXSW History," South by Southwest Music Conference and Festival, www .sxsw.com/about/sxsw-history (accessed June 26, 2014).

2. Larry Mizell Jr., "My Philosophy: Seattle Hip-Hop at SXSW: A Good Look." *The Stranger,* March 18, 2010.

3. Andrew Matson, "The Year in Local Hip-Hop: Double-Header Concert Go! Machine Wraps up 2009," *Seattle Times,* November 30, 2009.

4. Andrew Matson, "Adam Swan Explains 'Kevin Collabo,' Truckasaurus with 30+ Rappers," *Seattle Times,* August 3, 2010.

5. Andrew Matson, "'Stop Biting' Night at Lo-Fi Now an Album, Mini Doc," *Seattle Times,* December 31, 2012.

6. Andrew Matson, "Grand Groove: New Monthly Night by Seattle's Rap Vanguard," *Seattle Times,* August 1, 2011.

7. Larry Mizell Jr., "My Philosophy: Ladies Night 2.0," *The Stranger*, June 10, 2010.

8. 206 Zulu, "206 Zulu Helps Promote Awareness for Hip-Hop Issues and Culture," November 1, 2010, http://1st.206zulu.org/archive_12_10.html.

9. Michael F. Berry, "The Top 10 Moments in Seattle Hip-Hop History," *Seattle Weekly*, November 4, 2014.

10. *50 Next: Seattle Hip-Hop Worldwide*, www.50nextseattle.com (accessed August 18, 2014).

11. Larry Mizell Jr., "My Philosophy," *The Stranger*, February 19, 2014.

12. "The Legacy of Seattle Hip-Hop," Museum of History and Industry, 2014, www.mohai.org/component/content/article/730-the-legacy-of-hip-hop (accessed March 19, 2015).

13. "Our Story," Northwest Folklife, www.nwfolklife.org/about/our-story (accessed May 28, 2014).

14. "Cultural Focus: Beats Rhymes & Rhythms," Northwest Folklife Festival, www.nwfolklife.org/festival2015/cultural-focus-beats-rhymes-rhythms (accessed May 28, 2015).

15. Gwendolyn Elliot, "The Seattle Breakers Reunion—and Sir Mix-A-Lot's DJ Nes Rodriguez—This Friday at the WSCC," *Seattle Weekly*, May 12, 2011.

16. ZiggyFan2012, "4 Generations of B-Boys Come out to Celebrate 30 Years of Hip-Hop Culture at the 'Seattle City Breaker's Reunion,'" *King County News*, August 5, 2012, http://kingcountynews.org/2012/08/05/4-generations-of-b-boys-come-out-to-celebrate-30-years-of-hip-hop-culture-at-the-seattle-city-breakers-reunion.

17. Charles Lam, "Massive Monkees Light a Beacon—Seattle Dance Crew Builds Dreams," *Northwest Asian Weekly*," January 24, 2013, www.nwasianweekly.com/2013/01/massive-monkees-light-a-beacon-seattle-dance-crew-build-dreams.

18. Jevon Phillips, "What You're Watching," *Los Angeles Times*, September 24, 2009.

19. Charles Lam, "Massive Monkees Light a Beacon—Seattle Dance Crew Builds Dreams," *Northwest Asian Weekly*," January 24, 2013, www.nwasianweekly.com/2013/01/massive-monkees-light-a-beacon-seattle-dance-crew-build-dreams/.

20. Richter as quoted in Julie Pham, "B-Boy Crew Massive Monkees Build a Break Dancing Business," *Forbes Magazine*, April 23, 2013.

21. "New Class: Way of the B-Girl," Massive Monkees, www.facebook.com/massivemonkees/posts/10152974501485464 (accessed October 4, 2013).

22. Gabrielle Nomura, "Reign Supreme Brings International Break Dancing Talent to Seattle Competition," *Northwest Asian Weekly*, December 6, 2013, www.nwasianweekly.com/2013/12/reign-supreme-brings-international-break-dancing-talent-seattle-competition.

23. Kate Smith, "UW Hip-Hop Club Dances for Paul Lee," *The Falcon*, November 19, 2014, www.thefalcononline.com/2014/11/uw-hip-hop-club-dances-for-paul-lee.

24. Stephanie Klein, "Seattle's Iconic Eyesore Tubs Is Demolished," *My Northwest*, March 14, 2014, http://mynorthwest.com/11/2475025/Seattles-iconic-eyesore-Tubs-is-demolished.

25. Lily Cutler, "Seattle's Secretive Graffiti World Steps out of the Shadows," *Crosscut*, October 28, 2013.

26. Charles Mudede, "Rap Urbanism," *The Stranger*, February 22, 2012.

27. Kevin Capp, "206 Hip-Hop: Still about to Be Big," *Seattle Weekly*, January 5, 2010.

28. Charles Mudede, "Leave Home: Does Making It in Hip-Hop Mean Leaving Seattle?" *The Stranger*, August 26, 2010.

29. Larry Mizell Jr., "My Philosophy," *The Stranger*, March 16, 2011.

30. Frannie Kelley, "Crowd Funding for Musicians Isn't the Future; It's the Present," *NPR Music*, September 25, 2012, www.npr.org/sections/therecord/2012/09/25/161702900/crowd-funding-for-musicians-isnt-the-future-its-the-present.

31. Larry Mizell Jr., "My Philosophy," *The Stranger*, July 13, 2011.

32. Larry Mizell Jr., "My Philosophy: On *Watch the Throne* and the State of Rap," *The Stranger*, August 17, 2011.

33. Larry Mizell Jr., "My Philosophy," *The Stranger*, December 28, 2011.

34. Megan Jasper, personal communication with the author, December 2014.

35. Charles Mudede, "Taste That Crown: Shabazz Palaces' Monumental Hometown Debut," *The Stranger*, January 7, 2010.

36. Larry Mizell Jr., "My Philosophy," *The Stranger*, September 16, 2010.

37. Eric Grandy, "The Geniuses: 2010 Stranger Music Genius Shabazz Palaces," *The Stranger*, September 16, 2010.

38. Jon Caramanica, "Left-Field Hip-Hop Coherently Disjointed," *New York Times*, October 17, 2010.

39. Sasha Frere-Jones, "Organized Confusion: Shabazz Palaces' Sounds and Symbols," *New Yorker*, August 29, 2011.

40. Andrew Matson, "Concert Preview: THEESatisfaction at Neumos," *Seattle Times*, February 2, 2010.

41. Carrie Battan, "THEESatisfaction: awE naturalE," *Pitchfork*, March 29, 2012, http://pitchfork.com/reviews/albums/16444-awe-naturale.

42. Larry Mizell Jr., "My Philosophy: Get Heard out of the Hood," *The Stranger*, March 21, 2012.

43. Larry Mizell Jr., "Cloud Burst," *The Stranger*, December 21, 2011.

44. Larry Mizell Jr., "My Philosophy," *The Stranger*, January 9, 2013.

45. Jeff Weiss, "Nacho Picasso," *Pitchfork*, November 8, 2011, http://pitchfork.com/reviews/albums/15976-for-the-glory.

46. Paul de Barros, "Grammy Makes Few Nods to the Northwest," *Seattle Times*, December 7, 2012.

47. Larry Mizell Jr., "My Philosophy," *The Stranger*, January 27, 2011.

48. Andrew Matson, "Concert Review: Macklemore and Ryan Lewis at the Showbox 03/05/11," *Seattle Times*, March 6, 2011.

49. Larry Mizell Jr., "My Philosophy: Tech N9ne, Black Star, and Frat Rap," *The Stranger*, November 2, 2011.

50. Megan Buerger, "How Macklemore Tapped Major Label Muscle to Market an Indie Album," *Wall Street Journal*, January 28, 2014, http://blogs.wsj.com /speakeasy/2014/01/28/how-macklemore-tapped-major-label-muscle-to -market-an-indie-album.

51. Larry Mizell Jr., "My Philosophy: Macklemore & Ryan Lewis's #1 LP, Lots of City Arts Fest Hip-Hop," *The Stranger*, October 17, 2012.

52. Rauly Ramirez, "Macklemore & Ryan Lewis' 'Thrift Shop' Sets Record on Hot R&B/Hip-Hop Songs Chart," *Billboard*, April 5, 2013.

53. RIAA, "Gold & Platinum News: Record Month for RIAA Digital Awards," June 2013, www.riaa.com/newsitem.php?content_selector=riaa-news-gold -and-platinum&news_month_filter=6&news_year_filter=2013&id=EE58FB59 -98D3-423E-E1F4-EA274533B3B4.

54. Gary Trust, "Macklemore & Ryan Lewis' 'Can't Hold Us' Makes Hot 100 History," *Billboard*, May 8, 2013.

55. Macklemore as quoted in Larry Mizell Jr., "Fear and Loving," *The Stranger*, August 1, 2012.

56. Keith Caulfield and Gary Trust, "Macklemore & Ryan Lewis' 'Same Love' & Other No. 11 Hits," *Billboard*, September 17, 2013. James Montgomery, "Macklemore Weighs in on Teacher Suspended for Playing 'Same Love'," *MTV News*, November 30, 2012, www.mtv.com/news/1698189/macklemore -same-love-teacher-suspended. Alan Duke and Joe Sutton, "Teacher Suspended for Showing Class Macklemore's 'Same Love' Video," *CNN*, September 12, 2013, www.cnn.com/2013/09/12/showbiz/same-love-teacher -suspended.

57. Alan Duke, "Macklemore & Ryan Lewis Get Grammy Respect," *CNN*, December 7, 2013, www.cnn.com/2013/12/07/showbiz/56-grammy-nominations.

58. Charles Mudede, "Seattle Saves Hip-Hop, Again," *The Stranger*, January 30, 2013.

59. "We Are the 99 Percent," http://wearethe99percent.tumblr.com (accessed December 15, 2014).

60. Larry Mizell Jr., "My Philosophy: An Interview with Julie C of Hip-Hop Occupies," *The Stranger*, November 16, 2011.

61. Daudi Abe and Quintard Taylor, "From Memphis & Mogadishu: The History of African Americans in Martin Luther King County, Washington, 1858–2014," October 13, 2014, www.blackpast.org/memphis-and-mogadishu -history-african-americans-martin-luther-king-county-washington-1858-2014.

62. Naomi Ishisaka, "Changes in the Central District Affect the African-American Community," *Seattle Magazine*, March 2014.

63. Prometheus Brown, "Despite Flaws, OWS Deserves Our Participation," *Al Jazeera*. November 27, 2011, www.aljazeera.com/indepth/opinion/2011 /11/2011112316262171578 6.html.

64. Prometheus Brown, "Blue Scholars Prometheus Brown Writes a Song for the City," *Seattle Times*, June 9, 2012.

65. Washington State Liquor Control Board, "Fact Sheet: Initiative 502's Impact on the Washington State Liquor Control Board," www.liq.wa.gov/marijuana /fact_sheet (accessed February 4, 2014).

66. Larry Mizell Jr., "My Philosophy: Ten Years of My Philosophy," *The Stranger,* June 18, 2014.

67. Larry Mizell Jr., "206 Zulu Turns 10: Spreading Social Consciousness and the Transformative Elements of Hip-Hop," *The Stranger,* February 12, 2014.

68. Sean Jewell, "Roots and Branches: The Maraire Family," *Northwest Folklife Festival 2015,* www.nwfolklife.org/festival2015/cultural-focus/maraire -family (accessed June 18, 2015).

69. Daudi Abe and Quintard Taylor, "From Memphis & Mogadishu: The History of African Americans in Martin Luther King County, Washington, 1858– 2014," BlackPast.org, 2014, www.blackpast.org/memphis-and-mogadishu -history-african-americans-martin-luther-king-county-washington-1858-2014.

70. Larry Mizell Jr., "My Philosophy," *The Stranger,* August 22, 2012.

71. Quoted in Olivia Fuller, "Militia MaliMob Rapper Voices Somali American Struggles," *Seattle Globalist,* May 12, 2015, http://seattleglobalist.com/2015 /05/12/malitia-malimob-somali-rapper-stereotypes-seattle/36515.

72. Dan Buyanovsky, "The New New: 15 Seattle Rappers You Should Know," *XXL,* May 23, 2013, www.xxlmag.com/news/2013/05/the-new-new-15-seattle -rappers-you-should-know.

73. Charles Mudede, "The Hip-Hop List That Made 206 Butthurt," *The Stranger,* June 12, 2013.

74. XXL Staff, "The New New: 15 Female Rappers You Should Know," *XXL.* December 2, 2013, www.xxlmag.com/news/2013/12/new-new-15-female -rappers-know/6.

75. Melissa Locker, "The 7 Female Rappers You Should Be Listening to Right Now," *Time,* May 19, 2014.

76. Larry Mizell Jr., "My Philosophy," *The Stranger,* December 5, 2012. Larry Mizell Jr., "My Philosophy," *The Stranger,* April 2, 2014.

77. Larry Mizell Jr., "My Philosophy," *The Stranger,* May 15, 2013.

78. Clayton Holman, "Album of the Month: 'RSE GLD/WHT GLD' by Porter Ray," *City Arts,* August 29, 2013, www.cityartsonline.com/articles/album-month-rse -gldwht-gld-porter-ray.

79. Charles R. Cross, "Mike McCready, Seattle Symphony Team up for Annual Sonic Evolution,*" Seattle Times,* January 30, 2015.

80. Charles R. Cross, "Sir Mix-A-Lot Had a Lot of Fun with Seattle Symphony," *Seattle Times,* June 7, 2014.

81. James Oestreich, "Dutilleux and Ravel Mingle with Sir Mix-A-Lot," *New York Times,* June 8, 2014.

82. Daudi and Taylor 2014.

83. Lisa Loving, "'The Hood Ain't the Same': Draze Brings Seattle Together on Gentrification," *The Skanner,* March 6, 2014, www.theskanner.com/news /northwest/20909-the-hood-ain-t-the-same-draze-brings-seattle-together -on-gentrification.

84. Andrew Matson, "Download This: 'Hip-Hop Kitchen' by Seattle's Vitamin D," *Seattle Times,* August 24, 2011.

85. Larry Mizell Jr., "Enough about Their Rapping, How about Their Food?" *The Stranger,* August 27, 2014.

86. Charles Mudede, "Holistic Hip-Hop: The New Black Diet at Hillside Quickie's," *The Stranger,* January 15, 2004.

87. Andrew Matson, "At the Corner of Hip-Hop and Dinner: Seattle's Thuggin' Chef," *Seattle Times,* July 20, 2010.

88. Larry Mizell Jr., "Enough about Their Rapping, How about Their Food?" *The Stranger,* August 27, 2014.

89. Jenise Silva, "Food and Sh!t Pop-Up Returns to Beacon Hill Monday," *The Examiner,* January 18, 2014, www.examiner.com/article/food-and-sh-t-pop-up -returns-to-beacon-hill-monday.

90. Allison Austin Scheff, "A Filipino Food Movement Is Rising in Seattle," *Seattle Magazine,* February 2015.

91. Ryan Van Bibber, "Marshawn Lynch Wins Super Bowl Media Day," *SB Nation,* January 28, 2014, www.sbnation.com/lookit/2014/1/28/5354480/marshawn -lynch-wins-super-bowl-media-day.

92. Adam Schefter, "Marshawn Lynch Not Facing Discipline," *ESPN,* February 4, 2015, http://espn.go.com/nfl/playoffs/2014/story/_/id/12278859/marshawn -lynch-seattle-seahawks-complied-super-bowl-media-obligations.

93. "Jalen Testerman: Bio," www.jalentesterman.com/bio.html (accessed August 18, 2014).

94. Tricia Romano, "For 8-year-old Seattle Artist, Hip-Hop and Hoopla," *Seattle Times,* February 7, 2015.

95. Benjamin Sutton, "Yung Lenox, with Meme's Hip-Hop Portraitist, Is a Six-Year-Old Boy from Seattle," *Blouin ArtInfo Blogs,* May 10, 2013, http://blogs .artinfo.com/artintheair/2013/05/10/yung-lenox-wish-memes-hip-hop -portraitist-is-a-six-year-old-boy-from-seattle.

96. Quoted in Sarah Bennett, "Yung Lenox, a 7-year-old Artist Who Draws Rap Albums," *LA Weekly,* May 2, 2014.

97. Romano 2015.

Conclusion

The chapter title is inspired by Laura Kelley, "Central District," *Russell Simmons Def Poetry,* Episode #4.6, 2004.

1. Quintard Taylor, *The Forging of a Black Community: Seattle's Central District from 1870 through the Civil Rights Era* (Seattle: University of Washington Press, 1994), 158.

INDEX